BALANCING THE SKILLS EQUATION

Key issues and challenges for policy and practice

Edited by Geoff Hayward and Susan James

First published in Great Britain in October 2004 by

The Policy Press
University of Bristol
Fourth Floor
Beacon House
Queen's Road
Bristol BS8 1QU
UK

Tel +44 (0)117 331 4054
Fax +44 (0)117 331 4093
e-mail tpp-info@bristol.ac.uk
www.policypress.org.uk

British Library Cataloguing in Publication Data
A catalogue record for this book is available from the British Library.

Library of Congress Cataloging-in-Publication Data
A catalog record for this book has been requested.

ISBN 1 86134 575 5 paperback

A hardcover version of this book is also available

Cover design by Qube Design Associates, Bristol.
Front cover: photograph supplied by kind permission of Brand X Pictures/Alamy, www.alamy.com
Printed and bound in Great Britain by Hobbs the Printers Ltd, Southampton.

Contents

Acknowledgements

In the preparation of this book each of the authors was supported in some way by the Economic and Social Research Council (ESRC) Research Centre on Skills, Knowledge and Organisational Performance (SKOPE). We are grateful to the Director of the Centre, Ken Mayhew, for his continued support and interest.

We were greatly assisted in the preparation of the typescript by Stephanie Sturdy, and by ongoing conversations with Su-Ann Oh, Susannah Wright, Christophe Nordman and Richard Pring. We received helpful comments from two anonymous reviewers and support from Dawn Rushen and Laura Greaves at The Policy Press.

Preface

This book arose out of the work of Theme 3 of the ESRC-sponsored Research Centre on Skills, Knowledge and Organisational Performance (SKOPE). This theme was concerned with analysing the demand for skills in the economy, and the role of the education and training system in meeting such demands in the changing policy environment. What struck those of us working on the various projects within the Research Centre was how, at the turn of the 21st century, education and training continued to be a major focus of public policy across all the countries we investigated.

Balancing the skills equation brings together international authors who are in one way or another connected to SKOPE. All of us were concerned to understand the ways in which, and the extent to which, the supply and demand sides of the skills equation were linked. In addition, we also sought to understand how policy affected this linkage. We explored and developed our ideas through a series of seminars and SKOPE Working Papers. The outcome is a book that examines a related set of issues by authors writing from their own national perspectives.

Notes on contributors

Bill Bailey is Reader in Post-Compulsory Education and Training at the University of Greenwich. His research interests are in the historical and recent development of further and vocational education.

Stephen Billett is Associate Professor of Adult and Vocational Education at Griffith University (Brisbane, Australia). His research interests include the social and cultural construction of vocational knowledge; the role of individual agency in vocational knowledge construction; and how vocational expertise can be developed in workplace settings. In addition, he has a broad interest in policy and practice within adult and vocational education. He has recently published *Learning in the workplace: Strategies for effective practice* (2001, Allen & Unwin).

Cécile Deer is a Research Fellow of SKOPE and Lecturer at Balliol College, University of Oxford. Her areas of research interest are political economy; comparative public policy, particularly in the field of education; and the economics, history, sociology and philosophy of education.

Jean-Luc De Meulemeester is a Fellow of SKOPE and Associate Professor of Economics at the Free University of Brussels. His research interests include the economics and sociology of education; higher education systems and the role of policy; and comparative education policy.

Hubert Ertl is a Fellow of SKOPE and Lecturer at the University of Paderborn (Germany). His research interests include reform initiatives in the German dual system; EU policies in education and training; and issues of competence formation in a comparative perspective.

Rosa M. Fernández is a Research Fellow of SKOPE at the Department of Economics and a Lecturer at Worcester College, University of Oxford. Her research interests include applications on the fields of economics of education and labour economics; the interaction between educational decisions and labour market participation and performance; the impact of education and labour market experiences on crime participation; and the effects of technological change and growth on skill acquisition processes and decisions.

Alison Fuller is a Fellow of SKOPE and a Reader in the School of Education, University of Southampton. Her research interests include vocational education and training pedagogy, policy and practice; apprenticeship models of skill formation; workplace learning, patterns of adult participation and socioeconomic change; and qualifications. Among Alison's many publications is the recent edited collection, *Workplace learning in context* (2004, Routledge).

Suzanne Greenwald is a Fellow of SKOPE and the Educational Advisor for the Cambridge-MIT Institute at MIT. Her research interests include school-to-work transitions; higher education; experiential learning; and comparative educational policy.

Geoff Hayward is the Associate Director of the ESRC Research Centre on Skills, Knowledge and Organisational Performance (SKOPE) based at the Universities of Oxford and Warwick, and a Lecturer in Educational Studies at the University of Oxford. His research includes work on vocational education and training; workplace learning; education–work transitions; the changing role of higher education; and basic skills.

Guy Haug is an expert on higher education policies in a European and international setting. He started researching the issue of employability as a driving force of higher education reforms when he served as Principal Advisor to the European University Association (EUA) and was instrumental in shaping the move towards the European Higher Education Area (now known as the Bologna Process). He published a lot on various aspects of this process at the institutional, national and European level. He works currently as an adviser on higher education issues to the European Commission in Brussels. The views expressed in his chapter of this book are, however, only his own.

Susan James is a Research Officer at SKOPE, Department of Educational Studies, University of Oxford. Her areas of research interest include Vocational Education and Training (VET); VET systems; work-based learning; on-the-job and off-the-job training; school-to-work transitions; and theories of learning.

Ewart Keep is Deputy Director of SKOPE based at the Warwick Business School, University of Warwick. His research interests include national education and training policy; the impact of skills on organisational performance; the learning society and learning organisation; and personnel management within the education system.

Jonathan Payne is a Research Fellow of SKOPE based at the Warwick Business School, University of Warwick. His areas of research interest include social partnership; contemporary industrial relations; education, schooling and economic performance; the political economy of skill; and education and training in Norway.

Denis Rochat is a member of the THEMA Research Centre at the University of Cergy-Pontoise (France). His areas of research include education, transportation and marketing research.

Geoff Stanton is a Visiting Fellow at the University of Greenwich School of Education and Training, and also works as an independent educational consultant. He writes on the development and management of the further education curriculum and qualifications.

Lorna Unwin is a Fellow of SKOPE, and Professor of Vocational Education and Head of Department of the Centre for Labour Market Studies at the University of Leicester. Her areas of research interest are vocational education and training policy; adult education; the political economy of education; and workplace learning. Recent books include: *Working to learn: Transforming workplace learning* (2002, Kogan Page); *Teaching and learning in further education* (2002, Routledge); and *Young people's perspectives on education, training and employment* (2001, Kogan Page).

ONE

Producing skills: conundrums and possibilities

Geoff Hayward and Susan James

> Many believe that the workplace has changed dramatically in response to a new competitive business environment that is marked by flexibility, fast response time, and managerial and technological innovations. This new workplace is thought to require workers with higher and more varied skills, particularly general skills such as problem solving; unfortunately, schools are not perceived to be producing students who have such skills. The result, it is commonly argued, is a 'skills' gap that threatens ... productivity and competitiveness. (Stasz et al, 1996, p 2)

At the turn of the 21st century, education and training continues to be a major focus of public policy across practically all countries. However, such policy is now couched in terms that ring with evangelical zeal – a new 'educational gospel' (Lazerson and Grubb, 2004) – which espouses the importance of education and training to meet the skill demands of the 21st-century workplace while simultaneously curing a myriad of social ills. Thus, the gospel advocates the importance of more years of formal education, followed by an individual commitment to lifelong learning, as the means to achieve the twin aims of economic growth and social inclusion. This book critically examines the assumptions underpinning this 'educational gospel' from a variety of different perspectives.

In some countries, such as the UK and the US, the policy concern – economic growth and social inclusion – is underpinned by a sense of long-term crisis (see Chapter Four of this volume). In others, such as the Nordic countries, a rather more sober approach nonetheless involves a serious questioning of the purposes and arrangements being made for young people. In yet others, such as Germany, a long-cherished set of traditions, such as the dual system, which have apparently served the long-term economic interests of the country well, are being questioned (see Chapter Seven of this volume), while a sense that all was not well with the German general education system had been fostered by the PISA study (OECD, 2001). Furthermore, the concerns spanned the whole gamut of the education and training system from pre-school education through to higher education

(HE), although here we have focused on Vocational Education and Training (VET), and HE as it becomes increasingly integrated within VET systems.

In recent years, government policy across the world has focused on improving the skills of the workforce as a key strategy for improving national competitiveness. The perceived need to improve national competitiveness is in response to a number of challenges, as highlighted by Fuller and Unwin (2003):

- the linking of education and training to economic performance and the perceived need to up-skill the workforce (see, for example, Keep and Mayhew, 1988; Finegold and Soskice, 1990, 1998; Wolf, 2002);
- globalisation and competitive performance (Brown et al, 2001);
- the changing nature of national economies;
- increasing demand for a multi-skilled and knowledgeable workforce, emphasised by the status placed on gaining qualifications considered by society at large to be necessary to be successful at work and in life;
- encouraging more young people to stay in full-time education to higher levels; and
- coping with persistent problems of social exclusion.

The underlying theme of these challenges is the perceived need for reform from governments throughout the western world, as highlighted by the international authorship of this volume. However, recognising a need is one thing; changing systems to meet that need is quite another. The need for reform is usually articulated within a policy discourse that emphasises the need to bring national education and training systems and the labour market into closer alignment. It is this coupling that we refer to as the two sides of the skills equation: supply and demand. Typically, the policy rhetoric surrounding the reform process speaks of the need to prioritise employer demands in order to rebalance the skills equation. This is to be achieved through almost continual reform of the supply side, in order to make the training on offer more responsive to the perceived needs of employers.

Yet the 20th century was the century of educational expansion. The 'educational gospel' has been one of mass schooling and more education for all. Such expansion has been financed primarily through general taxation, with the justification for this expenditure from the public purse being that the skills and knowledge learnt in schools, colleges and universities would transfer to productive activities outside of educational institutions, especially the workplace. Increasingly, policy makers seem to be questioning whether this is happening, or happening to a sufficient extent to warrant the continued expenditure on general education for all. The upshot, so the argument goes, has been a turn to vocationalism, the over-promotion of the work-related learning aims of secondary and tertiary education at the expense of the civic, aesthetic and moral purposes of education.

In this book, the UK is taken as the paradigmatic case of this trend. Such developments are typically traced to the Ruskin College speech given by the then Prime Minister James Callaghan in 1976. However, vocationalism is much older than this. Indeed, Ryan (2003, p 147) argues convincingly that:

> [t]he past century can be termed the century of vocationalism, an era in which the expansion and vocationalisation of school-based education went hand in hand.

Thus, in the UK, the idea of the vocationalist imperative can be traced at least from the Samuelson Commission on Technical Instruction (1882-84) to the present day. In France, there was "a reconstruction of vocational preparation, not around apprenticeship, which had sustained it until the 18th century, but around full-time schooling with vocationally-oriented curricula", while in the US Lazerson and Grubb argue that "the development of vocational purposes in schooling led to its expansion – in that enrolment growth occurred only after vocationalisation had increased, with the upgrading of occupational goals relative to civic and moral ones" (Ryan, 2003, p 147). Such a long history speaks to an enduring set of problems in political economy that policy makers have been trying to solve, apparently with only a modicum of success, for well over a hundred years.

Education and training policy is also seen as the key lever through which to redress distributional imbalances. In the new politics of learning, the poor are supposed to learn their way out of poverty, with training seen as the primary means of alleviating economic distress and enhancing 'employability' skills. Lafer (2002, p 2)[1] provides the following as a summary of this policy perspective in the US:

> The consensus behind training as a solution to economic distress is captured in a New York Times editorial issued as a call to action during the 1992 presidential campaign. After noting the dramatic increase in income inequality over the course of the 1980s, the Times offers the following analysis:
>
> Economists are increasingly persuaded that this rising inequality cannot be explained by something as simple as greed [or] politics. They look to something more deeply ingrained in modern industrialized economies – call it technology for short. The days when high school dropouts could earn high wages in manufacturing are gone. Modern economies more than ever require skilled, educated labor. The modern industrial economy is calling out for skilled, educated workers. The right way for Congress to respond is to promote the education of sophisticated workers. That means massive new commitments to … training high school dropouts and welfare mothers.

The picture that emerges from the analyses presented in this book is one where the gaze of the reformer is increasingly firmly focused on the supply side of the skills equation. This is a position that is particularly pronounced in the context of the UK, and is one of the reasons why we have used so many authors from England (Stanton and Bailey, Keep and Payne, Fernández and Hayward, Fuller and Unwin, James and Hayward). These authors' chapters provide a central theme running through the book about attempts to reform the supply side of the skills equation via state steering. The other chapters of this volume then provide counterweights to this vision of reform, but also illustrate the ways in which, and the extent to which, there is convergence on a view that is conventional wisdom among education and training policy makers in the UK: that within economies, skill demand exceeds supply. As a result, the story goes, economies underperform in terms of labour productivity, thereby thwarting various versions of the high skills vision and a fairer society. According to this way of 'framing and naming' the issue (Keep and Mayhew, 1999), the solution to economic underperformance is to increase the supply of skills into the economy.

While ignoring the demand side, this ideological commitment to reform of the supply side of the skills equation seems to be growing. Increasingly, intervening on the supply side through education and training policy has become almost the only socially and politically acceptable way for government policy to be used to raise the economic competitiveness of organisations. The result is a sidelining of other issues such as "competitive strategies, labour market regulation, work organisation, job design, and the quality of working life" (Keep, 2002, p 458) as being beyond the remit of public policy.

The chapters in this book flesh out this vision in the English context and also provide an insight into the extent to which it is growing in other countries as they strive to deal with the perceived challenges of globalisation. However, the policy discourses, whether about the need for more and better training to improve aggregate economic performance, or for special provision to re-engage the socially excluded, rarely recognises the complexity of realigning the two sides of the skills equation. Figure 1.1 attempts to sketch the nature of the complexity that reform processes need to take account of.

At one pole, we have steering by demand from the labour market: actors, acting rationally, are supposed to pick up signals from the labour market about the sorts of skills they will need to maximise their wages and maintain their employability. They then invest in education and training in order to do this. At the same time, employers are supposed to identify the skills they need to maintain profitability and invest in their production. However, as is well known, this steering mechanism runs the risk of market failure, resulting in a less than socially desirable investment in skills both by employers and by individual workers. Correcting such market failure is the usual justification for state intervention. This may take a number of forms, including direct subsidies to support training, the provision of state-sponsored VET programmes, and reforms to the qualification system. Typically, this is steering at a distance and may take place within more or less well-regulated training systems. In the UK, for example, such steering takes place within a climate of extreme voluntarism, with history suggesting that employers will react negatively to any attempts to regulate the training market by the introduction of, for example, licences to

Figure 1.1: The complexity of reform

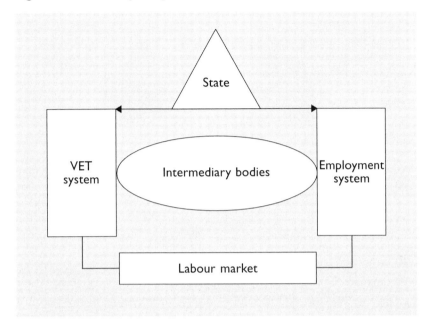

practice or requirements to train to minimum standards. France, by contrast, has a much more state controlled VET system (see Chapter Two of this volume). Thus the wider political, social and economic culture of a country affects the way VET reform is enacted within that country (Brown et al, 2001).

A third steering mechanism involves a collaborative model based around strong local associations between social partners. In the strongest model of this type, Germany, the state supports an arena in which the social partners decide on the nature of occupations and the training needed to join them. This model is now coming under attack as being too inflexible (see Chapter Seven of this volume).

Thus there seem to be problems with all three steering mechanisms sketched in Figure 1.1, and the chapters in this book speak to the complexity of drawing the two sides of the skills equation together in a number of different nations and across regions. Geoff Stanton and Bill Bailey (Chapter Two of this volume) place in context the many policy initiatives and changes that have occurred over the last 60 years in English VET, and also pave the way for the three chapters that follow. These authors, by guiding us through various attempts at state steering of the VET system, through the many schemes introduced in VET from the 1960s onwards, such as Unified Vocational Preparation (UVP), Youth Opportunities Programme (YOP) and the successor Youth Training Scheme (YTS), and the Technical and Vocational Education (TVE), lay out the foundations for the current qualification system of English VET: the competence-based National Vocational Qualifications (NVQs). Juxtaposed with the many VET changes, the academic route is described. The juxtaposition of the academic and VET routes leads Stanton and Bailey to question whether there has ever been a VET policy or simply a series of initiatives. Drawing from this hypothesis, these authors propose that there are a number of lessons to be learnt from the last 60 years of VET, and conclude by outlining their view of these lessons: the need for a regulatory framework and the development of attractive VET learning programmes that offer meaningful progression routes within occupations.

Jean-Luc De Meulemeester and Denis Rochat (Chapter Three of this volume) critically review the slew of recent documents regarding education and training reform in the EU, beginning with Articles 126 and 127 from the Maastricht Treaty. Their analysis starts by examining how EU experts 'frame and name' the policy problem. This is along the lines set out earlier in this chapter: a lack of competitiveness, which is a result of inflexible labour markets and an inadequate education and training system. They then proceed to dissect the assumptions underpinning this way of constructing the policy problem and how this leads to a variety of policy aims and objectives which involve substantially dismantling existing cultures of learning in order to realign them with the politics of learning set out in the official EU policy discourse. There then follows a critical assessment of the policy claims and their underpinning assumptions. The authors critique the diagnosis of the problem as being too superficial, question whether there is a real problem with the supply of human capital in the EU and bemoan the neglect of the demand side of the skills equation. They point out the extent to which the policy suggestions overstate the benefits of a narrower approach to VET, exaggerate the ability of individuals to construct their own curriculum and ignore the key role of teachers in education. They also consider whether Europe is the right decision-making unit in a globalised economy. They conclude that:

> The policy that the EU experts would like to see implemented is the corollary
> of their philosophical views regarding the optimal organisation of society.
> They are partisans of a free-trade and laissez-faire economy. (p 49)

This chapter reveals, therefore, the important role of ideology in constructing a new vision for VET in Europe.

A key term worldwide in debates about education and training reform, one that has almost totemic status, is 'skill'. Ewart Keep and Jonathan Payne (Chapter Four of this volume) discuss the changing meaning of skill in the UK policy context. These authors provide an overall picture of how the meaning of skill has changed in the last 20 years or so to encapsulate a definition that seems to mean all things to all stakeholders: government, employers and individuals. The authors argue that the prime place to develop the type of skill employers and governments are really talking about remains the workplace, and that the appropriation of 'skill' to cover a wide variety of meanings and to encompass a wide variety of attributes, is not only deceptive but precludes a much-needed debate regarding the responsibilities of skill development.

Rosa Fernández and Geoff Hayward (Chapter Five of this volume) take up the theme of skill, the qualification of skill and its supply and demand. The idea of skill typically gets finessed or operationalised into qualifications in policy discourse so that increasing the skill supply into the economy becomes equated with increasing the qualification supply. Using administrative data and nationally representative skill surveys, they conclude that government policy in England over the last 25 years has been successful in increasing the supply of qualifications but that this has led to overqualification of the workforce at intermediate skill levels. The implications of this for wages are then examined. Finally, they turn to the idea of the education system as being a site where generic skills can be developed and certificated. Their analysis suggests that this policy has largely been a failure because it has failed to take account of the wider economic incentive structures set up in the education system by the same policies that have resulted in an increase in qualification supply.

The two chapters that follow are concerned with the development of thinking about apprenticeship. In the first, Alison Fuller and Lorna Unwin (Chapter Six of this volume) present a concise and succinct overview of the development of apprenticeship in the UK through state-steering mechanisms in order to place in context Modern Apprenticeship (MA) schemes that developed after 1994. The state-steering mechanisms have meant that apprenticeship in the UK now has to bear additional aims and responsibilities, most notably those relating to social inclusion, in addition to those of producing a more skilled workforce. Furthermore, Fuller and Unwin demonstrate how the perverse incentive structures set up by the state-led approach to developing apprenticeship have led to poor participation and completion rates for young people entering the work-based learning route. Using examples from research in the banking and engineering sectors, these authors demonstrate the need for a flexible approach to the training of Modern Apprentices (MAs), particularly Advanced Modern Apprentices (AMAs), in order to produce quality learning outcomes. From the case studies provided, issues and challenges with regard to participation and provision are elucidated. Fuller and Unwin propose a number of challenges facing policy makers currently, and conclude that the wide variation of quality with regard to provision is hindering the growth and success of the MA programme.

The second chapter on apprenticeship by Hubert Ertl (Chapter Seven of this volume) focuses on the very different context of the German dual system but picks up on the idea of flexibility developed in Fuller and Unwin's chapter. The German system remains highly regarded both in the UK and overseas, but rarely has discussion of its inadequacies come to the fore; this is what this chapter seeks to do in the first instance. Ertl discusses the current debate surrounding the German dual system, and highlights the need for reform if the system is to meet the economic demands of the 21st century. He highlights the consensus of the relevant stakeholders of a concern for the need for modernisation of the system in order to increase its flexibility through the introduction of modularisation, and to speed up the process of reform. His argument is couched against a discussion of the system's underlying principles, and the perceived need for reform with some examples. Ertl puts forward three conceptualisations of conceivable types of modular structures for the German system of initial training, and concludes by giving his perceptions as to why the reform initiatives have been limited in their success but highlights one reform – areas of learning (*lernfelder*) – that promises to be successful in achieving the desired outcomes of all the stakeholders. Ertl's chapter also picks up another theme that runs through this book: the potential clash between the politics of learning – that is, how learning is articulated within political discourse – and the cultures of learning that are embedded in valued social practices and workplace cultures. This is epitomised by the rejection of modularity as a reform mechanism by those who place great value on the holistic nature of the German approach to apprenticeship.

Stephen Billett (Chapter Eight of this volume) completes our journey to the workplace. Drawing on over a decade of research on workplace learning, Billett provides a convincing argument about the need to legitimate workplaces as learning environments on their own terms. In so doing, he again picks up on this theme of the potential clash between the politics and cultures of learning. Thus, his analysis speaks against the current trend in policy discourse that conceptualises learning as the responsibility of individuals, and relocates that responsibility in a broader social sphere. Furthermore, his chapter is a celebration of the cultures of learning embedded in the ongoing social practices of work. Understanding this culture, and the social practices that constitute it, from the ground up, is essential if reform of VET is going to be successful, yet so much public policy seems to ignore this fact by emphasising the pragmatic purposes of learning at work rather than its pedagogic possibilities. Billett's chapter concludes with a helpful checklist of actions to be taken by different actors to foster high-quality learning at work.

An overarching message that Billett's recommendations send to us is the need for the different actors who share responsibility for promoting lifelong learning to collaborate with each other. Suzanne Greenwald (Chapter Nine of this volume) picks up on this theme by examining the costs and benefits of education–business partnership arrangements. Another leitmotif of the reform of education and training over the last century has been the belief among policy makers that business has a vital role to play in the reform of education systems. What this role might be emerges from Greenwald's comparative analysis of education–business partnerships in the US and the UK. She first traces out the history of fluctuating corporate involvement in education and then develops a typology of different partnerships. She documents the process of policy borrowing and imitation through which the UK took on many of the models of partnership developed in the US. The chapter then explores the twin themes of isolationism and exploitation that emerged from her analysis of surveys of school principals, head teachers, teachers and students in the US and the UK, before turning to provide an employer's perspective. This chapter captures, therefore, both sides of the skills equation: supply and demand. Her conclusions echo the level of uncertainty about the purpose and form of such partnerships revealed by her research, and raise the important issue of the role of business in paying for education and training.

Higher education (HE) has neither been immune to the increasing vocationalisation of education systems nor from the reforming zeal of public policy makers. Thus, two more chapters of this volume examine how this is playing out at the European level. First, Guy Haug (Chapter Ten) runs us through the intended process of reform of European HE, from the Sorbonne Declaration in 1998 via the Bologna Declaration, to its most recent review in Berlin in 2003. On first reading, the most striking feature of the so-called Bologna process is the sheer scale of the ambition of the proposed reforms: "the creation of a coherent, compatible and competitive European higher education area by the year 2010" (p 187) across 40 countries. The second is the extent to which these reforms are driven by the same basic set of concerns that underpin the reform of other parts of the VET system, for example, the employability and skills agenda in a developing European labour market with HE policy agendas being "less and less autonomous, and more and more driven by employment aspects" (p 190). In addition, there is recognition of HE itself as a commodity that needs to be sold in a global marketplace. All of this is revealed in Haug's comprehensive review of the underpinning aims of the Bologna process, and the needs that the process seeks to address. He then turns to consider progress to date, which focuses heavily on the reform of qualification systems, in particular the development of a more uniform two-tier Bachelor–Master degree structure of a standard size and length. It is clear that there is a growing acceptance of the need for these reforms and the main instruments chosen to pursue them. The chapter also provides a detailed insight into how the issue of employability in relation to higher education is being pursued in different countries. However, the chapter does conclude with an implicit question: to what extent are we seeing, despite all of this activity, convergent strands of action? In addition, there is the question of how to involve employers; that is, the demand side of the skills equation, more fully in this essentially supply-side reform.

Cécile Deer (Chapter Eleven of this volume) acts as a counterweight to Guy Haug, in that she questions the necessity of expansion of HE, which is an implicit assumption in the Bologna process. Deer first charts the history of the expansion of HE and distinguishes between different modalities of expansion. This provides a multiple set of lenses, from geographical ones through to pedagogical ones, with which to explore the expansionary process. She next turns to consider the economic rationale given for the expansion of HE, which leads to a consideration of the costs and benefits of investing in HE couched in human capital theory terms. Deer then turns to a more sociological consideration of expansion in terms of the selecting and screening functions and education's potential to promote meritocratic social mobility. This analysis,

Deer argues, suggests a loosening of the ties between academic titles and their traditionally associated social status. This calls into question the "certifying effect of university diplomas as the number of candidates joining the employment market outstrips the number of graduate jobs available" (pp 210-11). This point echoes the analysis presented in Chapter Five of this volume by Fernández and Hayward, and one which at least calls into question the employability argument that underpins the Bologna process described by Haug. Deer concludes by examining the complexity of the logic of HE expansion and argues that:

> The expansion process has laid bare the fact that what has been at stake in gaining a university experience are the social benefits that such an experience is supposed to confer. (p 214)

In this volume's final chapter, James and Hayward (Chapter Twelve) return to a central theme: the potential conflict between the politics and culture of learning. They ground their reflections in a case study of the learning of apprentice chefs, an occupation with a long tradition of apprenticeship embedded within a particular set of cultural practices, which reform has sought to modify through the introduction of competence-based qualifications located within a new definition of apprenticeship, as described by Fuller and Unwin (Chapter Six of this volume). The authors' reflections focus around the necessary conditions that need to be satisfied if the introduction of outcomes-led qualifications, a common feature in the policy discourse of VET reform, are to be adopted and implemented successfully in existing cultures of learning. Their analysis suggests that a top-down model of qualification development and implementation is unlikely to be successful unless it connects with the values of the key actors in the apprenticeship system. Forging such connections is likely to be a time-consuming business because it involves developing strong networks of social partners to mediate the introduction of new qualifications and render them meaningful inside traditional programmes of learning.

Note

[1] Lafer's critique is not aimed at the idea of providing people with better educational opportunities but rather at the idea that providing a better educated workforce will lead to both increased economic productivity and people to earn a better living in economies with an inadequate supply of decent, well-paid jobs.

References

Brown, P., Green, A. and Lauder, H. (2001) *High skills: Globalization, competitiveness, and skill formation*, Oxford: Oxford University Press.

Finegold, D. and Soskice, D. (1988) 'The failure of training in Britain: analysis and prescription', *Oxford Review of Economic Policy*, vol 4, no 3, pp 21-53.

Finegold, D. and Soskice, D. (1990) 'The failure of training in Britain: analysis and preparation', in D. Gleeson (ed) *Training and its alternatives*, Milton Keynes: Open University Press, pp 18-57.

Fuller, A. and Unwin, L. (2003) 'Fostering workplace learning: looking through the lens of apprenticeship', *European Educational Research Journal*, vol 2, no 1, pp 41-55.

Keep, E. (2002) 'The English vocational education and training policy debate – fragile "technologies" or opening the "black box": two competing visions of where we go next', *Journal of education and Work*, vol 15, no 4, pp 457-79.

Keep, E. and Mayhew, K. (1988) 'The assessment: education, training and economic performance', *Oxford Review of Economic Policy*, vol 4, no 3, pp i-xv.

Keep, E. and Mayhew, K. (1999) 'The assessment: knowledge, skills and competitiveness', *Oxford Review of Economic Policy*, vol 15, no 1, pp 1-15.

Lafer, G. (2002) *The job training charade*, Ithaca, NY: Cornell University Press.

Lazerson, M. and Grubb, W.N. (2004) *The education gospel: The economic power of schooling*, Cambridge, MA: Harvard University Press.

OECD (Organisation for Economic Co-operation and Development) (2001) *Education policy analysis 2001*, Paris: OECD.

Ryan, P. (2003) 'Evaluating vocationalism', *European Journal of Education*, vol 38, no 2, pp 147-62.

Stasz, C., Ramsey, K., Eden, R., Melamid, E. and Kaganoff, T. (1996) *Workplace skills in practice: Case studies of technical work*, Santa Monica, CA: RAND.

Wolf, A. (2002) *Does education matter? Myths about education and economic growth*, London: Penguin.

TWO

Fit for purpose? Sixty years of VET policy in England

Geoff Stanton and Bill Bailey

Introduction

This chapter assesses the aims and content of recent policy for Vocational Education and Training (VET) in England. Since 1945, the period covered here, VET policy has been discontinuous and piecemeal. We have therefore found it easiest to describe it in distinct sections.

Section One deals with a period of some 30-35 years after 1945, during which initial attempts to deliver policy aims by legislating for individual and employer participation were first diluted and then abandoned. Section Two covers a brief period during which government exerted some influence by means of entering into specific contracts for course delivery with VET providers. And Section Three describes a shift to control of VET through the regulation of qualifications.

In the light of these analyses and the overview in Section Four, Section Five identifies a number of assumptions upon which recent policy appears to have been based, but which continue to receive little if any scrutiny. Our concluding section briefly examines some current initiatives and considers whether or not they indicate that the right lessons have been learned.

Policy makers do not begin with a clean slate, and a consideration of recent history may help clarify the context in which policy makers are framing their proposals for the 'modernising' of VET for the 21st century. Also, a failure to take account of comparatively recent experience can lead to the repetition of avoidable mistakes, a failure to achieve intended purposes and unwanted but predictable outcomes.

Section One: The coming and going of legislation

The dominant characteristic of English VET, in contrast with that in many other industrialised economies, is that it is voluntary. There is no legal compulsion on employers to provide or support training for their employees, or (in most cases) on employees to have a vocational qualification; that is, a licence to practise their trade. This principle of voluntarism, an aspect of a wider laissez-faire approach to economic policy, has not been unchallenged. Critics have contrasted the lack of a clear and focused VET policy in England with the developed and mandatory systems of VET found in competitor economies like France and Germany.

Post-war ambitions

It is often overlooked that the British parliament twice legislated for a compulsory system of post-school education and training – in the Education Acts passed at the end of the First and Second World Wars. The failure to implement these acts reveals much about English attitudes towards the training of young workers and to vocational education in general. The Education Act of 1944 provided for compulsory day-release for all young workers from the ages of 15 to 18 in County Colleges, the development of vocational education in technical colleges and of adult education in community colleges. In 'Educational Reconstruction', the White Paper of 1943, the principles of post-school education were elaborated. The County Colleges (the successors of the Day Continuation Schools of the 1918 Education Act) were to be the foundations of post-war policy by providing continuing general education and civic and vocational training for young workers aged 15-18. Compulsory attendance at the County College was to be the means for better preparation of young workers for adult and working life and the encouragement for later involvement in technical studies and adult classes (Ministry of Education, 1943). Pre-war technical education had been very much a 'night school' affair for a minority of workers, many of who failed to complete their studies. Compulsory release from employment, for one day per week, was seen as a more efficient mode of study for all young people.

The shift from predominantly evening to daytime attendance at the new County Colleges would, it was thought, stimulate demand for advanced vocational courses at technical colleges which were also to become the focal points of local community education. This was an ambitious and generous scheme of post-school education and training with the potential to form the framework of a comprehensive and coherent provision. Its principles were worked through in Ministry of Education pamphlets to the local education authorities (LEAs) in the immediate post-war years. The most important of these were *Youth's opportunity* (1946) and *Further education* (1947), addressed to the LEAs to guide them in the preparation of their schemes for further education (FE) in their areas.

The effect of economic pressures

The LEAs submitted their plans to the ministry for approval during the next few years but none was approved and implemented. The Labour government was faced with the task of post-war reconstruction, and financial difficulties affected all educational plans. Priority was given to rebuilding schools and to the raising of the school-leaving age to 15. Developments in FE were restricted to those directly related to key industrial occupations. This approach was continued by the incoming Conservative government of 1951, which restricted FE building proposals to "the more essential industries, not … courses such as commerce, art or printing" (Ministry of Education, 1952a, p 3). These decisions meant, of course, that the momentum for a comprehensive and compulsory provision of post-school education was lost and that technical colleges were left to 'make do' in old premises. In many cases, they accommodated increased student numbers in often unsuitable buildings like former elementary schools vacated as part of the development of secondary schooling. Inevitably, this meant that the provision of technical education was patchy and variable between LEA areas. While more employers voluntarily allowed young employees to attend classes during the day, and this did lead to increased student numbers, there was no entitlement to further education for young people.

In short, the failure to implement wartime plans had left post-school vocational education largely in the same position as it had been before the war; dependent on the voluntary collaboration of both employers and the individual. We trace the importance of this later in this section.

The re-emergence of post-school policy

When government policy turned to post-compulsory education in the mid-1950s, it was not to the LEA schemes and the comprehensive plans of the immediate post-war years but to a more limited and narrow purpose. This was shown in debates about manpower and foreign competition and in particular a concern about the inadequate supply of technologists, which had been addressed in the Percy Report (1945) but not acted upon. Doubts about the building of County Colleges and the preference for encouraging increased voluntary day-release were strengthened by unfavourable comparisons with the US and USSR whose use of technologists was perceived to be critical in their industrial advance. David Eccles, Minister of Education, signalled the new policy in 1952 in a circular to LEAs when he stated the government's intention to develop advanced technical education in a number of the larger technical colleges through the introduction of a higher level of grant for advanced courses in technology (Ministry of Education, 1952b). Four years later the *Technical education* White Paper confirmed this adjustment of priorities with the designation of eight (later ten) major technical colleges as Colleges of Advanced Technology whose role would be to increase the supply of technologists to the economy. While other sections of the White Paper referred to other types of college and the need for technical education to include some liberal study, its strongest sections – and its subsequent importance – related to its argument for advanced technical education and the legitimisation of university level courses outside universities (Ministry of Education, 1956). The use of some colleges to supplement the supply of higher education (HE) places in industry-related courses was seen to be necessary for economic development and competitiveness. This marked a modification of the higher ideals of 1944 and the adoption of a priority within a more pragmatic and limited approach to technical education.

Also, in retrospect, this in turn implied the demise of the aim of compulsory day-release for all young workers. Increasing rates of voluntary release for technical courses by employers was now seen as the way forward – paralleled by an increased number staying on at school after age 15. Government was reminded of its duty to implement the County Colleges proposals by the Central Advisory Council's report *15-18* (Crowther Report) in 1959; but, significantly, the Committee gave first priority to raising the school-leaving age to 16. This was eventually implemented in 1972, more than a quarter of a century after the end of the Second World War, by which time economic conditions were much changed.

From the mid-1950s onwards, public policy with regard to VET was then piecemeal and reactive to current needs and crises. The vision of a place for all in a young people's college is replaced by instrumental measures to align VET arrangements and provision more directly with perceived economic and manpower needs. This is shown in the White Paper, *Better opportunities in technical education* (1961), which proposed what it called "a major reconstruction" (p 3) of the system of courses for technicians, craftsmen (sic) and operatives. This was followed in 1964 by the Industrial Training Act. Similarly based on the view that the quality and the quantity of training was inadequate for increasingly competitive markets, this measure reflected the demands of larger companies who complained that employees trained by them were being 'poached' by smaller companies at the end of their training. The Industrial Training Boards (ITBs) established for some industries under the act were charged with providing sufficient training for their sectors and ensuring that the costs of training were shared fairly among companies. This aim was to be achieved by the imposition on all firms in an ITB sector of a levy, which was repayable only to those firms providing satisfactory training. By 1970, 30 ITBs were in operation with best progress being made in those industries such as engineering, which had strong records of training. Interesting not only for their legal power to require employers to pay the training levy but also for their composition, representing the two 'sides' of industry, the ITBs even at the height of their influence did not cover all sectors of employment. In the absence of a past record of planning and consultation, it took time for some industries to set up their ITB. These delays reflected also the opposition of many small employers to the principles, the levy and the bureaucracy of the ITBs. This opposition was influential upon the Conservative government elected in 1970, which was committed to cutting back the role and activities of the ITBs. This it did in 1973 with the passing of the Employment and Training Act. Thus, with a few exceptions, the ITBs were wound up, and the short period, when in the industrial sectors affected there was a 'partnership' of the two sides of industry on bodies with the legal power to require employers to pay for training, came to an end.

The 1973 Act also set up the Manpower Services Commission (MSC) within the Department of Employment. Heralded at the time as a major national body with the responsibility for modernising employment and training arrangements, the MSC was composed of representatives of employers and employees (the CBI and TUC), with one FE member. Modelled on the Swedish Labour Board, the MSC's first important publication was *Towards a comprehensive manpower policy* (1976). Despite the ambitions reflected in its title, the MSC – as we shall see later in this chapter – soon became preoccupied with shorter-term measures required to address escalating youth unemployment, and the longer-term unemployment of adults.

The three post-war decades, therefore, had seen public policy for VET retreat from a determination to implement the comprehensive plans of the 1940s. Instead, when initiatives and changes were thought necessary they were selective and reactive and not consistently seen through, as in the case of the ITBs. While in the case of some employers in some industries there were some examples of good practice, based on the recognition of the necessity for training, the national record was patchy and admitted to be inadequate. Importantly, there had been no movement towards the need for skilled workers to have a 'licence to practise' their trades or a legal requirement or entitlement for them to receive training. Nor were employers legally obliged to support financially the training of their workforce. Finally, the MSC became more associated with remedial measures of various kinds than with the positive and planned development of a skilled workforce.

The impact on colleges

These policy failures had important implications for the public sector providers of VET: the technical colleges. They had been left without a clear role and purpose with regard to VET not only by benign neglect in official policy but also, during the 1970s, by the decline in the old industries which had traditionally provided students for vocational courses. The lack of a clear role for the colleges was evident in the White Paper, *A plan for polytechnics and other colleges* (DES, 1966). After the decision to raise the Colleges of Advanced Technology (CATS) to university status following the Robbins Report, the Labour government decided that major technical colleges would again be designated for a role in the provision of HE and this was carried through with the creation of the 30 'new polytechnics'. There was, however, no 'plan' for the other colleges which, in the absence of an official statement of an unambiguous VET or other role, were diversifying into other areas of post-school provision, driven by their view of local needs and markets. As a result, 'technical colleges' also began to prepare young people who had not succeeded in school (or otherwise wished to leave) for GCE O-level and A-level examinations, to prepare older students for HE and in some cases contribute to the teaching of HE programmes and to offer practical and other adult education classes. During the 1970s, new starts were made in provision for 16 year olds and adults with special educational needs, and in the form of vocational preparation schemes for school-leavers unable to obtain employment in the less buoyant youth labour market of the 1970s (see Section Two of this chapter).

While these developments raised the profile of the local colleges as providers for more groups within their communities, and could be justified as the college fulfilling social purposes by meeting demands unmet by other institutions, it necessarily involved a reduction of their vocational focus. This was often reflected by a change of name by the colleges: from technical college to College of Further Education, and later to, simply, college (Bailey, 2002).

Section Two: UVP, YOP, TOPS and TVEI: a curriculum-led interlude

In the mid-1970s, the newly formed MSC became a vehicle for another kind of control. In 1976 the government launched a pilot scheme of Unified Vocational Preparation (UVP) (DES/DoE, 1976). This was aimed at those young people who entered the labour market at age 16 but then received little in the way of FE or systematic training. They also tended to be those who had done least well at school, and by some estimates formed at least 40% of the school-leaving population.

The scheme was jointly sponsored by the MSC and the Department of Education and Science (DES). This was partly because one of the scheme's principles was that education and training elements should be inseparably combined, partly because the MSC, unlike the DES, was able to directly fund the provision. By law the DES could fund education only through its contribution to the general budget of local authorities. Local decisions then determined, first, how much of this allocation found its way into the local education budget, and, second, how much of that was spent on any particular form of provision. This militated against schemes that were of low status and aimed at learners who needed new forms of provision.

Although UVP was a small and short-lived scheme (at its peak in the early 1980s it had only 1,400 participants per annum from 550 companies), it had a number of features that either became more significant later or that make an interesting contrast with later developments:

1. As well as being able to directly contract with colleges, the MSC was also able to fund institutions that were not part of the education system as such. The single largest provider of UVP schemes was the Distributive Industries Training Board, and the YMCA also mounted some innovative schemes. In providing a mechanism for funding such agencies, this laid the foundation for the promotion of a 'market' in VET a decade later.
2. The learning programme for each scheme was locally designed, and funded against financial estimates submitted by its designers. The whole scheme was systematically evaluated by the National Foundation for Educational Research (NFER) (Wray et al, 1980) and supported by staff and curriculum

development (FEU, 1979a)[1]. The focus was on challenging and attractive methods of teaching and learning, usually not leading to a formal qualification. In these respects, UVP was similar to the later and much larger and more comprehensive Technical and Vocational Education Initiative (TVEI), launched in 1982, and in sharp contrast to the approaches adopted when the National Curriculum and National Vocational Qualifications (NVQs) were introduced later in the decade (Pring, 1994).

3. Finally, the scheme aimed simultaneously to develop the young person's confidence, an understanding of themselves, employment and their society, and to improve their educational and vocational skills. This integrated approach did not survive the introduction of the National Curriculum and NVQs: the former was built around conventional academic subjects and the latter concentrated on assessing workplace competence.

The Technical and Vocational Education Initiative (TVEI) was announced in November 1982 by Prime Minister Margaret Thatcher. In the words of the MSCs operating manual, TVEI was intended as:

> a pilot scheme; within the education system; for young people of both sexes; across the ability range; voluntary. Each project must provide a full-time programme; offer a progressive four-year course combining general with technical and vocational education; commence at 14 years; be broadly based; include planned work experience; lead to nationally recognised qualifications. (MSC, 1984, quoted in Dale, 1990, p 13)

Despite initial resistance from teachers and LEAs, on the grounds that TVEI represented an undesirable shift towards both centralisation and what came to be called 'vocationalism', many schemes were submitted and implemented. In September 1983, 14 pilot schemes were operational. By September 1987 the scheme had been extended with the aim of involving all secondary schools in the country and their linked FE colleges.

While one reason for LEA participation was undoubtedly financial, it also became apparent that those responsible were prepared to support innovation of various kinds as long as it was well planned. Many teachers called on their experience of UVP and of new schemes created for full-time students wishing to stay on post-school for another year, such as the City and Guilds Foundation Course, the RSA Vocational Preparation Course and the regionally operated Certificate in Further Education. The Further Education Unit (FEU) drew on the experience of these and other college-designed courses to produce the curriculum design that later formed the basis for the Certificate of Pre-Vocational Education (FEU, 1979b). In discussing these developments, Richard Pring (1994, p 65) has said:

> within the curriculum thinking exemplified by TVEI and other pre-vocational developments, there are the seeds of a defensible educational philosophy which

bridges the academic/vocational divide – by liberalising the vocational track and vocationalising the liberal one, without betraying the best that is within each.

The reason that it was possible for teachers to 'rescue' (in their terms) TVEI was that the model of development it used was one in which, although the centre specified what aims it wanted achieved, it allowed local consortia, usually involving both schools and colleges, to propose the best method of doing this in their context. Accountability to the centre was strong: detailed contracts were drawn up with the MSC and progress towards their implementation was reviewed every six months before the next payment was made. Proposals had to include planned staff and institutional development in support of the intended curriculum change. However, the contract was against locally defined objectives and methods, and those at the centre had the wisdom not to prescribe these too closely or uniformly.

Unified Vocational Preparation was aimed at young employees, and TVEI at full-time students, but the rapid rise in youth unemployment in the late 1970s necessitated the creation of the Youth Opportunities Programme (YOP), also managed and funded through the MSC. The MSC also established equivalent programmes for the older employed, such as the Training Opportunities Programme (TOP). The need to cope with rising unemployment distracted the MSC from any attempt to develop and implement a national manpower strategy, and also prevented the expansion of the UVP scheme.

Section Three: The era of assessment, qualifications and institutional reform

NCVQ and NVQs

What UVP, YOP and TVEI all had in common was an emphasis on innovative learning programmes aimed at reaching potentially reluctant learners, and the absence of any specially designed qualifications for those taking the programmes. The advent of NVQs was seen as a means of filling this qualifications gap. Also, NVQs were used as part of a mechanism for funding learning outcomes, instead of the previous approach, which had funded learning programmes. This may not have been altogether intentional but rather the result of the coincidence of a number of factors, including the much greater scale of operation then required and the need to reduce administrative costs.

Thus, the late 1980s marked the end of a curriculum-led phase of development and a decisive shift to the use of qualifications:

- to lead change;
- to hold providers accountable; and
- to trigger funding.

Although at the time TVEI was seen as a radical attempt by central government to interfere in the traditional autonomy of teachers, schools and LEAs, with hindsight it was also the last initiative in a tradition that assumed that new ideas would be developed locally, and that the role of the centre was confined to setting aims and seeing that good practice was disseminated. The 1988 Education Act introduced into England a National Curriculum, designed centrally and imposed by law on all state-funded schools. With it came a new assessment regime. Standard Assessment Tests (SATs) were to be taken by all pupils at ages seven, 11 and 14, and GCSEs were to test National Curriculum achievement at age 16. The National Curriculum Council (NCC) was given the responsibility of determining the curriculum content. Its sister body, the Schools Examination and Assessment Council (SEAC), not only designed the SATs but also had the authority to regulate all school qualifications, including A-levels.

The late 1980s can be seen as a watershed period in the control and use of qualifications, since two years before the 1988 Education Act, the National Council for Vocational Qualifications (NCVQ) had been set up. In origin this had nothing to do with training schemes for the unemployed, or with the funding and regulation of VET providers. However, it came to be very closely associated with both.

NCVQ was proposed by the earlier Review of Vocational Qualifications (MSC/DES, 1986) that concluded that existing vocational qualifications were confusing, too diverse and variable in quality. Therefore, it proposed that a framework be created into which qualifications would be admitted once they satisfied certain criteria. The framework would offer some quality assurance, and would show how qualifications related one to another. One of the criteria that qualifications would have to meet was that of relevance to the needs of employment, and in order to inform this the Standards Programme was established by the Department of Employment. This was tasked to define what it meant to be competent in specific occupational roles, and to do this in terms of performance required rather than of courses passed.

It is now often forgotten that: (a) 'NVQ' was intended to refer to a framework not a qualification; (b) that all vocational qualifications, taken on both full- and part-time routes, were intended eventually to fit within the framework; (c) that occupational standards were intended to be only one of several influences on vocational qualifications, and that others were to include the facilitation of progression; and (d) that it was anticipated that existing qualifications should evolve over time to meet the requirements of the framework.

What actually happened was that, in order to be approved by NCVQ, it was decreed that qualifications had to match exactly the newly defined standards and that wherever possible assessment should be via observation of candidates in the workplace. Among other things, this meant that:

- in effect, new and different qualifications had to be designed rather than old ones be adapted;

- vocational qualifications that required evidence of more than workplace competence (for instance evidence of the mathematical achievement required for progression but not for the current job) could not be approved by NCVQ;
- students who chose to take full-time courses, or who could not gain access to a relevant workplace for assessment purposes, could not easily take NVQs; and
- the assessment of NVQs placed new burdens on employers and workplace supervisors.

For all these reasons, most existing vocational qualifications continued alongside a new set of qualifications, which came to be called 'NVQs'. In some sectors, the NVQs remained relatively unused for existing employees. However, they became the required outcome for many of the training schemes developed by the MSC for the increasing number of unemployed.

After the demise of the MSC in 1988, many of these training schemes were managed by local Training and Enterprise Councils (TECs). As their name implies, these employer-led organisations were also responsible for promoting local economic development but, as had happened with the MSC, they too often became preoccupied with schemes for the unemployed. The NVQs became not only the key outcomes for such schemes but were also used as an indicator of quality and as a trigger for funding. Although TECs varied in their funding strategies, some of them linked 100% of provider funding to the achievement of NVQs, and most of them negotiated with training organisations to obtain the lowest possible price for provision. Not only were there no agreed course structures or nationally agreed funding rates, but also it was common for TECs to conceal what they were paying since they were set up as private sector companies and they regarded such information as being commercially sensitive.

In contrast, when the Further Education Funding Council (FEFC), the body set up to fund public-sector colleges, began work in 1993, it established a national and transparent funding methodology. It also created an inspectorate to report on quality of provision. The FEFC inspectorate gave significant weight to student achievement as measured by qualifications – but these did not have to be NVQs. Other factors, such as governance and responsiveness, were also taken into account, and lessons were observed and assessed. For many years, until 1998, there was no inspectorate for publicly funded training taking place outside colleges. The fact that an NVQ was achieved was regarded as sufficient evidence of the scheme's adequacy.

At best the TEC approach was intended to reward efficiency and, by focusing on outcomes, to liberate providers so that they could be flexible and innovative. However, although some providers did produce stimulating competition for more conventional institutions, many of them designed their schemes down to a price, and some, such as the Youth Training Scheme (YTS), gained a negative reputation. At worst, outcome-related funding was favoured because it was administratively more convenient for the TECs to operate, since it removed the need for regular checks on how many trainees were attending the schemes and for how long. Payment was based on a single auditable indicator – the achievement of the qualification.

All this had a damaging effect on the fledgling NVQs. They became linked in the public mind with low-level work, and with low status candidates on inadequate programmes. Also, NVQs were the worst possible type of qualification to be used as part of output-related funding (Stanton, 1996): assessment depended upon the observation of performance by a supervisor or trainer, often a person whose salary depended upon the candidates being deemed to have passed. Not surprisingly, cases of fraud began to emerge[2].

Nor were NVQs well suited to being used as a vehicle for the quality assurance of the learning programme. Indeed, they were deliberately designed to be independent of any particular learning programme. In order to implement NVQs, staff needed a qualification in NVQ assessment methodology; however, there was no requirement for a qualification in teaching or training, nor even in the occupational area being assessed. When eventually the Training Inspectorate began inspections of publicly funded training in 1998, over 40% of providers were found to be inadequate (TSC, 1999).

Since there was no support from a legal framework either for employee entitlement or for licences to practise, NCVQ had to keep employers on board through incentives and through being seen to meet their needs. This produced an expectation of subsidy for NVQs, and an acceptance in some cases of sets of standards because an Industry Lead Body (ILB) produced the standards, not because NCVQ thought them adequate.

The Further Education Funding Council, set up by the Further and Higher Education Act of 1992, considered linking funding to outputs in the form of qualifications, and its consultation paper, 'Funding Learning' (FEFC, 1992), carefully analysed the risks of doing so as well as the potential advantages. As a result, the FEFC funding system made the link only to a limited extent (less than 10% of total funding). The FEFC methodology applied to all college provision, both academic and vocational, but was applied neither to the equivalent academic courses in school sixth forms nor to equivalent vocational provision funded by TECs.

FEFC, the LSC and the new inspectorates

The Further Education Funding Council eschewed any role in the planning of provision. It funded whatever colleges found their local populations wanted to enrol for, or whatever parts of this demand the college found it economical to meet. Nevertheless, the FEFC *was* used as the instrument for some government policies:

- to increase student participation;
- to drive down unit costs;

- to introduce a national funding method with a common level of funding for similar courses in all FE colleges; and
- to move staff onto more flexible contracts of employment.

The FEFC Inspection Framework was also very influential. The headings under which reports were made affected not only college priorities but also their structures. Senior staff were appointed to be responsible for such things as Quality Assurance systems, college-wide systems for student recruitment, guidance and support and resources, all of which merited a section of their own in inspection reports (Harper, 2000). Financial audit was linked to inspection, and in the early days when principals resigned following an Inspection Report it was usually because they had lost control of the finances, or had been let down by a weak Finance Officer left over from the pre-incorporation era. In the late 1990s, the emphasis switched to the analysis of data on student retention and achievement, helped by the creation on a national basis of the Individual Student Record (ISR). This allowed comparisons to be made between colleges, and some colleges, whose management systems had passed earlier inspections, now found themselves criticised for failings in the area of teaching and learning.

In 2001, the national Learning and Skills Council (LSC), supported by its 47 regional councils, took over the responsibilities of both the FEFC and the TECs in England. It is also responsible for school sixth forms and adult and community education. Its remit is also wider than just funding: it has responsibility for planning, quality and the promotion of learning and skills. With the LSC came a new inspection regime for VET, or rather two of them: OFSTED was made responsible for the inspection of all age 16-19 provision wherever it took place, and whether it was academic or vocational; and a new Adult Learning Inspectorate (ALI) was set up to cover not only work-based learning and vocational education for adults, but also recreational and basic skills provision for those aged 19+. OFSTED also led new 'area inspections', looking at the adequacy and quality of provision made by a combination of providers in a locality.

This division of responsibilities on the basis of the learners' age, rather than whether their courses are academic or vocational, is reflected also in the LSC's committee structure. It has two major committees, one responsible for young people and the other for adults. The wider planning and policy responsibilities given to the LSC makes its structure particularly significant.

As we have argued elsewhere (Stanton and Bailey, 2001), this method of dividing up the LSC's work and responsibilities has the effect, whatever its advantages, of making it difficult to discern or develop a specific and all-age policy for VET. What is more, responsibility for other initiatives, such as the introduction of vocationally oriented Foundation Degrees (DfES, 2000), to be offered jointly by colleges and universities, or the recently conceived University for Industry (Ufi, 2000), are not within the ambit of the LSC although they are within that of the DfES. Yet, other important influences on VET, such as the requirement or otherwise for licences to practise, or consumer protection law that might stimulate the need for qualified staff, are the responsibility of other ministries such as the Department of Trade and Industry (DTI) or the Department of Health. In recognition of these differing responsibilities, the Performance and Innovation Unit (PIU) of the Cabinet Office has undertaken a cross-departmental review of what it calls 'workforce development' (PIU, 2002).

One disadvantage of the recent tendency to integrate provision 'laterally' (according to the age of the learner), rather than 'vertically' (according to whether it is part of an academic or vocational pathway), is demonstrated by the fate of General National Vocational Qualifications (GNVQs). In an attempt to give such provision parity of esteem with the 'academic' qualifications of GCSEs and A-levels, the government required, in 1999, that the same awarding bodies should offer both kinds of qualification, and that the regulatory body, the Qualifications and Curriculum Authority (QCA), should apply similar criteria when approving both. The result has been that GNVQs have become more academic in what and how they assess, and that their vocational content has become diluted. However, as David Raffe et al (2001) have pointed out, other countries within the UK have adopted different approaches to the creation of learning pathways, and it is possible to trace consequential differences in terms of the status and inclusiveness of VET.

Meanwhile, and in recognition that provision leading to NVQs alone does not provide adequately for young people entering the world of work, Modern Apprenticeships (MAs) are being developed. However, these require a cooperative employer willing to recruit to the scheme, and these are not available in every area or for every occupation. Also, the quality and thoroughness of the MA varies among the occupational sectors, often related to whether they have a tradition of such training (Fuller and Unwin, 2003). This demonstrates again the disadvantages of reliance upon the voluntary principle, and emphasises the need for a good quality and thoroughly vocational full-time alternative to be offered by colleges.

Section Four: Overview of the post-war narrative: change, inconsistency and instability

Of course, we would not expect VET policy to have remained the same during the last 60 years. The question is, has it evolved in the light of experience and economic and technological change, or has it been inconsistent, and subject to irregular attention and disruptive rather than supporting developmental changes? Unfortunately, discontinuity seems to have been a more common feature than consolidation. For instance:

- influence through legislating for employees' rights was provided for but not implemented;
- influencing firms through a training levy was tried, but then abandoned;

- influence through labour market planning was part of the remit of both the MSC and TECs, but in each case was lost among other priorities;
- a curriculum-led approach was tried, and influenced through direct purchase of provision by the MSC, but this was not accompanied by the complementary development of qualifications. Important things were learnt about both curriculum change and its management, but these were not followed up in the design or implementation of either NVQs or the National Curriculum (Stanton, 1997); and
- under both the FEFC and TEC regimes, provision was qualifications-led. However, in other respects the regimes diverged in almost every respect, although both funded VET that led to similar qualifications. Thus:
  - inspection was a powerful influence on FEFC-funded provision in colleges. Training and Enterprise Council-funded training went (for some time) without inspection;
  - the nature of provision was determined by individual learner choice or the 'learning market' in colleges, and by an official view of labour market trends in the case of TEC-funded provision;
  - Further Education Funding Council funding was transparent, TEC funding of provision was treated as commercially confidential[3].
- education and training targets were introduced, but despite much talk of skills gaps and shortages the targets are still expressed in terms of level rather than kind of achievement (NACETT, 1998);
- National Vocational Qualifications were introduced as a framework that would contain all VET qualifications (DfE, 1991). One and a half decades later, NVQs had become a 'niche' product for existing employees. General Vocational Qualifications have shifted towards academic criteria for excellence. Many VET qualifications, although influenced by unitisation and occupational standards, still lie outside the official framework that has been constructed; and
- having operated in parallel, FEFC and TEC provision was in 2001 united under the LSC. With the advent of LSCs, planning and partnerships replaced competition as the route to quality and sufficiency in the VET world. However, LSC merged VET and general education in its committee structure and government did so in determining the responsibility of the two inspectorates. It is now possible to distinguish differing trends in 16-19 age provision as opposed to adult provision (for instance, with regard to whether provision emphasises coherence or flexibility), but less easy to identify the strategy for VET provision, particularly when it crosses these boundaries (Stanton and Bailey, 2001).

Section Five: Tacit assumptions

Despite this instability, and perhaps as contributory factors to it, there are some ongoing (and English) assumptions that pervade this period. These assumptions are not usually made explicit in policy statements, consultative documents or action plans. Therefore, their implications, and the extent to which some ongoing problems are linked to them, remain largely un-debated. Important among these are the following:

1. *It is not appropriate to obtain participation and collaboration from employers and companies through legislation.* This has meant that it has been necessary to devise a series of incentives to voluntary collaboration, some of which are financial and others of which assume that any lack of employer commitment derives from their not being provided with what they want. The latter assumption has resulted in attempts to involve employers in planning and funding (through TECs and LSCs), provision (through governing bodies) and qualifications (through lead bodies, National Training Organisations [NTOs] and Sector Skills Councils). There is still little evidence that employers see this involvement as being a high priority (Keep, 2002). A further consequence is that who should pay for what in VET – the state, the firm or the individual – has never been properly analysed.

2. *Vocational licences to practise are justified only when concerns for public safety are strong.* Thus, installing a gas appliance requires a licence, although rewiring a house does not. (Cynics say that this is because gas explosions can put groups of people at risk, whereas faulty wiring only kills people one at a time!) There is no sense that successive governments have seen the need for licences to practise for general consumer protection reasons, or in order to prevent qualified trades-people from being undercut by the unqualified.

3. *Parity of esteem is primarily determined by the extent to which a qualification gives access to HE.* A corollary of this is that vocational qualifications need to establish lateral links with academic qualifications of the same level. This is leading to a qualifications framework that requires all vocational qualifications to fit into the same number of levels, whether or not this matches the structure of the trade or industry. As we have seen, the importance given to lateral rather than vertical links is also shown firstly by the committee structure of the national LSC, which is based on the age of the learner rather than by the type of learning, and secondly by the existence of two inspectorates that follow the same division.

4. *An infrastructure of state providers is not essential to effective VET policy implementation.* While the National Curriculum requires the existence of schools, and HE requires the existence of universities, it is often implied that whether or not colleges are required for VET depends upon them coming up to scratch. In practice, however, history has shown that even schemes designed primarily for delivery by the voluntary sector or in employment would often have failed without college support.

5. *It is not necessary to show how policy derives from research or analysis.* This is a general point, illustrated by the fact that although a number of the above assumptions are not shared by other countries, it is not felt necessary to justify them before making proposals that depend upon them. Similarly, research into the labour market is often quoted in VET policy documents,

but the link to the design, funding and implementation of VET policy is rarely teased out.

6. *Qualifications matter more than courses.* Qualifications have always been important in the world of VET, but they have become increasingly central in recent policy making. For instance, it is now thought appropriate for central government to regulate qualifications, but inappropriate for it to supervise the design of courses or to require providers to meet minimum standards with regard to facilities or expertise. Until recently, the only qualification required of a person helping a trainee to acquire an NVQ in the workplace has been one in assessment.

This assumption has also caused government to be increasingly concerned with the reliability of assessment, sometimes at the expense of its validity. Thus, when Key Skills are judged to have become important, centrally written tests are introduced into areas such as communications, even though this distorts what employers and others mean by this skill. It has also caused considerable resources to be devoted to the development of assessment regimes, while the issue of how to enable people to learn their vocation (or Key Skills) has (by implication) been seen as unproblematic. In other words, VET policy has been driven by a theory of assessment rather than a theory of learning.

Fitness for purpose and the role of VET qualifications

The emphasis on qualifications, linked with much talk about the need to 'strengthen the vocational route' makes this area worth some further examination. A persuasive definition of the quality of a service or product is that it is 'fit for purpose'. For this to be possible, the purpose needs to be debated, defined and agreed. The lack of clarity about the purpose and role of VET in the English system is symbolised by the ongoing lack of clarity about whether VET qualifications are intended:

- to aid selection and recruitment to the workplace and/or to HE;
- to recognise workplace competence;
- to motivate enhancement of workplace competence and help progression; and
- to be a vehicle for the enhancement of general education – 'education through training'.

There is also an unwillingness to recognise that these purposes may be in tension one with another.

As we have seen, the same qualifications are also used:

- as performance indicators for providers of VET;
- as national targets, for instance for the LSC;

- as a trigger for funding; and
- as a means of influencing course design.

Section Six: Recent developments

Government in England continues to work the policy churn and during the preparation of this chapter, four policy documents have been published. These are:

2002 November	*Success for all: Reforming further education and training our vision for the future* (DfES, 2002)
2003 February	*14-19: Opportunity and excellence* (DfES, 2003a)
2003 February	*The future of higher education* (DfES, 2003b)
2003 July	*21st century skills: Realising our potential* ('The Skills White Paper', DfES, 2003c)

It is too early to attempt to assess the impact of these, especially as not all the proposed measures will be implemented in the way intended (if history is any guide). It is possible, however, to offer some preliminary thoughts on the proposals with reference to our interpretation of VET policy since the Second World War, particularly our argument that policy has been discontinuous and piecemeal.

The first thing to say is that none of these documents is about VET as such. At first sight, what has come to be known as 'The Skills White Paper' (DfES, 2003c) comes closest to focusing on VET, and it does make a brave attempt to develop a cross-departmental approach. However, on closer examination it becomes clear that:

- the paper is more about desired and required outcomes, rather than the processes by which people can access and benefit from VET; and
- it focuses on post-19 adult education and training, making only token references to VET for 14-19 year olds or in HE.

A focus on 'skills' rather than VET allows the White Paper to neglect such crucial issues as:

- the *VET route* that someone might follow throughout their working life, and when preparing for work; and
- the *resources and capacity* required for delivering the desired outcomes – there is, for instance, little analysis of whether the country has the staff with the skills and experience necessary for training others, or is making the investment required to create and maintain the necessary physical plant and equipment.

Secondly, although each of the four policy documents published between November 2002 and July 2003 contains proposals for VET, these are nowhere considered together. If this were to be done, inconsistencies would become apparent. For instance:

- the 14-19 document argues for dropping the use of 'vocational' to describe qualifications on the grounds that it lowers their status, while *Success for all* advocates the creation in the LSC sector of Centres of Vocational Excellence; and
- while the White Paper does mention the role of HE, it does so in the context of the newly introduced Foundation Degrees, neglecting the large number (some say 50%) of conventional honours degrees that are vocational.

The lack of clarity about the role of HE in providing VET is particularly significant given the government's intention that 50% of the population should have experienced HE by the age of 30. A comprehensive skills strategy, let alone a comprehensive VET strategy, can surely not leave out of account such a large proportion of the age group, some 40% of whom will be taking conventional degrees.

Furthermore, when first announced in February 2000, part-time Foundation Degrees were seen, among other things, as providing a progression route for those who had completed apprenticeships. This meant that the predominant mode would be part-time, since apprentices were already employed. However, more recently the emphasis has switched to full-time Foundation Degrees recruiting from full-time Level 3 courses, in order to ensure that the 50% participation target for HE is met.

The compatibility of this HE target with that being set for MAs is therefore open to question. The Cassels Report suggested a target for MAs of 35% (DfES, 2001), but this has become a target of 28% of young people 'entering' MAs before the age of 21 by 2004 in the White Paper. No explanation is given for this change or for the unusual formulation of this target, the attainment of which will also depend on the voluntary willingness of employers to support their employees' further education and training.

Conclusions

All this might lead one to ask whether England has ever had a VET policy, as opposed to a series of initiatives. On the other hand, VET has never had a higher profile than at present, and the political recognition of its economic and social value has never been greater. This is shown by its current prominence in Treasury thinking as well as within the DfES, as demonstrated by the joint paper, *Developing workforce skills* (HM Treasury/DfES, 2002). That is why it is timely to review the experience of the last 60 years and to attempt to learn the appropriate lessons from it.

From our point of view, the key lessons are the following:

- We still do not have a coherent policy for VET, and one is required.
- There is a developing legal framework of employer–employee rights and responsibilities for such things as pensions, working hours, the minimum wage and parental leave. Without an equivalent legal framework for VET, it is unlikely to be given sufficient priority.
- Attractive and flexible vocational learning programmes are required, as well as rigorous and relevant vocational qualifications.
- These programmes should enable people to obtain an appropriate combination of general education, training for occupational competence and work experience, with provision for ongoing career and personal development.
- It needs to be recognised that the status of VET derives from the possibility of progression within an occupation as well as from parity of esteem with academic qualifications.
- There is a need to establish and maintain a properly resourced VET infrastructure in terms of premises, equipment and staff.

Notes

[1] The creation of the Further Education Curriculum Review and Development Unit (later to become the FEU) was announced in 1976 in an appendix to the pamphlet that proposed the UVP schemes.

[2] Ironically, traditional qualifications such as A-levels that were characterised by externally marked written examinations would have been much more suitable for the application of payment by results.

[3] We are not here debating which of these approaches was preferable, but pointing out that no rationale was offered for different approaches being simultaneously adopted.

References

Bailey, B. (2002) 'Further education', in R. Aldrich (ed) *A century of education*, London: Routledge Falmer, pp 54-72.

Dale, R. (1990) *The TVEI story: Policy, practice and preparation for the workforce*, Buckingham: Open University Press.

DES (Department of Education and Science) (1966) *A plan for polytechnics and other colleges*, London: HMSO.

DES/DoE (Department of the Environment) (1976) *Unified vocational preparation: a pilot approach*, London: DES.

DfE (Department of Education) (1991) 'Press release', Tim Eggar MP, 21 March, London: DfE.

DfES (Department for Education and Skills) (2000) *Foundation degrees consultation paper*, London: DfES.

DfES (2001) *Modern apprenticeships: The way to work*, Cassels Report, Nottingham: DfES.

DfES (2002) *Success for all: Reforming further education and training our vision for the future*, London: DfES.

DfES (2003a) *14-19: Opportunity and excellence*, Cm 5342, London: DfES.

DfES (2003b) *The future of higher education*, London: DfES.

DfES (2003c) *21st century skills: Realising our potential – individuals, employers, nation*, Cm 5810, London: DfES.

FEFC (Further Education Funding Council) (1992) *Funding learning*, Coventry: FEFC.

FEU (Further Education Unit) (1979a) *Experience, reflection, learning*, London: FEU.

FEU (1979b) *A basis for choice*, London: FEU.

Fuller, A. and Unwin, L. (2003) 'Creating a "modern apprenticeship": a critique of the UK's multi-sector, social inclusion approach', *Journal of Education and Work*, vol 16, no 1, pp 5-25.

Harper, H. (2000) 'New college hierarchies? Towards an examination of organisational structures in further education in England and Wales', *Educational Management and Administration*, vol 28, no 4, pp 433-45.

HM Treasury/DfES (2002) *Developing workforce skills: Piloting a new approach*, London: HM Treasury.

Keep, E. (2002) *The English VET policy debate*, Oxford: SKOPE.

MSC (Manpower Services Commission) (1976) *Towards a comprehensive manpower policy*, Sheffield: MSC.

MSC (1984) *TVEI operating manual*, Sheffield: MSC.

MSC/DES (1986) *Review of vocational qualifications*, London: HMSO.

Ministry of Education (1943) *Educational reconstruction*, London: HMSO.

Ministry of Education (1945) *Higher technological education*, Percy Report, London: HMSO.

Ministry of Education (1946) *Youth's opportunity*, London: HMSO.

Ministry of Education (1947) *Further education*, London: HMSO.

Ministry of Education (1952a) *Capital investment in 1952: Educational building*, Circular 245, London: Ministry of Education.

Ministry of Education (1952b) *Advanced technology*, Circular 255, London: Ministry of Education.

Ministry of Education (1956) *Technical education*, London: HMSO.

Ministry of Education (1959) *15-18: a report of the Central Advisory Council for Education*, London: HMSO.

Ministry of Education (1961) *Better opportunities in technical education*, London: HMSO.

NACETT (National Advisory Council for Education and Training Targets) (1998) *Fast forward for skills*, London: NACET.

PIU (Performance and Innovation Unit) (2002) *In demand: Adult skills in the 21st century*, London: PIU.

Pring, R. (1994) *Closing the gap: Liberal education and vocational preparation*, London: Hodder & Stoughton.

Raffe, D., Brannen, R., Faurgreive, J. and Martin, C. (2001) 'Participation, inclusiveness, academic drift and parity of esteem: a comparison of post-compulsory education and training in England, Wales, Scotland and Northern Ireland', *Oxford Review of Education*, vol 27, no 2, pp 173-203.

Stanton, G. (1996) *Output related funding*, London: Institute of Education.

Stanton, G. (1997) 'Patterns of development', in P. Tomlinson (ed) *Education 14-19: Critical perspectives*, London: Athlone Press, pp 37-54.

Stanton, G. and Bailey, B. (2001) 'VET under review in England: trends and developments', *European Journal of Education*, vol 36, no 1, pp 7-22.

TSC (Training Standards Council) (1999) *Reaching new standards: Annual report of the Chief Inspector*, London: TSC.

Ufi (University for Industry) (2000) www.ufi.com

Wray, M.J., Moor, C. and Hill, S. (1980) *Unified vocational preparation: An evaluation of the pilot programme*, Windsor: NFER.

THREE

The European policy regarding education and training: a critical assessment

Jean-Luc De Meulemeester and Denis Rochat

Introduction

The aim of this chapter is to highlight the philosophy governing European policy regarding education and training. It is mainly concerned with a critical assessment of the official discourse as it appeared in the texts produced by the Commission.

Education has become a new field of intervention of the EU following the Maastricht Treaty and the creation of a specific General Division of the EC, DG XXII (now Education and Culture [EAC]). Indeed, it is currently thought that we are facing "an overall transition to a knowledge society, whose economic basis is the creation and exchange of immaterial goods and services" (CEC, 2000c, p 7). In such a world, knowledge and skills are of primary importance in maintaining both individual and national competitive advantage. In other words, education and training become key *economic* issues.

The legal basis of educational policy is organised by Articles 126 (education) and 127 (training) of the Maastricht Treaty. In Article 126, one finds the statement of an objective: "the Community contributes to the development of an education of quality", but without any definition of the latter term. Article 126 §2 gives some insights. One means to achieve the objective of quality would be the development of the European dimension in education, inter alia through the teaching of the languages of the member states and favouring the increased mobility of both students and teachers. Such mobility also implies measures ensuring the academic recognition of diplomas all over Europe. Besides mobility, another dimension stated in the Maastricht Treaty is the promotion of cooperation between educational establishments, as well as the development of exchange of information and experiences on issues common to the education systems of the member states. Besides those two elements, the action of the European Community should be directed towards the development of distance education. One should bear in mind that EU actions must take account of the subsidiary principle. It is indeed explicitly stated in §1 of both Articles 126 and 127 that:

> the Community wishes to contribute in the development of quality education by encouraging cooperation between the Member States and, if necessary, by supporting and completing their action while fully respecting the responsibility of the Member States in the contents of education and in the educational systems organisation, just as much as their cultural and linguistic differences.

Besides this rather general legal basis, EU experts and officials have expressed their general views either through official publications such as *Teaching and learning: Towards the learning society* (CEC, 1995)[1] (henceforth referred to as the *White Paper*), or through less official (although influential) publications such as *Accomplishing Europe through education and training* (CEC, 1996), the report to the General Commissioners Flynn and Cresson carried out by a group of 25 experts led by J.L. Reiffers[2] (henceforth referred to as the *Report*), or the Proceedings of the International Conference organised by the Groupe Ampère, supervised by the EU (CEC, 1997)[3]. If the most recent contributions tend to stress more specific issues such as the promotion of Information and Communication Technology (ICT) or international cooperation in education and training, there are exceptions such as the *Memorandum on lifelong learning* (CEC, 2000c). European Union officials are also influenced by lobbying groups such as the European Roundtable of Industrialists (ERI)[4].

In this chapter, we outline the ideas put forward in these documents and discuss their internal logic. Section One begins with a summary of the perspective of European institutions concerning the dangers allegedly faced by the EU, and of the responsibility of Education and Training institutions. In Section Two, we present the type of evolutions advocated by the EU, and in Section Three we subject them to a critical review. The final section, Section Four, is devoted to some concluding remarks.

Section One: The issue at hand

Lack of competitiveness of the EU economy

The EU experts point to a severe and potentially dangerous competitiveness problem for Europe. Competitiveness has now become a key objective of the European construction, as is illustrated by its adjunction to the list of the objectives to be pursued by the EU in the Treaty of Amsterdam (1997)[5]. The experts stress this problem in a dynamic perspective, pointing to the increasing pressure that currently less-developed economies may exert in the near future on European economies, and foremost on their labour markets. Many countries could indeed offer unskilled but also increasingly skilled manpower at a very low cost when compared to Europe (CEC, 1996) – hence the requirement of fostering the quality dimension of goods[6]. The competitiveness issue is not analysed very thoroughly in the European reports published by the DG XXII, as it is a topic mainly dealt with by another General Division, the DG III (Industry). The competitiveness issue (that is, an external problem) is implicitly related to internal problems, more specifically to a deficiency in the working of labour markets. This deficiency reflects itself also through severe unemployment (particularly among the young). The causes are essentially similar. On the one hand, labour markets are seen as very institutionalised. Wages cannot adjust in order to clear the market because of regulations and impediments to free competition. On the other hand, there is a problem of quality in the supply of skilled manpower, due to deficiencies in the education and training system. The consequences are that EU exports suffer from excessive labour costs and that the products cannot respond to new demand because of bottlenecks in the supply of skilled manpower[7]. The solutions to these two problems lie, according to the EU, in the deregulation of labour markets and in a reform of the Education and Training (ET) systems[8]. The last publications of the DG Enterprise (CEC with Karl Aiginger, 2000d) increasingly stress the quality dimension as a rational response to high labour costs. Education therefore becomes a central issue as there exists a direct link between the level of human capital and the quality of goods produced (Gabszewicz and Turrini, 2000).

The responsibility of education systems

For the EU experts of DG XXII, we are now moving towards a knowledge-based economy; that is, an economy where national and even individual competitiveness relies more and more intensively on the human capital held by the individual actors:

> the White Paper acknowledges that investment in skills is a prime factor in competitiveness and employability. (CEC, 1995, p 73)

It is not the accumulation of knowledge per se that is important; rather, it is the ability to learn quickly and to use the acquired knowledge productively:

> employers are increasingly demanding the ability to learn and acquire new skills rapidly and to adapt to new challenges and situations. (CEC, 2000c, p 11)

Unfortunately, the EU experts point to several deficiencies of current ET systems:

• *ET systems ignore the requirements of competitiveness*
The current ET systems appear much too conservative and are still characterised by a culture largely cut off from the world of the enterprise:

> In the context of profound socio-economic changes, a conservative system
> will find it difficult to produce innovative individuals. (CEC, 1996, p 23)

Moreover, "ET systems are insufficiently aware of the constraints of competitivity" (CEC, 1996, p vii). It is only "in adapting to the characteristics of future-oriented enterprise [that] education and training systems could contribute to European competitiveness and to the maintenance of employment" (CEC, 1996, p vii).

- *ET systems are too heavily institutionalised*

The institutionalisation of ET systems[9] poses a set of problems, essentially linked with the implied lack of flexibility and adaptiveness in a world where skill requirements are constantly changing. European Union experts around the DG XXII indeed believe that competitiveness and growth will be favoured if capital (including human capital) can be produced and allocated where it pays off the most, as rapidly as possible. Any hindrance to the mobility of human capital is a hindrance to economic performance. The current level of institutionalisation of ET systems has now become an impediment to growth.

- *ET systems rely too heavily on formal accreditations*

Formal credentials do not promote risk-taking behaviour as large European organisations (such as large firms, administrations) often tend to link wage schedules with degrees obtained (see, for example, CEC, 1995, pp 33-4), as well as with experience; that is, years worked with the same employer. Such a system bases compensation on early acquisition of degrees but not at all on the job performance. The EU experts of DG III also stress that if educational degrees help in making the labour market more transparent, they also encourage formal learning early in life, while rendering the access to qualification much more difficult later in life. This might both reduce the chances of unemployed workers of finding another job by updating their skills, and reduce the chances of employers to find the skills they urgently need (CEC, 1997, p 95). Moreover, the cross-sectoral and cross-national mobility is reduced by the low transferability of degrees both from one country to another and from one educational sector to another[10]. Finally, degrees are sometimes used as an entrance requirement for an occupation. It may sometimes be in the public's best interest (for example, with medical degrees), but sometimes also only serve the interests of a profession (reducing competition) (CEC, 1997, p 95).

- *ET systems develop an elitist structure that drives the entire system away from economic needs*

European ET systems are generally characterised by an elitist structure. Their main objective is to filter out an executive elite through a rather long, and (initially) largely general and non-vocational education. This heavily selected elite who gain access to top positions in society also enjoy the highest income. A large share of the student population hopes to become part of this elite, with the consequence that too large a share of the student population follows a general educational path with few connections to the economy. If they fail to survive in this 'elitist track', they either drop out and try to find employment with no solid vocational training, or follow a vocational or technical education which is brought into disrepute as a failure track. The consequences are twofold: an elite too academically oriented and "not truly representative of the available human resource potential" (CEC, 1995, p 33), and an excessively large share of students following general orientations instead of more technical or vocational ones (CEC, 1996, §74, p 26). Moreover:

> a number of recent surveys show that over a long period the more elitist types of training are more often than not the prerogative of the upper managerial or intellectual strata. (CEC, 1995, p 34)

• *ET systems make individuals less responsible through their sequential organisation*
In the current organisation, students follow much too standardised curricula along a prespecified order. The current ET system has a sequential structure, leaving no room for students to build their own competencies freely:

> most of what our education and training systems offer is still organised and taught as if the traditional ways of planning and organising one's life had not changed for at least half a century. (CEC, 2000c, p 14)

There are few nodes where crucial decisions have to be made, with long lasting and irreversible effects. Students are therefore often trapped in certain educational paths with no opportunity to switch to other ones. Moreover, some educational paths are dead ends, impeding any return to higher or further education. This can lead to huge personal and social waste.

Section Two: Towards a new educational system

The ideal new system advocated by EU experts reflects the criticisms exposed earlier in this chapter; it is defined by its promise to correct the majority of the aforementioned shortcomings:

An ET system more responsive to the market needs through more information and transparency

European Union experts consider that a good educational system is one where any formation is open to everybody who wants it and is able to acquire it. They want to render the existing ET system more open by simply making the whole structure more transparent through diffusion of information among prospective students. This policy might help the students in avoiding irresponsible and non-motivated choices, as is often the case in higher education today:

> Once the [cognitive] basics have been secured, two conditions would appear
> to be necessary if individuals are to be able to exercise responsibility in
> building up their abilities: adequate information and guidance; access to
> training along with all the opportunities available for mobility. (CEC, 1995,
> pp 35-6)

The experts put forward a clear objective:

> ensure that everyone can access good quality information and advice about
> learning opportunities throughout Europe and throughout their lives. (CEC,
> 2000c, p 16)

An ET system that recognises informal ways of learning in order to promote lifelong learning

European Union experts believe that a good ET system should be less centred
around the acquisition of degrees (even if they do not advocate their suppression,
CEC, 1995, p 34[11]; 1996, p 42) and that it should give real chances (and
incentives) for informal acquisition of skills and abilities to be recognised. Greater
external efficiency could be attained by putting less emphasis on formal degrees
and accumulation of knowledge and more emphasis on informal learning and
experiences. This objective could be met, inter alia, through the setting up of
a system of personal cards of skills and competencies, where all validated
fundamental, technical or vocational competencies would be reported –
notwithstanding the way these competencies have been acquired (CEC, 1995,
p 39). Such a system will "return a measure of initiative to the responsibility of
the individual, in enabling each person – no matter where or when – to try as
often as she or he wishes to secure accreditation for partial competencies,
howsoever these have been acquired" (CEC, 1996, p 42). The recent
Memorandum on lifelong learning (CEC, 2000c, p 15) also stresses that:

> innovative forms of certification for non-formal learning are also important
> for widening the recognition spectrum altogether, regardless of the type of
> learner at hand.

Improving the quality of ET systems products: Towards a new curriculum?

The willingness of EU experts to improve the quality of educational products is
reflected in their concern for curricular reform. On the one hand, the nature
of the curriculum should be made more relevant to the needs of the economy
by stressing problem-solving ability rather than mere knowledge accumulation
and developing the ability of learning to learn rather than merely learning
contents (CEC, 1996, p viii). This should be eased by a systematic use of
information technologies. This could help the teacher in his task, and
simultaneously give more weight to personal initiative of the students during

the learning process, resulting in a real "pedagogy of innovation" (CEC, 1995, p 29). While the world of learning should be closer to the values of entrepreneurship and the world of economy (this was the second objective stated in the *White Paper*, CEC, 1995, pp 60-3), a solid knowledge basis should also be imperatively cultivated (CEC, 1995, pp 28, 30). The main idea is that such a new curriculum, instilling problem-solving abilities, general cultivation, and innovation abilities (CEC, 1996, §93, p 33) should provide workers with competitive advantages allowing them to survive in an ever-changing economy. The Lisbon European Council (March 2000) defined the 'basic skills' in this sense as "IT skills, foreign languages, technological culture, entrepreneurship and social skills" (CEC, 2000c, p 10).

Improving the adaptiveness of ET systems through decentralisation and evaluation

The overall organisation of ET systems could be made more responsive to the needs of society by increasing the degree of autonomy of and the degree of competition between schools:

> Experience has shown that the most decentralised systems are also the most flexible, the quickest to adapt and hence have the greatest propensity to develop new forms of social partnership. (CEC, 1995, p 48)

> In Member States whose systems are more decentralised or allow more competition among educational establishments, or where private sector education is more developed, it is already more natural to respond to users' needs. The clear danger is that this will encourage an educational elitism which benefits those able to pay; children with special needs end up in state-run schools of inferior quality. (CEC, 1996, p 78)

Moreover, evaluation procedures should be encouraged:

> The evaluation is indispensable, as it provides key pieces of information allowing the questioning of accepted practices. However, evaluation has a second and equally important function. Publicly accessible, comprehensible and well-founded evaluation provides a clear picture of the types of education and training available. This greater transparency is necessary so that users know what they are doing when they choose a particular field, establishment or training course. Thus, sound evaluation will greatly improve the average productivity of the education and training systems, since the learner can exercise free choice. (CEC, 1996, p 83)

Increasing the levels of investment in human resources at all levels

European Union experts point out the necessity of raising levels of investment in human resources (CEC, 2000c, p 12):

> This means not only that current investment levels are regarded as too low to ensure the replenishment of the skills pool, but that it is necessary to re-think what counts as investment altogether. (CEC, 2000c, p 12)

Inducing firms to increase their investments in training

European Union experts are aware that there exists a kind of market failure as far as investment in training is concerned[12]:

> The overall training effort remains too modest. (CEC, 1995, p 37)

Therefore, in order to favour training within firms, the EU experts suggest a favourable fiscal treatment and incentives for firms employing high-skilled employees in large proportions:

> The approach to be explored is how to consider know-how and skills acquired by employees during the course of their duties as adding value to the company, so that part of the expenditure on training and salaries during the training period can be considered as depreciable intangible fixed assets and transferred accordingly on the balance sheet. (CEC, 1995, p 73)

Inducing individuals to update their skills (lifelong learning)

EU experts consider that the first condition for lifelong learning lies in the individuals themselves:

> [P]eople will only plan for consistent learning activities throughout their lives if they want to learn. They will not want to continue to learn if their experiences of learning in early life have been unsuccessful and personally negative. They will not want to carry on if appropriate learning opportunities are not practically accessible.... And they will not want to invest time, effort and money in further learning if the knowledge, skills and expertise they have already acquired are not recognised in tangible ways, whether for personal reasons or for getting ahead at work. (CEC, 2000c, p 8)

Besides these elements, "incentive measures must be more fully developed", for example, through "individual learning accounts" – "encouraging people to contribute to the cost of their own learning through special savings and deposits that attract matching or supplementary grants or benefits from public or private funding sources" (CEC, 2000c, p 12) or schemes allowing them to combine work with learning activities.

• *Increasing the funding in order to ensure a successful reform*
It is also clear that such a deep reorganisation of ET systems will require important financial means, and that an increase of the current levels of public funding seems unavoidable, at least in relative terms, in order to achieve ratios of public spending on ET systems in the GDP a little bit higher (8%) than the US (CEC, 1995, p 48; 1996, pp 78, 87).

• *The EU as a pertinent level of intervention for comparing and evaluating the ET systems*
In order to achieve such a curriculum and organisational reform of ET systems, EU experts think that the European level is a very relevant level of decision or, at least, initiative (even if subsidiarity principles require that the real implementation should be left to states or regions of the EU)[13]. Indeed, the EU has a broad view across all the experiences all over Europe, and it can compare them (see CEC, 2000c, p 20) in order to identify the most successful experiments and suggest their application elsewhere. Evaluation procedures should also be encouraged by the EU in order to foster the overall efficiency of the system and to improve the average productivity of ET systems (CEC, 1996, p 83). The authorities at the European level could also play a significant role in the homogenisation of degrees and training schemes all over Europe (see CEC, 1997, p 96).

Promoting a system that brings benefits to the whole society

Enabling individuals besides employability

The new educational system should not solely promote economic and technical competencies. The objective is not to transform people into mere robots but into autonomous, entrepreneurial actors ("educating citizens, not robots", ERI, 1995, p 15):

> The main aim of education is to help each individual to fulfill his/her own potential, and to become a complete human being, not a tool for the economy. (CEC, 1995, p 27)

Solid foundations in numeracy and literacy, and beyond that in sciences (CEC, 1995, p 28) and arts and humanities, particularly history and history of sciences (p 30), should therefore be provided.

Creating a new citizenship

This education could also be the cornerstone of a new sense of European citizenship. It should foster the European feeling through the awareness of the shared heritage of the European civilisation. However, this new citizenship should also be an active, participative, one. In this sense, the new, active citizenship is not merely an issue of values; it is also a question of methods (*The Report*, 1996, §57, p 19). In this respect, the EU experts suggest that the very same pedagogical tools that are used to foster information processing and problem-solving abilities (that is, economically useful abilities) should also help in creating more civic attitudes. Creating a European citizenship – that is, an active, participative one – should be considered as a task very complementary to the one seeking to foster individual competitiveness through increased productive skills. "Labour market competitiveness can therefore be enhanced by encouraging a well-developed sense of citizenship" (*The Report*, 1996, §57, p 20), as "both employability and active citizenship are dependent upon having adequate and up-to-date knowledge and skills to take part in and make a contribution to economic and social life" (CEC, 2000c, p 5).

Fostering social cohesion

Another clear objective of the educational reforms, explicitly stated in the *White Paper*, is to increase social cohesion. On the one hand, increasing individual competitiveness through a better education (as described earlier in this chapter) should help people in preserving their social status in an increasingly competitive world. On the other hand, the educational system, by allowing for upward social mobility, plays a key role in social stability:

> All European countries have affirmed these principles, which are at the heart of the contract that exists between our societies and their education and training systems. These principles legitimate both the formation of elites and make the corresponding existence of less advantageous social positions acceptable. A serious and permanent dysfunction at this level would without doubt be a significant obstacle to European development, including its economic development. (CEC, 1996, p 46)

Coping with the requirements of a new economy

The main aim is to make the whole system more responsive to market needs and more flexible and adaptive. The system should deliver the economy with the right quantity of people with the right skills as rapidly as possible, in order to cope with the changing demands of the economy. Briefly stated, the strategy put forward by EU experts is twofold:

- improving the quality of the products of ET systems as well as the speed of the production process; and
- simultaneously creating incentives for firms to invest in training.

Section Three: A critical assessment

The arguments put forward by EU experts to advocate a reform of ET systems are not always convincing because of a lack of explicit connection with the major objective stated; that is, restoring EU competitiveness. On the one hand, the means of practical implementation of the wishes expressed is not clearly elaborated. This may be linked with the broad coverage of their analysis and its ambition to encompass all levels of education as well as training. On the other hand, the experts are not always explicit about the link between the problems they stress and the relatively imprecise solutions they suggest. This might be due to the institutional division between the DG XXII (EAC), specialised in education and training issues, and the DG III (Enterprise) focusing inter alia on the competitiveness of the European industry (see, for example, CEC, 1997). There may also be some internal conflicts within the DG XXII itself, resulting in some ambiguity in the published reports. One can infer from the published documents (as well as from documents of lobbying groups such as the European Roundtable of Industrialists [ERI]; see later in this chapter) that what EU experts believe is that education should evolve in parallel with the changes observed in the economy and the world of the enterprise. Time has become increasingly important in defining competitiveness in the world economy, and to produce just in time what the consumer demands is now a real imperative (Sennett, 1998; see also ERI, 1995, p 9, "industry has had to respond quickly in order to remain competitive"). In such a world, ET systems should not constitute a form of bottleneck.

A much too superficial diagnosis concerning the current organisation of ET systems

European Union experts tend to consider the current organisation of ET systems as a potential hindrance to the enhancement of European competitiveness. Therefore, the ET system should be made more vocational on its lower ends, and more technological and scientific on its higher levels (shortage of scientists and engineers) in terms of contents taught. It should also promote autonomy, information-processing and problem-solving abilities. It should narrowly serve the economy, even if EU experts also contend that developing such abilities may also promote a new active citizenship and increase the probability of avoiding unemployment.

Is there a real problem with the supply of human capital?

Such a view may be too simplistic. On the one hand, it assumes that ET systems systematically do not respond adequately to the new demands of human capital emanating from the economy. Recent analyses tend to suggest that, if there seems to be a "clear sign of a net relative demand shift towards skilled labour in Britain, France, Germany, Italy, Spain and the United States" (Manacorda and Petrongolo, 1999, p 188) during the last two decades (idea of a skill-biased technological change, see Juhn et al, 1993), the potential concomitant problem that this tendency in the evolution of relative demand for skills would not be matched by an equal increase in relative supply is not a homogeneous phenomenon. The problem of skill mismatch may be serious in the US or UK, but not in continental Europe where "skill mismatch did not cause serious labour market problems, where wage differentials did not widen and the bulk of the rise in unemployment could not be blamed on an unbalanced evolution of the demand and supply of skills" (Manacorda and Petrongolo, 1999, p 203). It is true that the European countries as well as the EC often stress a lack of graduates in science and technology; for example, the DG Research Group stressed that in Germany there was a halving in the number of physics students since 1991 (CEC, 2000a, p 21). However, this often quoted shortage of engineers and scientists may for example be linked with the lack of market incentives due to a relatively lower demand for their services, as compared with lawyers and financial analysts (on this topic see Vishny et al, 1991), even if this movement away from sciences might be harmful for long-term growth potential. More generally one can regret the absence of econometric or modelled approaches supporting the arguments put forward by experts from DG XXII.

The EU approach neglects the importance of the demand side

European Union experts have a very clear supply-side perspective; that is, they locate the source of the competitiveness problem mainly in the inadequate supply of human capital. Briefly stated, the European economy suffers from a shortage of qualified workers. It is implicitly assumed that once ET systems have been reformed, the new graduates will be hired and correctly used by the firms, contributing to the production of quality (high-tech), and hence competitive, goods. There is little interrogation regarding the demand side of the market. This piecemeal approach may be misleading, as some recent economic-historical or socio-economic analyses have pointed out (Fox and Guagnini, 1993; Ashton and Green, 1996; Sanderson, 1999). An economy can indeed be competitive by producing low quality products with low-skilled workers. If such a strategy has proven successful in the past, it is very difficult to change the behaviour of employers (see Finegold and Soskice, 1988, on low-skill–low-wage equilibria), even if experts contend that it might be dangerous in the future. Only a sharp drop in profitability might convince employers to change their strategy, and not merely the availability of high-skilled workers.

The latter will simply be underemployed, as the example of many less-developed countries (LDCs) suggests.

It must be pointed out that EU experts from DG III are more cautious than those of DG XXII, and that, if they recognise that ET systems can certainly contribute to the development of a qualified and adaptive workforce, the key factor in ensuring high levels of productivity and competitiveness is the way those competencies produced are used. It is also clear for them that the latter element cannot be influenced solely through reforming ET systems (CEC, 1997, pp 95-6).

The EU experts overstate the benefits of a narrow vocational ET system

The approach stressing a vocationalisation of ET systems in terms of the nature of the courses may lose sight of some important dimensions of education, even from the narrow economic viewpoint. Fostering information-processing and problem-solving abilities means fostering technical abilities rather than broader capacities of judgement, self-criticism and distantiation from narrow technical details. Briefly stated, it seems that EU experts stress what the current system mainly lacks; that is, technical education for workers. They do not point out that managers and leaders should also receive a broader education, less directly vocational, providing them with analytical, interpretative and synthetical abilities. This is important for people having to manage complex systems and take very rapid decisions within a fuzzy and uncertain context. The EU experts also disregard the importance of a broader education for the average worker: some authors (for example, Streeck, 1992) have indeed stressed the importance of such an education to foster adaptiveness of people and ability to learn. More generally, it seems difficult to advocate an active citizenship without stressing at the same time a broader notion of the role of education.

The EU experts exaggerate the ability of the individual to build his own curriculum

The EU experts also want to complement the existing formal educational system with a new one based upon informal on-the-job learning or even self-learning. The former should be fostered in order to ensure the command of a solid knowledge (mathematics, sciences, languages), while the latter should be the locus of more vocational learning. The new system also wants to emphasise the role of personal responsibility, in order to ensure a greater flexibility. As employees live in a very competitive world, they know that, in order for them to survive, they must constantly take the best decisions both in terms of career orientation and learning of skills. In their liberal philosophy, no state agency could take better decisions than individuals in situ, who possess the most relevant information for the problem at hand. The overall efficiency of the system is held to be guaranteed by the fact that people will face the cost of their decision if they fail. Even if it is contended that ET opportunities will be open to everybody, and that information will be made available to everybody, it remains that people are in fact unequal as far as information processing abilities are concerned (not to speak of the attitudes towards risk. See Mingat and Eicher, 1982; De Meulemeester and Rochat, 2001). Nothing in the proposed reorganisation of ET systems seems capable of counteracting this.

The EU experts tend to neglect the key role of teachers in education

The EU experts advocate a reform of the curriculum intended to give people information-processing and problem-solving abilities. They do not give any precise advice beyond that general statement, with the exception of suggesting a widespread use of information technology. In this sense, they appear quite attached to the belief that techniques alone might solve all problems: educational processes will become more efficient just by introducing more physical capital (that is, computers) complementary to the existing human capital (that is, teachers). More generally, EU experts seem to rely more on physical capital than on human capital, except the efforts of the (learning) individual, in the learning process. They stress the role of the free individual, they advocate the widespread use of information technology to liberate people from the role of the teachers:

> Teaching as a professional role faces decisive changes in the coming decades: teachers and trainers become guides, mentors and mediators. Their role – and it is a crucially important one – is to help and support learners who, as far as possible, take charge of their own learning. (CEC, 2000c, p 14)

This approach, again reflecting some anti-authoritarian stance of May 1968 thinkers (see Le Goff, 1999), may be misleading. As often pointed out in the literature, there are role models who also play a key role in the development of the personality of the young learners – let alone the problem of motivation (see the survey by Haveman and Wolfe, 1995).

Is Europe the most appropriate and effective locus of decision in a globalised economy?

Besides this very 'free-market' view, one may question the implicit assumption that the European level would be the most appropriate level of decision (or, at least, of initiative).

Europe is too heterogeneous an entity

On the one hand, it is very difficult to accept the idea that the EU level could identify the best practices only by making international comparisons, the latter being sufficient to secure their implementation everywhere else. Europe is indeed still a very heterogeneous set of countries and a successful experiment in a given context of economic development, but also of cultural attitudes, will not necessarily prove successful in a completely different environment (see Scharpf, 1999).

The role of policy in a globalised environment

On a more fundamental level, there seems to be an internal contradiction between the idea that the EU should promote competitiveness through a reform of education. Reforming education is simply reforming the process that leads to a supply of skills. Nothing guarantees that the latter will be compatible with the demands expressed by firms. These demands are indeed determined by the nature of the products they produce and sell (high-tech, low-tech). In a free-market economy, the latter decisions are left to profit-maximising firms and should not be induced by the state. And even if the European level would like, for example, to promote the production and export of high-tech products, it would be difficult to implement this in the context of firms which are now increasingly transnational. The perspective of the EU experts is contradictory with the universal conception of free-marketeers, for which nations become obsolete concepts in a unified global economy.

Section Four: Concluding remarks

The policy that the EU experts would like to see implemented is the corollary of their philosophical views regarding the optimal organisation of society. They are partisans of a free-trade and a laissez-faire economy. The material benefits linked with this choice are held to far outweigh the (inter alia) social costs. For them, this argument is decisive, because they are utilitarian and consider the (material) social welfare (intimately coupled with competitiveness) of the majority as the only goal that policy makers should be allowed to pursue. However, participating in a free market requires considerable reforms in order to secure competitiveness. These reforms aim at fostering individual responsibility (as liberalism is mainly an individualistic philosophy) and flexibility (the society will be prosperous only if it allows for continuous change). This leads the EU reformers to a very interventionist attitude towards existing educational institutions in order, if not to dismantle them, at least to complement them with much more flexible and less rigidly institutionalised new systems. They want to make the overall ET system structure much more responsive to market needs. In this sense, they consider the latter just as a tool in promoting material welfare and competitiveness. In this way, they introduce short-termism and economic concerns in a world which was initially devised to prepare for the long-run adaptiveness of society and individuals, not solely from an economic point of view, but also from a social, moral and political one. The judgement made on such a programme heavily relies upon the faith one has in the idea that social welfare is just equal to material welfare and that the best way to promote it is linked with the maintenance and the development of a free trade and laissez-faire society, where the sum of the (short-run) decisions taken by interest-maximizing individuals always leads to the best of all the worlds possible, and where as a consequence policy makers only ensure the greatest flexibility by partly removing or at least decreasing the importance of many institutions. As this judgement heavily relies upon one's ideological preconceptions, one can question the neutral basis on which these policy recommendations are based. If the existence of such proposals could nevertheless promote a new policy debate on the necessary institutional changes implied by the globalisation of ET systems, the EU would have played a very positive role of catalyst.

Notes

[1] A complete English version is available at www.europa.eu.int/en/record/white/edu9511/index.htm

[2] A complete English version is available at www.europa.eu.int/en/com/dg22/reflex/en/en1.doc

[3] We also refer to the report carried out by the DG III (Industry) (CEC, 1997).

[4] For example, the *Report* makes explicit references to the ERI's latest reports (CEC, 1996, § 66), as well as the *White Paper*, for example: "the report from the European Roundtable of Industrialists (February 1995) stressed the need for flexible training with a broad knowledge base, advocating a 'learning to learn' approach throughout life" (CEC, 1995, p 10).

[5] The EU should aim at a "very high degree of economic competitiveness" (Treaty of Amsterdam, Article 2).

[6] "These competitors will always have lower absolute costs and usually, after correcting for productivity differences, also lower unit labour costs. The consequence for a high wage country is to compete in quality" (CEC with Karl Aiginger, 2000d, p 1).

[7] "Skills gaps and mismatches, particularly in ICT, are widely recognised as a significant reason why unemployment levels are persistently high in particular regions, industrial branches and for disadvantaged social groups" (CEC, 2000c, p 11).

[8] "Europe's education and training systems are at the heart of the coming changes. They too must adapt" (CEC, 2000c, p 3).

[9] Through a learning process which takes place within formal organisations (schools, universities), and along very formal procedures (examinations, degrees, prescribed times for obtaining such or such qualifications).

[10] The European member states (not the EC) have taken initiatives in order to close the gap. See the Joint Declaration on a *European space of higher education*, signed on 19 June 1999 in Bologna by the representatives of 29 countries (Kaufmann, 2000).

[11] "This is not, of course, to say that the paper qualification is not a valid route.... But in parallel with this, we need to make the best use of skills and abilities, irrespective of how they were obtained and to enhance everyone's potential by catering more closely for the needs of the individual, business and industry" (CEC, 1995, p 15).

[12] This is the well-known problem of poaching externalities, analysed inter alia by Stevens (1996).

[13] One should point out here that the subsidiarity principle is stressed much more in the recent EU publications, for example *Memorandum on lifelong learning* (CEC, 2000c, pp 3, 5, 22).

References

Ashton, D. and Green, F. (1996) *Education, training and the global economy*, Cheltenham: Edward Elgar.

CEC (Commission of the European Communities) (1995) *Teaching and learning: Towards the learning society*, DG V and XXII, White Paper on Education and Training, Luxembourg: CEC.

CEC (1996) *Accomplishing Europe through education and training*, Luxembourg: CEC.

CEC (1997) *Report on the competitiveness of European industry*, Luxembourg: CEC.

CEC (2000a) *Better but not yet the best. Enterprise policy action to improve Europe's competitiveness*, Commission Staff Working Paper, 9 November, Brussels: CEC.

CEC (2000b) *Vers un espace européen de la recherché*, Luxembourg: CEC.

CEC (2000c) *A memorandum on lifelong learning*, 30 October, Brussels: CEC.

CEC with Karl Aiginger (2000d) *Europe's position in quality competition: Background report for the "European competitiveness report 2000"*, DG Enterprise Luxembourg: Enterprise Policy.

De Meulemeester, J.L. and Rochat, D. (2001) 'Rational choice under unequal constraints: the example of Belgian higher education', *Economics of Education Review*, vol 20, pp 15-26.

ERI (European Roundtable of Industrialists) (1995) *Education for Europeans. Towards the learning society*, Brussels: ERI.

Finegold, D. and Soskice, D (1988) 'The failure of training in Britain: analysis and prescription', *Oxford Review of Economic Policy*, vol 4, no 3, pp 21-53.

Fox, R. and Guagnini, A. (eds) (1993) *Education, technology and industrial performance in Europe*, Cambridge: Cambridge University Press.

Gabszewicz, J.-J. and Turrini, A. (2000) 'Workers' skills, product quality and industry equilibrium', *International Journal of Industrial Organisation*, vol 18, no 4, pp 575-93.

Haveman, R. and Wolfe, B. (1995) 'The determinants of children's attainments: a review of methods and findings', *Journal of Economic Literature*, vol 33, no 4, pp 829-78.

Juhn, C., Murphy, K. and Pierce, B. (1993) 'Wage inequality and the rise in returns to skill', *Journal of Political Economy*, vol 101, pp 410-42.

Kaufman, C. (2000) 'L'enseignement supérieur en Europe: état des lieux', in A.-M. Dillens (ed) *L'université dans la tourmente*, Brussels: Publications des Facultés Universitaires Saint-Louis, pp 125-69.

Le Goff, J.P. (1999) *La barbarie douce. La modernisation aveugle des entreprises et de l'école*, Paris: La Découverte (Sur le vif).

Manacorda, M. and Petrongolo, B. (1999) 'Skill mismatch and unemployment in OECD countries', *Economica*, vol 66, pp 181-207.

Mingat, A. and Eicher, J.C. (1982) 'Higher education and employment markets in France', *Higher Education*, vol 11, pp 211-20.

Sanderson, M. (1999) *Education and economic decline in Britain, 1870 to the 1990s*, Cambridge: Cambridge University Press.

Scharpf, F. (1999) *Governing in Europe, effective and democratic*, Oxford: Oxford University Press.

Stevens, M. (1996) 'Transferable training and poaching externalities', in A.L. Booth and D.J. Snower (eds) *Acquiring skills. Market failures, their symptoms and policy responses*, Cambridge: Cambridge University Press.

Streeck, W. (1992) *Social institutions and economic performance. Studies of industrial relations in advanced economies*, London: Sage Publications.

FOUR

'I can't believe it's not skill': the changing meaning of skill in the UK context and some implications

Ewart Keep and Jonathan Payne

All art is at once surface and symbol.
Those who go beneath the surface do so at their peril.
(Wilde, 2000, preface, p 4)

Everyone knows what a skilled worker is …. (Institute of Directors, 1991, p 23)

When talking to employers about their skill needs, the discussion nearly always focuses to a large extent on the personal attributes and attitudes sought in employees. (Dench et al, 1998, p 91)

Employability is the most vital skill needed by the nation's workforce. (BCC 1998, cited in Hyland, 1999, p 73)

Our evidence has required us to consider and accept the implication that 'skill' is a 'humpty-dumpty' word; it means just what the user wants it to mean. (Oliver and Turton, 1982, p 198)

Introduction

For at least two decades, UK policy makers have insisted that national economic competitiveness and social well-being depends upon a suitably skilled, flexible and motivated workforce (see Mansfield, 2000). At the same time, it is increasingly apparent that the term 'skill' has a much broader application today compared to 30 years ago, when it tended to be equated mainly with the physical dexterity and technical 'know-how' of the manual craft worker (Rainbird, 1997; Keep and Mayhew, 1999; Payne, 2000). The reports of the National Skills Task Force (NSTF) reveal that 'skills talk' now incorporates a whole new language of 'generic skills', 'reasoning skills', 'work process management skills' as well as "personal values and attitudes such as motivation, discipline, judgement, leadership and initiative" (NSTF, 1998, p 15). Today, technical or occupational skills are only the tip of a veritable skills iceberg comprising what, on closer inspection, would appear to be a vast array of personal characteristics, attitudes, dispositions, values and behaviours (see Hyland, 1999).

Of course, British employers have always been interested in the prospective behaviour and attitude of those they recruit, and have a long-established reputation for blaming the education system for failing to produce the kind of young people needed for industrial success (Aldcroft, 1992). One can go back at least as far as the 1906 government investigation into Higher Elementary Schools and discover that:

> what employers wanted from these more advanced schools for the children of the working class was a good character, qualities of subservience and general handiness. (Reeder, 1979, p 184)

In the early 1980s, Oliver and Turton (1982) also found that when employers complained of 'skills shortages', what they often had in mind was the lack of suitable job candidates possessing the requisite qualities of reliability, responsibility and stability of work record. Indeed, attempting to ascertain what type of skills employers think they want is a notoriously difficult exercise. Not only do employers' own views on the subject tend to be vague and confused, but they are also frequently contradictory, with one set of employers wanting one thing and another demanding nearly the opposite (see Finn, 1990; Guy, 1991; Huddleston and Keep, 1999). Whereas in the past, however, most managers would have regarded motivation, discipline and responsiveness to change as personal characteristics, attitudes or dispositions, what we find today is that they are increasingly being redefined as 'skills'.

The partial transformation that has taken place over time in the UK of how skill is conceptualised and defined is a matter of real importance to academics, policy makers and practitioners. Not only does it change what we think a 'skilled workforce' *is*, it also renders more problematic and contestable the means by which such a workforce might be produced. One consequence is to open up a political space where responsibility for such a project becomes subject to relocation and displacement. In the UK context, as this chapter argues, it is increasingly the education system that is now being asked to shoulder a growing burden of responsibility for pre-socialising young entrants to the workforce. While this makes the task of those responsible for educating and training young people much more problematic, it also raises the question of whether education can realistically be asked to do all that is now being demanded of it.

In this chapter, we expand on these themes by exploring some of the many implications that flow from the broadening definition of skill as it relates to UK Vocational Education and Training (VET) policy and, in particular, to the role of the education system. The chapter is divided roughly into three parts. Section One briefly outlines some of the main changes that have taken place in how skill is officially conceptualised in the UK and the forces that have been driving this process. Section Two then moves on to discuss some implications of this more diffuse usage of the term 'skill'. And Section Three presents our conclusions.

Before embarking upon the main purpose of this chapter, however, it is necessary to sound a note of caution. While the broadening definition of skill is an international trend that is not confined to the UK, it does not follow that all countries approach, understand and conceptualise 'skill' or 'training' in the same way. The new global discourse(s) of skill are filtered through nationally specific cultural frames of reference and disciplinary perspectives that are often very different to our own and which bear the broader imprint of particular national VET systems (Jobert et al, 1997). Our concern here is specifically with the changing meaning of skill as it has played out in the UK context and the implications for VET policy and practice.

Section One: The changing meaning(s) of skill(s) in the UK

As we have already attempted (see Payne, 1999, 2000), it is possible to trace the historical evolution of the changing meaning of skill across the relevant UK policy literature. Rather than repeat the same detailed mapping exercise here, we have chosen instead to highlight some of the more controversial dimensions of this change along with the forces that have been propelling it (see especially Keep, 2001).

Economic factors said to be driving the changing meaning of skill

Policy makers in the UK have tended to cite a number of broad economic factors that have been driving the changing meaning attached to skill in recent times. The NSTF's *Research report* (2000a), for example, specifically highlights the following:

- the shift from manual to non-manual employment and an associated belief in the rising importance of cognitive and interactional skills as opposed to physical forms of skill;
- the massive decline in the proportion of the workforce employed in manufacturing and the shift towards a more service-based economy, together with changes in the gender balance of the workforce;
- intensifying international competition in what is seen as an increasingly 'globalised' economy;
- the introduction of new forms of technology, for example, IT and Computer Numerically Controlled (CNC) machine tools; and
- new forms of work organisation linked to 'high-performance work systems' (HPWS), which are said to place a premium on a range of analytical and interactional capabilities such as problem solving, team working, initiative, judgement, leadership, creativity and, above all, the capacity to learn and relearn[1].

As this chapter goes on to argue, there is a need to exercise extreme caution when it comes to ascribing relative weightings to the previously mentioned factors. In particular, we would stress the danger of overly optimistic policy scenarios concerning the future of work and the spread of 'the high-performance work model' not least in the UK, a point we return to later (see Keep, 2000; Lloyd and Payne, 2002a, 2002b). In addition to the previous explanations, we would also highlight a number of other trends and influences that have shaped official perceptions of 'skill'.

Mass unemployment and the use of VET as a response

It was against the backdrop of economic recession and high youth unemployment in the UK during the late 1970s and early 1980s that our official conceptions of skill became loosened from their traditional moorings and were allowed to drift more freely. The need for government-sponsored schemes to tackle the 'problem', notably the Youth Training Scheme (YTS), along with the curriculum work carried out by the Further Education Unit (FEU), would have a profound impact on the way 'skill' was defined and understood (see FEU, 1979; MSC, 1984). Starting out from the premise that unemployed youth 'lacked' the personal qualities that employers were looking for, they would spawn new conceptual frameworks aimed at delineating the skills, competencies and personal attributes needed if trainees were to make themselves marketable to employers (see Jonathan, 1987; Hyland, 1999; Payne, 1999). In terms of the way the concept of skill was now being redefined, two overlapping and intertwined developments stand out. The first of these involved the search for 'generic' or 'transferable' skills that might help develop a 'flexible, multi-skilled' workforce able to respond to an increasingly uncertain and changing labour market. The second revolved around the development of a competence-based training model in the UK.

The rise of generic or transferable core/key skills

The first change of consequence concerns the meteoric rise of what have been variously labelled 'generic', 'transferable', 'core' or 'key' skills. These are often seen as having a broad application across a wide range of employment contexts and as transcending individual subjects. As Green (1998, p 23) notes, key skills acquired "an almost totemic status" within UK VET policy in the 1990s by offering a universal basis for 'employability' and 'success' within a flexible labour market and a potential unifying device for England's divided 14-19 curriculum (see Hodgson and Spours, 1997; Young, 1998). Today, 'key skills' continue to be accepted as a basis for UK VET policy, with the current Labour government committed to embedding them in all education and training programmes aimed at young people, including higher education.

Surveying the evolution of core/key skills, one sees a chameleon-like concept that has meant different things to different people at different times (see Lawson,

1992; Halsall, 1996; Hyland, 1999). Various bodies have come up with different checklists of what should go into the generic/core/key skills 'box', with a tendency in some formulations to include such nebulous items as 'values', 'integrity', 'leadership' and 'motivation'. The NSTF, for instance, chose to group under the heading of 'generic skills' not merely the six key skills originally developed by the National Council for Vocational Qualifications (NCVQ) – they are communication, application of number, IT, team working, improving own learning and performance and problem solving – but also "such additional transferable skills as employers may need over time" (NSTF, 2000b, p 23). With respect to the latter, it gave the following examples:

> ... reasoning skills (scheduling and diagnosing work problems), work process management skills ... and personal skills and attitudes such as motivation, discipline, judgement, leadership and initiative. (NSTF, 1998, p 15)

By contrast, the Confederation of British Industry (CBI, 1989, pp 9, 21), in its 1989 report on youth training, identified the following "Common Learning Outcomes to be applied to all stages of the education and training of 14-19 year olds":

> Values and Integrity, Effective Communication, Applications of Numeracy, Applications of Technology, Understanding of Work and the World, Personal and Interpersonal Skills, Problem Solving, and Positive Attitudes To Change.

However, work on graduate employability undertaken for the Association of Graduate Recruiters (AGR) suggested a very different take on the 'generic skills' required for labour market success. Here, the emphasis was on "self-reliance skills" (Whiteways Research, 1995, pp 18-19) including, among others, self-awareness, self-promotion, exploring and creating opportunities, action planning, networking, coping with uncertainty, negotiating and self-confidence.

As noted in the introduction to this chapter, key skills embody the growing tendency on the part of both employers and government to indiscriminately attach the label of 'skills' to what in the past would have been regarded as personal characteristics, dispositions, behaviours or attitudes. The question is whether in conflating what may be essentially very different things we run the risk of spreading the concept of skill so widely that it becomes essentially meaningless (Hyland, 1999). To what extent, therefore, does it really make sense to talk of 'motivation', 'integrity' and 'responsiveness to change' as 'skills' in the same manner as the diagnostic capabilities of an electrician or the combined knowledge and surgical proficiency of a brain surgeon? To this can be added the question of whether a general willingness to accept change is a desirable state of mind per se, let alone a skill, a question that can only truly be answered once one knows what the proposed change actually involves. One could argue, for example, that the German judiciary when confronted with the rise of Nazism in the 1930s displayed a remarkable flexibility to accommodate legal change although one would be hard-pressed to suggest this was a positive quality in the circumstances.

A further problem relates to the issue of transferability itself and whether it is possible to speak of truly 'generic' or 'transferable' skills that are, in some sense, portable across different occupations. The claim that there exist broadly applicable generic skills that are context/domain independent has long been regarded as highly contentious within the philosophy and psychology of education (see Dearden, 1984; Barrow, 1987). It is not our intention to delve into these highly complex debates here (for a good overall discussion, see especially Halsall, 1996; Hyland, 1999). However, we remain deeply sceptical as to whether there really is such a thing as a generic skill of problem solving. Although it may be possible to teach people the process elements of problem solving – problem identification, the acquisition of requisite knowledge, marshalling the necessary resources, deployment of knowledge in sequence and so on – and perhaps thereby instil a general propensity or readiness to undertake such activity, the ability to solve any given problem, above and beyond the most simple, relies on expertise and specialist bodies of knowledge. The same may be true of any higher order human activity such as 'reasoning' or 'critical thinking'. Thinking is always about X and, as such, requires the thinker to have some grounded knowledge of X before real thinking or analysis can take place (Gardner and Johnson, 1996). While we may claim to have some analytical reasoning or problem solving capabilities in the domain of UK VET policy, it would be unwise to assume that we could simply transfer this ability to the problems presented by a broken-down car, invasive heart surgery or an overheating nuclear reactor!

As Jonathan (1987, p 113) once remarked, "there is no Holy Grail of skills or competences which can substitute for broad knowledge, understanding and experience". Notwithstanding policy makers' unshakeable belief in the existence of generic transferable skills, as Hyland (1999, p 71) points out, even the former Employment Department was forced to concede:

> Numerous studies that have looked for evidence of transfer of various skills and knowledge across domains reveal a preponderance of negative findings, leading many researchers to conclude that learning is inherently context specific. (ED, 1993, p 10)

However, by presenting policy makers with the prospect of an education system that can turn out ready-wrapped 'flexible' and 'skilled' employees responsible for their own labour market fate, key skills may be "simply too good not to be true" (Hyland and Johnson, 1998, p 170). Not surprisingly, policy makers have remained fixated upon what, on closer inspection, turns out to be another instalment of the Emperor's New Clothes.

Skill as competence

No discussion of skill in the British context would be complete without some reference to the notion of competence, which from the early 1980s came to leave such an abiding mark on UK VET policy and practice. The establishment of the National Council for Vocational Qualifications (NCVQ) in 1986 and the competence-based qualifications it produced – National Vocational Qualifications (NVQs) – has already attracted lengthy commentary (see Jessup, 1991; Hyland, 1994, 1999). Here, we confine ourselves to the impact these developments have had on the way skill is conceptualised.

As Hyland (1994) argues, the competence-based approaches to education and training that underpinned the NVQ model were heavily reliant upon a functionalist methodological analysis derived largely from 'discredited behaviourist learning principles', originally imported from the US and Canada. In much the same way as 19th-century botanists wandered the planet collecting, examining and assigning to a particular order of species much of the extant plant life, so the competence movement descended on skill. Its attempt at a form of extreme technicist reductionism, based on task analysis and behavioural psychology, might be described as either Taylorism taken to its extreme or even Hobbesian in its treatment of the human mind (there is a long passage in Hobbes' *Leviathan* describing the working of the brain in terms of a simple clockwork mechanism) (Hobbes, 1986, pp 85-222). In the context of the UK's low-skill economy, its particular 'virtue' was that it would permit almost any demonstrable low-level work task or activity to be certified as an acquired competence or quasi-skill.

Competence-based approaches in the UK have left at least two enduring legacies in terms of the way 'skill' is now visualised and understood. First, they have encouraged an Anglo-Saxon 'practical man' approach to skill that tends to neglect the importance of underpinning knowledge and theory. As Green (1998, p 28) notes:

> Competence-based learning ... defines skill as the ability to perform prescribed tasks with predictable accuracy. Knowledge and theory are important only so far as they are necessary to competent performance, and may be 'tacit' or non-articulated. So long as the student can 'do' there is no need to know 'how', or to be able to articulate 'why'.

A historically 'lean' notion of skill in the UK, involving little theory or general education, now became even thinner. In effect, NVQs downgraded knowledge in favour of competent task performance, while 'core skills' acted as an impoverished surrogate in English vocational programmes for the general education normally available to European vocational students in preparation for active citizenship. As Green (1998) argues, the UK's 'core skills paradigm' has proved itself unable to deliver even minimum basic skills, let alone provide sufficient educational breadth, depth and rigour to support more expansive lifelong learning or citizenship goals. Furthermore, because core/key skills are derived from the world of work and underpinned by assumptions about the 'relevant and useful knowledge' deemed 'suitable' for vocational students, they fail to offer a common foundation for both academic and vocational studies necessary to construct a unified 14–19 curriculum. The conclusion he reaches (1998, p 40) is that:

> only some notion of general culture, addressing the future needs of adults as both workers and citizens, can fulfil this function.

The second legacy bequeathed to us by the competence movement concerns its stress on the universality of competencies. The implicit belief is that these are the property of the individual and are capable of being demonstrated and utilised with equal effect regardless of the wider organisational environment or surroundings. Such a view effectively denies a wider social or contextual dimension to learning or skill acquisition, and is, therefore, almost diametrically opposed to the work of the 'situated cognition' school (see Vygotsky, 1978; Rogoff and Lave, 1984; Lave and Wenger, 1991; Engeström et al, 1995; Gott, 1995). Furthermore, it discounts the importance of the specific organisational context or culture – the overlapping elements of product strategy, job design, work organisation and human resource management approaches – that are central to the processes of skill creation and utilisation (Thurly and Lam, 1990; Eraut, 2001).

Aesthetic labour

A further development, which has implications for the changing meaning and definition of skills, concerns the emergence of what has been termed 'aesthetic labour' (Nickson et al, 1998; Warhurst and Nickson, 2001). New research into Glasgow's 'trendy' wine bars, restaurants, hotels and boutiques suggests that, in parts of the 'upmarket' service sector, employers are now looking to recruit accessorised employees whose 'embodied capacities and attributes' can be used to deliver a particular company image or 'style' of service. The result is the emergence of a style labour market where the emphasis is upon age, grooming, deportment, dress sense, accent, body size/shape and general stylishness.

To some extent, of course, employers have always been concerned with the personal presentation of their staff, particularly those in front-line clerical occupations, like banking or sales for instance, that deal directly with the customer/client. However, aesthetic labour describes a new development that goes beyond the normal requirement for 'general cleanliness and tidiness' in the search for employees whose very corporeal being can be used to sell a particular image or lifestyle and, with it, the product itself. As one recruitment manager for a Glasgow hotel put it:

> They had to be pretty attractive looking people … with a nice smile, nice teeth, neat hair and in decent proportion. (Nickson et al, 1998)

Moreover, as Warhurst and Nickson (2001) argue, many of these characteristics are open to development and improvement through instruction. Their possession constitutes a new facet of what it means to be 'skilled'.

Paradoxically, the broadening meaning of skill can be seen as a label for the fact that employers are now demanding more from their workforce; although it is not clear that what they are demanding is always more skill. Indeed, 'skill' has become so elastic a term that it can now be applied to more or less any attitude or attribute that employers desire in their workforce. At the lower end of the labour market, skill is equated with motivation, enthusiasm, punctuality, obedience and an appropriate 'work ethic', effectively robbing the term of any real meaning (Payne, 2000). Similar trends have also been identified in the US context (see Lafer, 2002). The corporate-funded American Enterprise Institute, for example, argues that:

> Any entry-level job teaches the important skills of showing up for work, regularly and on time, suitably clothed and prepared to cooperate with other workers and to attempt to please customers. (Stelzer, 1997, cited in Lafer, 2002, p 21)

Against the backdrop of a shortage of decently-paying jobs in the US, Lafer (2002, pp 30, 28) also highlights the "skills-as-discipline curricula" of much welfare-to-work 'training', the purpose of which "appears to be getting poor people to embrace hard work at low wages, with little chance for advancement, and to suffer this fate willingly". Here 'skill' is about following orders, deferring to the boss and accepting 'your lot'. Project STRIVE, which is aimed at welfare recipients, recommends 'tough-love' interventions for people who have a problem with authority. People like:

> Gloria [who] … leans back with her arms crossed over her chest – just the kind of subtle gesture of defiance bound to irritate a supervisor on the job. Other participants will be challenged to recognize their own resistance to authority, displayed in their bored facial expressions, smirks, slouching and unconscious clucks of disgust. (Hymowitz, 1997, cited in Lafer, 2002, p 29)

Section Two: Implications

The broadening meaning of skill described above has far-reaching consequences for UK VET theory, policy and practice, together with the conduct and design of the firm's training and personnel management function. Limitations of space prevent a full discussion of all these various aspects and readers seeking a broader ranging treatment than is possible here are referred to our earlier work (see Payne, 1999, 2000; Keep, 2001). In this section, we highlight what we see as some of the most important implications for UK VET policy in general and, more specifically, for the education system itself.

Implications for VET policy and practice

The broadening meaning of skill carries at least two broad implications for the way policy debates in the UK are conducted. The first concerns the reinforcement of middle-class advantage in the labour market, while the second highlights the danger of defining skill so widely that the notion of what it means to be skilled, en-skilled or up-skilled becomes progressively diluted and meaningless.

Social capital and the reinforcement of middle-class advantage

Current trends in the redefinition of skill have serious implications in terms of labour market closure and the strengthening of middle-class advantage. Ainley (1994, p 80), for example, reminds us that the call to integrate key skills into higher education programmes forgets that these:

> are neither personal, transferable, nor skills; they are social and generic competencies.… It ignores the fact that middle-class students already possess many of these competencies as a result of their previous education and family socialisation.… For at rock bottom the real 'personal' and 'transferable' skills required for preferential employment are those of whiteness, maleness and traditional middle-classness.

The same may also be true of the new aesthetic skills which Warhurst and Nickson (2001) indicate are now at a premium in the new 'upmarket' service economy, such as personal presentation, accent, grooming and deportment. One possible danger is that young people from more socially disadvantaged backgrounds will find themselves squeezed out of such 'preferential' employment niches by university students now looking to pay their way through higher education. The more skill becomes about 'looking good and sounding right', the more it becomes bound up with the social and cultural capital of particular groups, and the greater the danger that it will reinforce class divides within the labour market.

When it comes to tackling this problem, however, the responses currently being advanced display all the characteristics of a complex moral dilemma. Warhurst and Nickson (2001) have argued that a strong case exists for training interventions designed specifically to target the aesthetic being and self-image of unemployed youth in a bid to put them on a more competitive labour market footing. They insist that:

> middle class concerns about social engineering – what might be termed the Eliza Doolittle syndrome – should not be allowed to cloud the issue. Equipping

unemployed people with aesthetic skills enhances their self-confidence and, importantly, employability. (Warhurst and Nickson, 2001, p 34)

The Wise Group, a leading charity that aims to help the unemployed get back into work, has already piloted one such scheme in Glasgow.

An alternative view, however, would be as follows. Let us first of all leave aside whether such 'training' is optional or compulsory (backed up by the threat of benefit withdrawal) or, for that matter, how 'decent' these 'upmarket' jobs really are in terms of pay, working conditions, security, pension provision, trade union rights, and so on. The fact still remains that every aspect of the trainee, from the way they speak and deport themselves to the shape and size of their body, is now considered a legitimate target for intervention, manipulation and control. Suddenly, the entire 'self' is up for grabs (Casey, 1995). Despite the good intentions of the style counsellors (Warhurst and Nickson, 2001) – and presumably one would avoid telling people they are 'too fat' or 'too common' – the subliminal message is that one must learn to give up one's own individual or class-based identity at least for the duration of the working day. Whether this is simply 'a bridge too far' or the necessary price to be paid in order to escape life on the dole is a tough one to call.

We are all skilled now

At a more general level, 'skill' is now being used so broadly that it means almost anything employers want it to mean and can be applied to almost any job. With everything from 'enthusiasm', 'responsiveness to change' and 'discipline' gathered together in the name of skill, everyone gets to share in the illusion that they are part of the new skilled workforce and that their jobs are already in the process of being 'up-skilled'. Thus, the sales assistant who has learnt to swipe barcodes and smile pleasantly for the shopper, can claim to have learnt new IT and customer service skills. This can be counted as 'up-skilling' even though they may now have less use for mental arithmetic than before, their product knowledge and ability to inform customer choice remains as limited as before, and the quality of the service encounter itself leaves much to be desired. The new discourse of skill thereby ensures that all jobs, including the very low skilled, can be revalued upwards in terms of their skill content, even to the point where such perceptions come to be internalised and reported by the very workers themselves. In a sense, we are all skilled now regardless of the type or quality of the job we do or the degree of personal control or discretion we have over our work (see Payne, 2000). This, then, is the most fundamental difference in how skill is officially conceptualised today as compared with the past, when to be skilled implied some level of real market power and personal discretion over one's work. Lafer (2002, p 19) makes a similar point, noting that:

If discipline is a 'skill', we have defined away any possibility for a class of 'unskilled' occupations.

The new discourse of skill provides UK policy makers, therefore, with a convenient cover for the dehumanising reality of many people's working existence in an economy where large numbers of jobs remain mind-numbingly mundane, low skilled, low waged and insecure, and require little training to perform them. The most recent Skills Survey indicates, for example, that while there were fewer jobs in 2001 requiring under one month "to learn to do the job well" compared with 1986, the actual proportion still remains high at 20% (Felstead et al, 2002, p 54). The survey also estimated that some 6.5 million people, or 27% of the UK workforce, were in jobs that did not require a single qualification to gain entry, more than double the number of economically active people currently without a qualification of any kind (Felstead et al, 2002, pp 31-2).

Despite finding "a consistent pattern of generally increasing skills in recent years" (Felstead et al, 2002, p 10), the same report also discovered, paradoxically, that there had been "a marked decline in task discretion" (Felstead et al, 2002, p 13). The proportion of employees reporting a great deal of choice over the way they do their work fell from 52% in 1986 to 39% in 2001. The steepest declines were most noticeable in professional occupations such as 'Education', 'Public Administration' and 'Finance'. While the report found some evidence of greater external supervision and control, it also highlighted increased constraints arising from fellow workers and customers/clients (Felstead et al, 2002, pp 67-73). These findings can be added to others, notably Dench et al's (1998) investigation into employers' perceptions and usage of key skills. This investigation revealed that while employers did indeed want all six of the government's key skills, the actual level of skill required was often very low. Indeed, rather than looking for the highly skilled, polyvalent and autonomous workforce so beloved of UK policy makers, the study concluded that "in reality most employers simply want people to get on with their job and not challenge things" (Dench et al, 1998, p 61).

When we look at the evidence, what we find is that the 'take-up' of the so-called high-commitment, high-performance workplace model has been extremely limited in the UK. There are both case studies (West and Patterson, 1997; Ackroyd and Procter, 1998; Guest, 2000) and surveys (Cully et al, 1998) to suggest that many jobs remain highly routinised, relatively low skilled and subject to hierarchical managerial control and discipline. Indeed, data from the Department of Trade and Industry (DTI)/ESRC's Workplace Employee Relations Survey (WERS) found that as few as one in 50 firms, or 2% of the sample, had fully-blown high-performance work systems in place (Cully et al, 1998). On this evidence, large swathes of the UK workforce would appear to be a million miles away from what might realistically be described as a 'knowledge economy' (see also Keep and Mayhew, 1999; Keep, 2000; Lloyd and Payne, 2002a, 2002b). As the next section of this chapter argues, such realities need to be kept firmly in mind when considering that the education system in the UK is now increasingly being asked to shoulder a growing burden of responsibility for creating the 'skills', attitudes or attributes that employers seek.

Implications for education

The changing meaning and definition of skill also carries a number of implications for the education system. Here we highlight two, neither of which may be considered benign. The first relates to the problems created for those responsible for managing the UK VET system. The second concerns the balance of responsibility that now exists between the education system and employers in the UK when it comes to the provision of initial VET for young entrants to the workforce.

Management by Objective (MBO): Trying to face both directions at once?

It can be argued that the broadening meaning of skill renders the task of those responsible for managing the UK VET system much more problematic. Here there is a cruel paradox. Skill has fragmented and shifted away from notions of 'hard' technical knowledge, just at the time when policy makers have decided that they want simple, unambiguous and 'rigorous' performance measures, mainly in the form of certification, in order to ensure the dreamed-of 'parity of esteem' with academic qualifications. A neat example of the kinds of problem this creates is provided by the fate of the three 'softer' key skills: problem solving, team working and improving own learning and performance. Since the Qualifications and Curriculum Authority (QCA) concluded that these skills did not lend themselves to standardised written assessment, their importance within Curriculum 2000 as well as Modern Apprenticeships (MAs) has been downplayed. More recently, the Department for Education and Skills (DfES) announced that the three wider key skills would henceforth be regarded as non-essential for employability (*Times Educational Supplement*, 20 July 2001). Paradoxically, survey evidence suggests that team working and problem solving are the two skills said to be most highly prized by employers (DfEE, 1999).

What we now have in the UK is a VET system driven by the managerialist maxim, 'if you can't measure it, you can't manage it', as former Secretary of State for Education and Employment, Gillian Shepherd, once remarked. The depth of the elephant trap of Management by Objective (MBO) deepened further once policy makers latched on to the competence movement's claim that 'outcomes' were everything and the process of learning mattered relatively little (Jessup, 1991). Moreover, provided those outcomes were measurable, it was then possible to direct funding accordingly, thereby pursuing sought-after 'efficiency gains' or unit cost reductions in the context of shrinking budget allocations. In this model, quantifiable performance measures stand as poor proxies for the quality or richness of the learning experience, the most important dimensions of which cannot readily be captured by crude testing and certification. The gulf between what can be measured and therefore planned and funded, and the broadening meaning of skill, may in fact be getting worse. The latest National Learning Targets for England for 2002 relate to the achievement of qualifications or skills standards (www.dfes.gov.uk/nlt/). The fact that many of the so-called 'softer' skills that employers now claim to be important lie well outside the current systems of certification has not been addressed.

The shifting balance of responsibility between education and employers

A quarter of a century ago, Bowles and Gintis's (1976) pioneering study, *Schooling in capitalist America*, launched a highly controversial debate about the relationship between education and the economy. Their claim was that schools were implicated in a process of social control and reproduction aimed at fitting pupils into a hierarchical workplace and society by means of a 'hidden curriculum' that tended to inculcate passivity, conformity and obedience in the majority of its products. More recently, others have argued that changes in the nature of work, linked to theories of 'post-Fordism', 'the knowledge economy' and the 'high-performance workplace' have begun to open up a new and very different 'correspondence' principle (Brown and Lauder, 1992; Young, 1998). High value-added, knowledge-based production is seen to require semi-autonomous teams of employees with the cognitive, emotional and collective intelligence to apply knowledge, solve problems and pursue 'continuous improvements' in product quality, design and innovation (see Carnoy, 1998; Bentley, 1998; Brown, 2001). Writing from a US perspective, Cappelli (1995) has suggested that the high-performance workplace fashions a new role for schools in teaching the "pro-social behaviour and attitudes" (by which he means 'motivation', 'initiative', 'persistence', 'cooperation', 'self-discipline' and 'personal responsibility') that are said to be increasingly bound up with organisational performance. Thus, he concludes (1995, p 118):

> These arguments suggest that it is time to think about systematic attempts to include work attitudes and behaviour as part of the public policy agenda. In particular, the sooner a discussion of workplace attitudes and behaviours can be brought into the more general debate about education reform, the easier it will be to produce a system that aligns and reinforces the interests of schools and of the workplace.

The problem with this view is that it tends to be based on a vision of an emerging high-performance workplace model, the evidence for which, both in the UK and US, remains extremely thin on the ground (Milkman, 1998). Only two years later, Cappelli et al (1997, p 168), while acknowledging that low-skill, low-wage service work remained prevalent in the US economy, were beginning to hedge their bets, suggesting that whether schools should assume greater responsibility for developing higher order skills was an 'open question'. Nevertheless, once the heady optimism surrounding the high-performance workplace model is replaced with the bleak reality of the UK's predominantly low-skills economy, asking schools to get into the business of producing appropriate skills, attitudes and behaviours takes on altogether more sinister connotations. Not only do we end up with a ready-made justification for an instrumentalist view of education's role in producing the kind of young people employers want, but what employers want may, in many cases, be little different from the simple 'compliance with authority' that Bowles and Gintis had in mind. The danger is that teachers and lecturers find themselves being told to create a flexible, cooperative, motivated and self-disciplined workforce which can also translate as being obedient, quick to fit in, unquestioning of its superiors and willing to accept low-wage, dead-end jobs and demotivating employment conditions.

For all these reasons, we would do well to be on our guard against bringing 'workplace attitudes and behaviours' into a 'debate about education reform'. Yet, in public policy terms, the UK is already some way down the track that Cappelli describes. Since the late 1970s, employers have made much headway in persuading government and public opinion that the education system should shoulder an increasing burden of responsibility when it comes to preparing students for the 'world of work' (Esland, 1996; Tomlinson, 2001). This shift in emphasis has taken place at a time when some of the pre-existing forms of skill acquisition and structured socialisation in the workplace, such as apprenticeship and graduate training programmes, have been pruned back to cut costs. Indeed, one has to search long and hard now to find examples of what employers are actually contributing to initial VET, beyond the small percentage who are currently participating in an increasingly marginalised work-based route (via MAs) itself renowned for its highly uneven quality (see Unwin and Fuller, 2000; Keep and Payne, 2002). Furthermore, the Labour government's objective of having 50% of the 18-30 age cohort going through higher education by 2010 may only serve to marginalise the work-based route still further, so that it comes to be seen increasingly as the 'provider of last resort' for those who have 'failed' in the education system.

In seeking to shift the burden of cost and responsibility for initial VET back onto education and the state, employers have been assisted by the tendency to relabel certain skills, attributes or attitudes as 'generic' or 'key' skills, which, it is assumed, can then be supplied by the education system. Graduates provide a good example of this in action. As mentioned earlier in this chapter, AGR, for example, has recently begun to up the ante in terms of the 'self-reliance' skills they believe it is reasonable to expect higher education institutions to create among undergraduates (Whiteways Research, 1995). Faced with a massive expansion in student numbers and cuts in unit resource provision, universities are under mounting pressure to include key skills, enterprise/entrepreneurship skills and social and presentational skills within the academic curriculum.

Nevertheless, while the rhetoric of key skills may be 'too good not to be true' from an employer and policy perspective, feeding the idea that the education system can contribute more and more to workforce pre-socialisation, the reality is very different. One immediately runs up against the aforementioned 'transferability' problem that has haunted core/key skills from their inception. While such 'skills' may be generic at a very general level, they remain heavily context/domain dependent and do not travel well between different occupations.

Furthermore, as many commentators now recognise, the primary location for the creation and development of higher order work skills remains the workplace (Crouch et al, 1999; Ashton et al, 2001). This is because such skills often require in-depth knowledge of work systems and technological requirements and are articulated in the context of routines, procedures, norms and cultural practices – in short, 'ways of doing things' – which tend to be highly company- or firm-specific (Koike and Inoki, 1990; Thurly and Lam, 1990; Crouch et al, 1999; Eraut, 2001; Lauder and Mehralizadeh, 2001). The idea, therefore, that education can ever be more than a complement to in-firm skill development and acculturation, or worse still, that it can equip students to enter any number of different jobs ready from day one to, as it were, 'hit the ground running', is deeply problematic. Leaving aside then whether education should develop the skills and attitudes employers want, there is also the question of whether it can realistically deliver what is increasingly being asked of it.

Much the same assessment applies to the tendency to describe 'motivation' as a skill, and the assumption that the creation of a motivated workforce is something that can now be partly 'outsourced' to the education system. In the past, if employees lacked motivation or commitment at work, this might have been seen to reflect failings in job design, work organisation, people management systems, reward structures and involvement and communication systems. Today, the buck has been passed to schools, colleges and universities for allegedly failing to imbue young people with the appropriate skills and attitudes. In light of the UK's poor record when it comes to adopting the high-commitment, high-performance model promised by Human Resource Management (HRM) (Bach and Sisson, 2000), British management might indeed welcome this opportunity to shift some of the blame for having failed to put their own house in order. The issue remains, however, as to whether schools and colleges can realistically be expected to act 'in loco decent personnel management' as would increasingly appear to be the case.

All of this suggests that the time has come for a serious rethink of what is reasonable to expect both employers and education to contribute to initial VET. If the current situation displays an imbalance of responsibilities, getting UK employers to accept their fair share of these will be far from easy. Furthermore, despite the concerns raised by WERS over the quality of management action and strategies, workplace issues such as job design, work organisation and people management approaches have occasioned little public policy debate. The reasons for this are perhaps not so hard to discern. One is the obsessive UK policy disorder of redefining all such problems as a 'skills issue', of which the reports of the NSTF are a clear example. Another is the Labour government's reluctance to clash with business interests by intervening inside 'the black box' of the firm, coupled with an almost evangelical faith that 'globalisation' will eventually do the trick as far as the diffusion of 'best practice' employment relations is concerned. Finally, shifting the focus of attention onto skills and VET as the answer to what might otherwise be seen as management or employment relations issues chimes well with the government's predilection for regarding VET as one of the few remaining areas where state intervention is still deemed legitimate (see Keep, 1999; Lloyd and Payne, 2002b).

Section Three: Conclusion

The chapter has explored the changing meaning of skill as it has played out in the UK and attempted to highlight some possible implications for VET theory, policy and practice. Like our own universe, the concept of skill seems to have entered a state of almost continual expansion and now incorporates a seemingly endless galaxy of generic skills, competencies, attitudes, dispositions and personal characteristics. For UK policy makers, there have been both advantages and disadvantages in all of this. On the debit side, the 'softening' of skill has made life more difficult for those wishing to manage the VET system in accordance with 'hard' measurable outputs, and now threatens to play havoc with the National Learning Targets.

At the same time, the broadening meaning of skill has provided policy makers with a useful ideological device. Indeed, it is hardly an exaggeration to say that 'skill' has now become a universal grab bag for any attribute that employers and policy makers deem desirable in their 'ideal-typical' flexible employee, whether it is creative problem solving, simple obedience or general malleability. As Avis (2002) suggests, beneath the surface of 'skill' lurks a 'moral economy' or 'etho-politics' (Rose, 1999), which seeks to shape worker/learner subjectivities in accordance with the needs of the economy, while simultaneously pressing education into the service of such needs. Change, flexibility and responsiveness now become immutable facts of life. The worker is asked to be a self-regulating individual, ultimately responsible for their own labour market fate, surviving by dint of their learning, ingenuity and wit, and requiring limited state support when the job runs out and the going gets tough (see also Coffield, 1998). By the same token, an expanded concept of skill offers policy makers a moveable feast that can be applied virtually to all sectors and all workers. People suddenly discover they now have 'skills' they never knew they had, the skill content of even the most routinised of jobs becomes inflated upwards, and policy makers find they have a useful rhetorical smokescreen for obscuring aspects of many people's working lives they would rather see hidden. In what is an interesting 'turn', the new aesthetics of skill colonises not only aspects of personality and behaviour but also the body itself, thereby legitimising education and training interventions that threaten to play with our very identities and understanding of 'self'.

The broadening meaning of skill has also become a label for the fact that the market is now demanding more and more of education in terms of pre-socialising young entrants to the workforce. Meanwhile, like the vanishing Cheshire cat in *Alice in Wonderland*, British employers have been busily absenting themselves from their own responsibilities in the area of initial VET, leaving behind only the 'grin' that is MAs. This chapter has argued that the primary location for the creation of higher order work skills remains the firm, with the corresponding danger that schools, colleges and universities now find themselves being presented with a task that resembles 'mission impossible'. Worse still, there is the danger that the agenda for up-skilling the future workforce turns out to be about enlisting teachers and lecturers in the creation of a subservient workforce willing to do whatever employers demand, even if this means accepting low-wage, dead-end jobs or working all hours. There is an urgent need, therefore, for a much fuller and franker public debate in the UK about what might be an appropriate balance of responsibilities as regards the role of the education system and employers in the creation of skills. Unfortunately, the current political, ideological and policy constraints render the prospects for such a debate rather remote.

Nor will it be easy for educationalists to take the initiative and draw a line in the sand when it comes to delineating more precisely what the education system can legitimately be expected to contribute to preparing young people for work. It is not just that shifting responsibility for the embedded structural weaknesses and performance woes of the British economy onto education suits employers and politicians rather well (Lloyd and Payne, 2003). It is also the case that many within education have gradually come round to the new rules of the game. Twenty-five years ago, the slightest suggestion that education should act as an 'outpost of capital', or that there was some simple symmetry between the needs of employers, young people and society, was sufficient to send shock waves through the British educational establishment (Esland, 1996). Today, with the help of more user-friendly language, those same assumptions have become part of the cultural furniture of education, and are increasingly accepted as such by senior management in schools, colleges and universities. Having drifted this far, the feeling may be that there is now no turning back. If so, we might imagine a time, perhaps not so very far away, when schools and colleges may be asked to provide classes in grooming, deportment and style for those from less privileged backgrounds. Commenting on the 'earnings gap' between middle-class and working-class graduates, Richard Brown, chief executive of the Council for Industry and Higher Education (CIHE), has enjoined universities to give greater attention to developing the social and life skills of the 'unwashed':

> At the moment, the thinking seems to be that if you can recruit the unwashed, then all will be fine. But social skills still count for an awful lot.... These skills are often bred into you if you come from a certain social class, but they are not if you were born on the wrong side of the tracks. Institutions need to think about how individuals' life skills can be developed where they are absent as a result of upbringing. (*Times Higher Educational Supplement*, 17 May 2002, p 3)

It remains highly questionable whether many of those who work in higher education would accept this as a legitimate part of their role, or whether they would wish to target certain students in this way, leaving aside whether they themselves would have the requisite skills, time or resources to deliver such programmes.

To return to the quotation by Oscar Wilde with which this chapter began, current policy discourses surrounding 'skill' in the UK are, in large measure, about 'surface and symbol'. Skill, it will be recalled, has always been a socially constructed phenomenon with both subjective and objective properties (Attewell, 1990; Noon and Blyton, 1997). However, as our concepts of skill have grown broader, bigger and fuzzier at the edges, so too the political and ideological dimensions have assumed greater significance. At the level of appearances, as Hyland (1999, p 58) argues, 'skills–talk', like 'lifelong learning' and 'standards', possesses all the hallmarks of a great political and educational 'slogan', sufficiently vague and blurry to rally diverse constituencies to make common cause behind the 'high skills vision'. This chapter has sought to probe beneath the surface of such rhetoric in an attempt to highlight some of the many consequences, contradictions and conflicts that remain buried at the heart of 'skill'. We ignore them at our peril.

Note

[1] For a more detailed discussion of the forces underlying this process of change, see Whiteways Research (1995), Gerber and Lankshear (2000) and Brown et al (2001).

References

Ackroyd, S. and Procter, S. (1998) 'British manufacturing organisation and workplace industrial relations – some attributes of the new flexible firm', *British Journal of Industrial Relations*, vol 36, no 2, pp 163-83.

Ainley, P. (1994) *Degrees of difference*, London: Lawrence and Wishart.

Aldcroft, D.H. (1992) *Education, training and economic performance 1944-1990*, Manchester: Manchester University Press.

Ashton, D., Sung, J., Raddon, A. and Powell, M. (2001) 'National frameworks for workplace learning' in *Workplace learning in Europe* London: ECLO/ETDF-FEFD, SKOPE, CIPD, pp 35-60.

Attewell, P. (1990) 'What is skill?', *Work and Occupations*, vol 14, no 4, pp 422-48.

Avis, J. (2002) 'Imaginary friends: managerialism, globalisation and post compulsory education and training in England', *Discourse: Studies in the cultural politics of education*, vol 23, no 1, pp 75-90.

Bach, S. and Sisson, K. (2000) 'Personnel management in perspective', in S. Bach and K. Sisson (eds) *Personnel management* (3rd edn), Oxford: Blackwell, pp 3-42.

Barrow, R. (1987) 'Skill talk', *Journal of Philosophy of Education*, vol 21, no 2, pp 187-99.

BCC (British Chambers of Commerce) (1998) *Skills for competitiveness*, London: BCC.

Bentley, T. (1998) *Learning beyond the classroom: Education for a changing world*, London: Routledge.

Bowles, S. and Gintis, H. (1976) *Schooling in capitalist America*, London: Routledge and Kegan Paul.

Brown, P. (2001) 'A strategy for skill formation in Britain', in F. Coffield (ed) *What progress are we making with lifelong learning? The evidence from the research*, Newcastle: Department of Education, University of Newcastle, pp 111-26.

Brown, P. and Lauder, H. (1992) 'Education, economy and society: an introduction to a new agenda', in P. Brown and H. Lauder (eds) *Education for economic survival: From fordism to post-fordism?*, London: Routledge, pp 1-44.

Brown, P., Green, A. and Lauder, H. (2001) *High skills: Globalisation, competitiveness and skill formation*, Oxford: Oxford University Press.

Cappelli, P. (1995) 'Is the "skills gap" really about attitudes?', *California Management Review*, vol 37, no 4, pp 108-24.

Cappelli, P., Bassi, L., Katz, H. and Knoke, D. (1997) *Change at work*, Oxford: Oxford University Press.

Carnoy, M. (1998) 'The changing world of work in the information age', *New Political Economy*, vol 3, no 1, pp 123-8.

Casey, C. (1995) *Work, self and society: After industrialism*, London: Routledge.

CBI (Confederation of British Industry) (1989) *Towards a skills revolution – A youth charter*, London: CBI.

Coffield, F. (1998) 'A tale of the three little pigs: building the learning society with straw', *Evaluation and Research in Education*, vol 12, no 1, pp 44-58.

Crouch, C., Finegold, D. and Sako, M. (1999) *Are skills the answer? The political economy of skills creation in advanced industrial countries*, Oxford: Oxford University Press.

Cully, M., O'Reilly, A., Millward, N., Forth, J., Woodward, S., Dix, A. and Bryson, A. (1998) *The 1998 workplace employee relations survey: First findings*, London: ESRC/ACAS/PSI.

Dearden, R. (1984) 'Education and training', *Westminster Studies in Education*, vol 7, pp 57-66.

Dench, S., Perryman, S. and Giles, L. (1998) 'Employers' perceptions of key skills', *IES Report 349*, Sussex: Institute of Manpower Studies.

DfEE (Department for Education and Employment) (1999) 'Helping graduates into employment', *Skills and Enterprise Briefing*, February, issue 1, no 99.

ED (Employment Department) (1993) *Development of transferable skills in learners*, Sheffield: ED Methods Strategy Unit.

Engeström, Y., Engestrom, R. and Karkkeinen, M. (1995) 'Polycontextuality and boundary crossing in expert cognition: learning and problem solving tasks in complex work activities', *Learning and Cognition*, vol 5, pp 319-36.

Eraut, M. (2001) 'Learning challenges of knowledge-based organisations', in *Workplace learning in Europe*, London: ECLO/ETDF-FEFD/SKOPE/CIPD.

Esland, G. (1996) 'Education, training and nation-state capitalism: Britain's failing strategy', in J. Avis, M. Bloomer, G. Esland, D. Gleeson and P. Hodkinson (eds) *Knowledge and nationhood: Education, politics and work*, London: Cassell, pp 40-70.

Felstead, A., Gallie, D. and Green, F. (2002) *Work skills in Britain, 1986-2001*, Annesley: DfES.

FEU (Further Education Unit) (1979) *A basis for choice*, London: FEU.

Finn, D. (1990) 'The great debate on education, youth unemployment and the MSC', in G. Esland (ed) *Education, training and employment, vol 2*, Wokingham: Addison-Wesley Publishing Co/Open University Press, pp 35-58.

Gardner, P. and Johnson, S. (1996) 'Thinking critically about critical thinking', *Journal of the Philosophy of Education*, vol 30, no 3, pp 441-56.

Gerber, R. and Lankshear, C. (eds) (2000) *Training for a smart workforce*, London: Routledge.

Gott, S. (1995) 'Rediscovering learning: acquiring expertise in real world problem solving tasks', *Australian and New Zealand Journal of Vocational Education Research*, vol 3, no 1, pp 30-68.

Green, A. (1998) 'Core skills, key skills and general culture: in search of the common foundation in vocational education', *Evaluation and Research in Education*, vol 12, no 1, pp 23-43.

Guest, D. (2000) 'Piece by piece', *People Management*, vol 6, no 15, pp 26-30.

Guy, R. (1991) 'Serving the needs of industry', in P. Raggatt and L. Unwin (eds) *Change and intervention: Vocational education and training*, London: Falmer Press, pp 47-60.

Halsall, R. (1996) 'Core skills – the continuing debate', in R. Halsall and M. Cockett (eds) *Education and training 14-19: Chaos or coherence?*, London: David Fulton, pp 73-88.

Hobbes, T. (1986 edn) *Leviathan*, London: Penguin.

Hodgson, A. and Spours, K. (1997) 'From the 1991 white paper to the Dearing report: a conceptual and historical framework for the 1990s', in A. Hodgson and K. Spours (ed) *Dearing and beyond*, London: Jonathan Cape, pp 4-24.

Huddleston, P. and Keep, E. (1999) 'What do employers want from education? A question more easily asked than answered', in J. Cramphorn (ed) *The role of partnerships in economic regeneration and development – International perspectives*, Coventry: Centre for Education and Industry, University of Warwick, pp 38-49.

Hyland, T. (1994) *Competence, education and NVQs: Dissenting perspectives*, London: Cassell.

Hyland, T. (1999) *Vocational studies, lifelong learning and social values: Investigating education, training and NVQs under the new deal*, Aldershot: Ashgate.

Hyland, T. and Johnson, S. (1998) 'Of cabbages and key skills: exploding the mythology of core transferable skills in post-school education', *Journal of Further and Higher Education*, vol 22, no 2, pp 163-72.

Hymowitz, K. (1997) 'Job training that works', *Wall Street Journal*, 13 February.

Institute of Directors (1991) *Performance and potential*, London: Institute of Directors.

Jessup, G. (1991) *Outcomes: NVQs and the emerging model of education and training*, Brighton: Falmer.

Jobert, A., Marry, C., Tanguy, L. and Rainbird, H. (eds) (1997) *Education and work in Great Britain, Germany and Italy*, London: Routledge.

Jonathan, R. (1987) 'The youth training scheme and core skills: an educational analysis', in M. Holt (ed) *Skills and vocationalism: The easy answer*, Milton Keynes: Open University Press, pp 68-119.

Keep, E. (1999) 'UK's VET policy and the "third way": following a high skills trajectory or running up a dead end street?', *Journal of Education and Work*, vol 12, no 3, pp 323-46.

Keep, E. (2000) 'Creating a knowledege-driven economy – definitions, challenges and opportunities', *SKOPE Policy Paper 2*, Coventry: University of Warwick.

Keep, E. (2001) 'If it moves, it's a skill – the changing meaning of skill in the UK context', Paper presented to ESRC's 'Future of Work' seminar, UMIST, October.

Keep, E. and Mayhew, K. (1999) 'The assessment: knowledge, skills and competitiveness', *Oxford Review of Economic Policy*, vol 15, no 1, pp 1-15.

Keep, E. and Payne, J. (2002) 'Policy interventions for a vibrant work-based route – or when policy hits reality's fan (again)', in K. Evans, P. Hodkinson and L. Unwin (eds) *Working to learn: Transforming learning in the workplace*, London: Kogan Page, pp 187-211.

Koike, K. and Inoki, T. (eds) (1990) *Skill formation in Japan and South East Asia*, Tokyo: University of Tokyo Press.

Lafer, G. (2002) 'What is "skill"? Training for discipline in the low-wage labor market', Paper presented to Labour Process Conference, University of Strathclyde, April.

Lauder, H. and Mehralizadeh, Y. (2001) 'Globalisation, multinationals and the labour market', in P. Brown, A. Green and H. Lauder (eds) *High skills: Globalisation, competitiveness, and skill formation*, Oxford: Oxford University Press, pp 204-34.

Lawson, T. (1992) 'Core skills: 16-19', in T. Whiteside, A. Sutton and T. Everton (eds) *16-19: Changes in education and training*, London: David Fulton, pp 85-94.

Lave, J. and Wenger, E. (1991) *Situated learning – Legitimate peripheral participation*, Cambridge: Cambridge University Press.

Lloyd, C. and Payne, J. (2002a) 'Towards a political economy of skill', *Journal of Education and Work*, vol 15, no 4, pp 365-90.

Lloyd, C. and Payne, J. (2002b) 'On the political economy of skill: assessing the possibilities for a viable high skills project in the UK', *New Political Economy*, vol 7, no 3, pp 367-95.

Lloyd, C. and Payne, J. (2003) 'The political economy of skill and the limits of educational policy', *Journal of Education Policy*, vol 18, no 1, pp 85-107.

Mansfield, B. (2000) 'Past imperfect', *PRIME Research and Development Ltd*, Harrogate: PRIME.

Milkman, R. (1998) 'The new American workplace: high road or low road?', in P. Thompson and C. Warhurst (eds) *Workplaces of the future*, London: Macmillan, pp 25-39.

MSC (Manpower Services Commission) (1984) *Core skills in YTS, Part 1: Youth training scheme manual*, Sheffield: MSC.

Nickson, D., Warhurst, C., Witz, A. and Cullen, A-M. (1998) 'Aesthetic labour in the service economy: an overlooked development', Paper presented to the Third International Labour Market Conference, Aberdeen, June.

Noon, M. and Blyton, P. (1997) *The realities of work*, London: Macmillan.

NSTF (National Skills Task Force) (1998) *Towards a national skills agenda: First report of the National Skills Task Force*, Sudbury: DfEE.

NSTF (2000a) *Skills for all: Research report from the National Skills Task Force*, Sudbury: DfEE.

NSTF (2000b) *Skills for all: Proposals for a national skills agenda: Final report of the National Skills Task Force*, Sudbury: DfEE.

Oliver, J.M. and Turton, J.R. (1982) 'Is there a shortage of skilled labour?', *British Journal of Industrial Relations*, vol 20, no 2, pp 195-200.

Payne, J. (1999) 'All things to all people: changing perceptions of skill among Britain's policy makers since the 1950s and their implications', *SKOPE Research Paper, No 2*, Oxford and Warwick Universities.

Payne, J. (2000) 'The unbearable lightness of skill: the changing meaning of skill in UK policy discourses and some implications for education and training', *Journal of Education Policy*, vol 15, no 3, pp 353-69.

Rainbird, H. (1997) 'The social construction of skill', in A. Jobert, C. Marry, L. Tanguy and H. Rainbird (eds) *Education and work in Great Britain, Germany and Italy*, London: Routledge, pp 177-91.

Reeder, D. (1979) 'A recurring debate: education and industry', in G. Bernbaum (ed) *Schooling in decline*, London: Macmillan, pp 177-203.

Rogoff, B. and Lave, J. (1984) *Everyday cognition: Its development in social context*, Cambridge, MA: Harvard University Press.

Rose, N. (1999) 'Inventiveness in politics', *Economy and Society*, vol 28, no 3, pp 467-93.

Stelzer, I. (1997) *Lessons of the US job machine*, America Enterprise Institute, May.

Thurly, K. and Lam, A. (1990) 'Skill formation of electronic engineers: comparing the learning behaviour of British and Japanese engineers', *Comparative Industrial Relations* (Discussion Paper Series), vol 90, no 211.

Tomlinson, S. (2001) *Education in a post-welfare society*, Buckingham: Open University Press.

Tysome, T. (2002) '"Unwashed" must brush up on their social skills', *Times Higher Educational Supplement*, 17 May, no 3, p 3.

Unwin, L. and Fuller, A. (2000) *National report on apprenticeships – Great Britain*, Leicester: Centre for Labour Market Studies (mimeo).

Vygotsky, L. (1978) *Mind in society: The development of higher psychological processes*, Cambridge, MA: Harvard University Press.

Warhurst, C. and Nickson, D. (2001) *Looking good, sounding right – Style counselling in the new economy*, London: The Industrial Society.

West, M. and Patterson, M. (1997) *The impact of people management practices on business performance*, London: Institute of Personnel and Development.

Whiteways Research (1995) *Skills for graduates in the 21st century*, London: AGR.

Wilde, O. (2000 edn) *The picture of Dorian Gray*, London: Penguin.

Young, M. (1998) *The curriculum of the future: From the 'new sociology of education' to a critical theory of learning*, London: Falmer Press.

FIVE

Qualifying for a job: an educational and economic audit of the English 14-19 education and training system

Rosa M. Fernández and Geoff Hayward

Introduction

A dominant international theme in vocational education and training (VET) policy discourse continues to be the need to boost skill supply to meet both the requirements of emerging knowledge economies and to reduce social exclusion by increasing the employability of socially disadvantaged groups. For example, the Commission of the European Communities (CEC, 2003, p 3) warns that while:

> efforts are being made in all European countries to adapt education and training systems to the knowledge-driven society and economy ... the reforms are not up to the challenges and their current pace will not enable the Union to attain the objectives set.

The objectives referred to are those set at the Lisbon European Council held in March 2000 where:

> the Heads of State and Government acknowledged that the "European Union is confronted with a quantum shift resulting from globalisation and the challenges of a new knowledge driven economy" and set the Union a major strategic goal for 2010 'to become the most competitive and dynamic knowledge-based economy in the world, capable of sustainable economic growth with more and better jobs and greater social cohesion.' (CEC, 2003, p 3)

To achieve these aims it is envisaged it will require a radical programme to modernise education systems, thereby placing education and training policy at the heart of the Union's economic and social policy (see Chapter Three of this volume).

Such a discourse argues for the need to steer education and training systems to meet both the needs of individuals and the labour market. However, the linkage between the education and training system, on the one hand, and the demands of individuals and the labour market, on the other hand, is complex and developing mechanisms to steer an education and training system to meet individual and labour market demands is highly problematic for policy makers. As Descy and Tessaring (2002, p 4) point out in the context of the EU:

> State-managed planning and demand-led steering by the market represent two opposite extremes among the mechanisms by which VET systems can be coordinated. Both types of steering are found in every system in differing degrees.... State-led steering, through centralised planning, generally acts on the education supply. VET systems cannot, however, be steered solely by a State system as it is impossible to forecast changes in the demand beyond a certain point.

This chapter seeks to address the issue of balancing the supply and demand side of the skills equation using England as a case study. England represents an opportunity to assess the extent to which centrally driven state-led steering has had a significant impact on skill supply because of the large number of education and training policy initiatives over the last 25 years. Furthermore, suitable data sets exist to assess the hypothesis that this has led to overqualification of the workforce, which Descy and Tessaring (2002) acknowledge as being of increasing importance for European labour markets.

The English patient

Conventional wisdom among education and training policy makers in England echoes the sentiments of the Lisbon Council: that within the English economy, skill demand exceeds supply[1]. As a result, the story goes, the English economy underperforms in terms of labour productivity compared with competitor nations, thereby thwarting the high skills vision for the English economy and a fairer society. According to this way of 'framing and naming' the issue (Keep and Mayhew, 1999), the solution to economic underperformance is to increase the supply of skills into the economy. Education and training policy is consequently focused upon:

> a range of supply-side solutions ... that are dependent upon a number of managerial technologies. Examples include target setting and its associated planning mechanisms, and funding systems and their associated methodologies and incentive structures. The visible manifestation of a belief in the ability of these devices to deliver a high skills vision rests in the creation of the new Learning and Skills Council (LSC) and its statutory duty to set and pursue a fresh set of National Learning Targets. These targets form the overarching

strategic focus for the management of the English [Education and Training] system. (Keep, 2002, p 458)

This ideological commitment to the reform of the supply side of the skills equation, while ignoring the demand side, has a long history in England. Indeed, intervening on the supply side through education and training policy has become almost the only socially and politically acceptable way for government policy to be used to raise the economic competitiveness of organisations. The result is a sidelining of other issues such as "competitive strategies, labour market regulation, work organisation, job design, and the quality of working life" (Keep, 2002, p 458), and as being beyond the remit of public policy. The 'black box' of the firm has remained firmly and tightly shut for the last two decades and, notwithstanding more recent policy analyses such as that undertaken by the Performance and Innovation Unit (PIU, 2001), is likely to remain so for the foreseeable future.

The supposed imbalance between skill supply and demand is usually explained in terms of failures in the allocative role of the labour market. A lack of communication between employers, on the one hand, and education and training providers, on the other hand, is often highlighted as a particular weakness in the English system. Compared to many of its European neighbours, England has very poorly developed employer networks and organisations that can mediate the development of education and training policy at a local level. Consequently, the demand for skills is primarily communicated to the supply side via the state and, in the process, messages are refracted by state concerns about accountability into an emphasis on formal qualifications and graduation from formal programmes of education and training. Following the logic outlined by Keep (2002), performance targets are then set in terms of particular proportions of a population achieving certain levels of qualifications. For example, the National Learning Targets for England required that, by 2002, 60% of 21 year olds should be qualified to Level 3 (see Table 5.1) and 85% of 19 year olds should be qualified to Level 2. The assumption, then, is that the skills acquired within the formal education and training system will then transfer into the workplace.

The dominant policy view in England remains, therefore, that the route to a more prosperous and equal society lies through education and training, and, thereby, the acquisition by individuals of qualifications that are supposed to have both use and exchange value in the labour market (see Chapter Twelve of this volume). In particular, the view expressed by Tony Blair, that "[i]n the long run, schools must play the central role in preparing people better for work and careers" (PIU, 2001, p 3), has been central to education and training policy for the last quarter of a century. As a result, the English education and training system has been subject to wave after wave of reform. Qualifications have changed repeatedly, funding mechanisms adjusted and complicated, targets set and regulatory organisations established with increased levels of competition between institutions implemented through the 'marketisation' of the education and training system, with the overall aim of matching skills supply more closely to the perceived demand for skills revealed, for example, by employer surveys.

Our purpose in this chapter is to audit how successful such education and training policy has been in terms of increasing the supply of qualifications into the economy over the last two decades and the economic consequences of this. We focus on the English 14-19 education and training system and the supply of intermediate qualifications at Levels 2 and 3 of the English National Qualification system taken in the main by young people aged 14-19 (see Table 5.1). We first provide a statistical overview indicating how the performance of the 14–19 education and training system has changed over time in terms of participation and certification rates. We then examine the qualifications mix being produced by the system. Finally, we consider economic arguments for supply side education and training policies, and their potential consequences for labour market performance. In particular, we investigate the extent to which over-education is now emerging in the English labour market at the level of intermediate skills, an issue recognised to be of growing importance in European labour markets (Descy and Tessaring, 2002).

Qualification supply

The English qualification system is both complex and subject to continual and rapid change. Nonetheless, all qualifications are being accommodated within a National Qualifications Framework (NQF) on the basis of their level and their location within one of three more or less distinct pathways (see Table 5.1). For the purposes of this analysis, we focus on qualifications located at Levels 2 and 3 in the NQF. We also adopt the tripartite division of qualifications provided by the NQF to explore participation and attainment in the education and training system.

Table 5.1: Locating major qualifications within the NQF

Level of qualification	General	Vocationally-related	Occupationally-related
5	Higher level qualifications eg degrees and postgraduate qualifications		Level 5 NVQ
4		`	Level 4 NVQ
3 Advanced level	GCE A level	VCE A level (Advanced GNVQ)	Level 3 NVQ
2 Intermediate level	GCSE A*-C	(Intermediate GNVQ)	Level 2 NVQ
1 Foundation level	GCSE D-G	Foundation GNVQ	Level 1 NVQ
Entry level	Certificate of Educational Achievement		

Source: QCA (2003)

The last two years of compulsory education

In theory, all young people in England are required to stay at school until the age of 16. In England, the main examination taken by students at the minimum school leaving age is the General Certificate of Secondary Education (GCSE). This is awarded at eight grades, A*-G. Achieving five or more GCSE passes at grades A*-C is deemed equivalent to achieving a Level 2 qualification, while achieving five GCSE passes at grades D-G equates to a Level 1 qualification. In addition, students may also take vocationally related courses such as the Intermediate General National Vocational Qualification (GNVQ) or the Foundation GNVQ. Passing the intermediate GNVQ is equivalent to four GCSE passes at grades A*-C, while a pass in the Foundation GNVQ equates to four GCSE passes at grades D-G. Thus, a student could be considered to have achieved a Level 2 qualification by either passing five or more separate GCSEs at grades A*-C, or by passing an Intermediate GNVQ plus one GCSE pass at Grade A*-C.

Starting from a low level of attainment in comparison with other OECD nations, there has been a steady increase in the proportion of English students achieving a Level 2 qualification by the end of compulsory schooling – from 32.8% in 1989 to 51.2% by 2002. The rise has been particularly pronounced for young women (from 35.8% to 55.6%) compared to young men (from 29.8% to 46%).

This change in the proportion of students achieving a Level 2 qualification by the age of 16 also translates into a steady increase in the total number of young people achieving at this level. In 1990, approximately 220,800 young people obtained a Level 2 qualification by the end of compulsory schooling. By 2002, this number had grown to approximately 310,700, an increase of 54%. This means that, between 1990 and 2002, approximately 3.24 million young people achieved a Level 2 qualification by the end of compulsory schooling. In addition to increasing the potential supply of Level 2 skills, this increase in attainment at the end of compulsory schooling has also had a major impact on participation in 16-19 education and training, whereby an increasing number of young people convert their Level 2 qualifications into Level 3 qualifications.

Participation 16-19

At the end of compulsory schooling, young people have to make a choice about the education and training pathway they wish to follow and, in the case of full-time courses, the institutions in which they wish to study. Essentially, there are four choices available to young people at this stage:

- full-time education which includes both the academic/general and vocationally-related pathways described earlier in either a school sixth-form or a college;

- government-sponsored training which falls into the third, occupational route and involves both employers and private training providers;
- employment (either full- or part-time), with or without employer-funded training; and
- unemployment without benefits.

Analysis of administrative data sets[2] and data derived from the Youth Cohort Study (YCS)[3] reveal an increase in participation in education and training for 16-18 year olds from the mid-1980s until the early 1990s, followed by a slow decrease in participation followed by a more recent increase. Table 5.2 shows the main activity of young people in their first three years following compulsory schooling as revealed by the YCS. In 2000, the last year for which verified administrative data are currently available, approximately 87% of 16 year olds, 79.3% of 17 year olds and 60.4% of 18 year olds were in some form of education and training. Thus, taken together, some 75.4% of 16-18 year olds were in some form of education and training in 2000.

The major factor underpinning this increasing participation rate has been increased participation in full-time education (FTE) in both the general and vocationally-related routes (see Table 5.1). Participation in these routes by 16 year olds increased from 47.3% in 1985 to 72.6% in 1993, followed by a slow decline to 69.4% in 1997. Participation in FTE then started to increase again reaching 71.4% among 16 year olds in 2000.

Government-supported training (GST), which includes Modern Apprenticeships (MAs), Life Skills and other training for young people, is the main component of the third pathway (the occupational route) which young people can follow after the end of compulsory schooling. Such training for 16 year olds reached a peak in the second half of the 1980s with just over a quarter of 16 year olds and a fifth of 17 year olds participating. Participation among 16 year olds has declined rapidly since then, reaching 8% in 2000. The decline has been less rapid for 17 year olds, with approximately 11% participating in GST in 2000. The same pattern is also observed for those undertaking Employer-Funded Training (EFT).

Data from the Spring 2002 sweep of the YCS (DfES, 2003a, 2003b) provides the most recent information on participation. This study indicates that 71% of 16 year olds were in FTE and 9% were in GST, values that are very close to the official estimates of 71% and 7% participation in FTE and GST respectively. The YCS indicates that 40% of 18 year olds were still in FTE in spring 2002 (official estimate 37%) with a further 8% in GST (official estimate 8%).

The YCS data (Table 5.2) also demonstrates that the proportion of 16-18 year olds in employment (excluding those involved in GST) has declined over time. As Raffe et al (1998) point out, this trend partly reflects the economic cycle, with a boom in the late 1980s being followed by a recession in the early 1990s. However, the economic growth of the mid- to late 1990s does not seem to have reversed the trend.

Table 5.2: The proportion of young people in different activities 16-19 based on the YCS

	1985	1986	1987	1988	1989	1990	1991	1992	1993	1994	1995	1996	1997	1998	1999	2000
At age 16+																
FTE	37	39	41		48		58	66		72				69		71
GST	17	28	26		24		16	14		12				11		10
Full-time job	29	22	23		23		16	10		8				10		8
Out of work	15	10	8		4		7	7		6				5		5
Other	2	1	2		2		3	2		3				5		5
At age 17+																
FTE		32	29	33		41		52	57							
GST		3	12	19		19		16	15							
Full-time job		45	43	38		33		20	15							
Out of work		15	13	8		4		9	9							
Other		4	3	2		3		3	4							
At age 18+																
FTE			18	16	20		27		39	40		43		42		44
FT higher education									29	19		23		22		23
GST			4	3	3		3		7	7		7		8		11
Full-time job			59	64	64		54		34	33		29		31		29
Out of work			14	12	8		10		14	11		11		7		6
Other			5	4	6		6		8	9		10		12		12

Source: DfEE (1998, 1999a, 1999b; DfES, 2001a-2001e, 2002a, 2002b)

Raising participation rates in post-compulsory education in either the FTE or GST pathways is only the first step to meeting the political desire to increase the supply of qualified young people entering the labour market. Young people also have to stay in the system and to achieve qualifications.

Retention and survival rates

Compared to 1995, school expectancy in the UK (the expected years of schooling under current conditions) had increased by 10% by 2002 (OECD, 2002). However, as Table 5.2 indicates, participation in education and training in England and Wales fell in a step-like manner, so that participation at 18 still remains below the levels found in most other OECD countries. As the OECD (2002, p 9) points out:

> Drop-out and survival rates provide some indication of the internal efficiency of education systems. Students leave educational programmes before their completion for many reasons – they realise that they have chosen the wrong subject or educational programme, they fail to meet the standards set by their educational institution, or they want to work before completing the programme. Nevertheless, high drop-out rates indicate that the education system is not meeting the needs of clients. Students may find the educational programmes do not meet their expectations or their needs in order to enter the labour market, or that the programmes require more time outside the labour market than they can justify.

At the time when post-16 participation was increasing rapidly (1985-92), the difference between the percentage of young people participating at 16 and 17 was approximately 16%. This figure had decreased to 7% by 2001. The cross-sectional evidence suggests, therefore, that retention rates in the 16-19 part of the English education and training system have improved over time. Evidence from the YCS (DfES, 2003), a longitudinal study, supports this view. Furthermore, the YCS suggests that the majority of young people are in the same activity at 17 and 18 years of age as they were in at 16. For example, for those aged 16 in 1998-99, 86% of those in FTE at 16 were still in FTE at 17 years of age. This trend persists for 18 year olds though a greater proportion of the young people surveyed changed activities between 17 and 18 than between 16 and 17. For those changing activities, a job was the most common destination. Thus retention rates in the English education system have also improved over time, though retention still varies between the types of courses young people take following completion of compulsory schooling. In particular, retention rates are much higher on two-year Level 3 courses for young people who have been academically successful at the end of compulsory schooling compared to those taking one-year Level 2 courses, such as Intermediate GNVQ, post-16 (Payne, 2003).

The level of attrition on one-year, Level 2 vocational courses can be very high. For example, Huddleston (2002) reports that in the academic year ending in

July 1999, nationally only 60% of students who registered on Intermediate Business GNVQ courses passed the course. The figure for the Intermediate GNVQ in Leisure and Tourism in the same year is 56%. Furthermore, among the admittedly small sample of 140 students studied by Huddleston (2002) in four further education (FE) colleges, only 53% of Intermediate GNVQ Business students and 46% of students on Intermediate GNVQ Leisure and Tourism courses, remained on the programme until the end of the academic year. Not only do such courses have lower internal efficiency than two-year Level 3 courses, they also have essentially zero rates of return in the labour market (see later in this chapter).

The evidence presented so far shows an increasing proportion of 16-19 year olds participating in post-compulsory education in England. Furthermore, retention and certification rates within the English education and training system have also improved. This has had a significant impact on the level of qualifications held by the English workforce. Thus by the autumn of 2003, 76.1% of 19 year olds held a qualification at Level 2 or higher compared to 72.3% in 1997. However, disaggregating these data by level reveal that the greatest increase has been among 19 year olds holding Level 3 qualifications (from 41% in 1997 to 45% in 2003) rather than among those holding Level 2 qualifications (from 25% in 1997 to 24% in 2003). Furthermore, the increase at Level 3 is largely in terms of academic rather than vocational qualifications, with young people opting for the academic route, as an increasing proportion of the age cohort aim for entry to higher education (HE) at 19 years of age, and not direct entry into the labour market.

The qualification mix

The final stage of this audit is to examine the choices made by 16-19 year olds who are studying full time. Those involved in FTE from 16 to 19 years of age are participating in two main pathways – the general and the vocationally related – at a number of different levels (see Table 5.1). Taking GCE A Level and GCSE to constitute the general route and VCE A level/GNVQ/NVQ to constitute the vocationally-related route, then the administrative data indicate that there has been an increase in participation in both the general and the vocational pathways from 1985 to the present day. However, participation in the general pathway always exceeds participation in the vocational pathway. This reflects an underlying issue in the English education and training system compared with other European countries such as Germany, Austria, Denmark and Switzerland: lower participation in the vocational route in the UK. Furthermore, the growth in participation in the vocational pathway for 16 year olds is almost wholly due to substitution effects: rather than retaking the GCSEs they failed at the end of compulsory schooling, 16 year olds began to take Intermediate and Foundation GNVQs in increasing numbers following their introduction in 1992.

Despite the provision of these alternative vocational courses, total participation in courses leading to Level 2 qualifications, post-16 in FTE has fallen over time. This is probably due to the increasing percentage of young people gaining a Level 2 qualification at the end of compulsory schooling. They can then opt either to take a Level 3 qualification or to enter the labour market at the end of compulsory schooling, such as through the GST pathway on, for example, an Advanced Modern Apprenticeship (AMA). However, uptake of the AMA option by 16 year olds is not a particularly popular choice, with over 50% of all people starting an AMA being over the age of 19 (Fuller and Unwin, 2003).

The disparity in participation between the general and the vocationally-related route becomes even greater if we examine qualifications at Level 3: GCE A-levels, Advanced GNVQ/VCE A-levels and NVQs at Level 3. In 2000, of the 16 year olds in England taking full-time Level 3 courses, 76% were taking GCE A/AS compared to 15% taking the Advanced GNVQ/VCE A/AS option, and 10% taking the NVQ Level 3 or other equivalents. In other words, at Level 3, three times as many English 16 year olds in FTE were taking GCE A-levels than were taking either GNVQ/VCE or NVQ Level 3.

Overall, then, it appears that the sequence of policies implemented over the last 25 years or so, aided by a wide range of other social factors, have been successful in increasing the proportion of young people accessing and completing intermediate level qualifications in England. In particular, there has been a sharp increase in the number of young people studying in the academic route at Level 3 with their progression being primarily into HE rather than into the labour market. However, simply counting the number of graduates, or the number of qualifications achieved, does not necessarily inform us about the quality of the education outcomes with respect to the demands of the economy for skills. It is to this that we now turn.

Qualifications and the labour market

The economic case for supply side education policies follows the literature on economic growth where education plays a fundamental part in the process of economic growth (Temple, 2001; Sianesi and Van Reenen, 2002). On the basis of this evidence, supply side education policies aim at providing the appropriate environment for sustainable development. These theories rely on the assumption that the use of acquired skills in the labour market will boost productivity and ensure long-term economic growth. Within this framework, the use and value of education in the labour market appears to be a better means to assess supply side education policies aimed at guaranteeing economic growth. In England, the situation is such that the labour market dictates the quantity and quality of skills at use or on demand, whereas the supply of skills is centralised through public sector policies. The interaction between the two sides of the market for skills may result in aggregate imbalances, indicating difficulties in the production of the right skill mix and therefore casting doubt on the success of supply side education policies. In what follows, we analyse the prevailing equilibrium between qualifications supply and demand in the British labour market.

Qualifications demand and supply in the UK

The standard approach to identifying what skills are in high demand is to estimate the returns to education. Wages summarise the value that the labour market places on skills. Wage premiums on particular skills can be regarded as a signal that either those skills are in short supply or else that their contribution to the productive side of the economy outweighs the cost of obtaining them[4]. In any case, the interpretation of the wage premium signal is that those skills are worthwhile investing in, hence justifying the use of the returns to education technique as a means to identify them.

There is a wealth of empirical evidence on the returns to qualifications by level of attainment, sometimes distinguishing between academic and vocational qualifications and by subject of degree[5]. The message from this literature is clear: acquiring qualifications pays off. Furthermore, the higher the level of qualification, the better the return compared to not having qualifications. Estimates of the returns to education vary themselves depending on the data set and the technique used to estimate them. Considering broad qualifications, the returns to obtaining O-Levels or GCSE qualifications (Level 2) pay some 8-20% more than not having them. An additional 17-23% accrues to those acquiring two or more A-levels (Level 3). However, lower vocational qualifications (up to and including Level 2) earn no return in the labour market compared to not having them while Level 3 Vocational Qualifications earn some 7-12% higher wages than those who do not have them (Dearden et al, 2000). More important than the existence of handsome dividends to acquiring qualifications is the fact that these returns do not show a clear tendency to decline in recent times (Walker and Yu, 2001), despite the increase in qualifications held by the labour force.

Although conventionally accepted, the use of rates of returns to identify skills in high demand in the labour market is not a perfect technique. Wages are the result of the interaction between labour demand and supply, and therefore wage premiums could be capturing the effect of various characteristics of workers other than qualifications. The most cited example of this kind of problem is innate ability. More-able people are more likely to obtain qualifications. More-able people are also likely to be more productive and earn higher wages. Therefore, a positive correlation between qualifications and wages can be observed independently of the value of education itself. Most studies on returns to education acknowledge this possibility and different techniques have been developed in order to reduce the noise that the wage signal contains as a measure of the value of qualifications (Blundell et al, 2001). The conventional method to remove the effect of variables other than education on wages is to include controls for them in the estimation of rates of return. The quantity and quality of controls depends on the data set but it is common to include individual characteristics such as gender, ability and family background, and firm characteristics such as size or sector. Nevertheless, the extent to which the wage signal is 'clean' after controlling for other effects remains uncertain.

An alternative way of assessing the balance between the supply and demand of qualifications in the labour market is to compare the qualifications held by the labour force with those required for the jobs available. There is probably no objective way to disentangle the qualifications required to perform a particular job from those actually held by the job holder, not least because in many cases the person who is performing the job shapes it. One approach is to directly ask workers what qualifications they think would be needed in order to get the job they hold. This was the approach taken by Felstead et al (2002) for their report, *Skills in Britain 1986-2001*. Taking the job holder's judgement of qualifications requirements for that job as demand, and considering how many people there are in the labour force holding those qualifications as supply, the authors come up with a sizeable excess supply of qualifications at Levels 2 and 3. There seem to be many more people in the labour force holding these qualifications than available jobs that would require these qualifications. The excess supply exceeds two million people for Level 3 qualifications and it is of the order of 1.5 million for Level 2 qualifications. Considering the trends, these authors illustrate how this excess supply of qualifications held by the labour force arose as a result of widespread educational upgrading in the population, as described in the previous two sections of this chapter. This emerging excess supply shows that education policies have indeed achieved their goal of raising the educational attainment of the labour force.

Objections can also be raised to the use of workers' perceptions as an approximation for the demand of qualifications (Hartog, 2000). Following from the fact that demand seems to be lower than supply, it could be argued that workers perceive their jobs as less demanding due to experience, for example. The extent to which workers reported a required qualification below the one they held gives an idea of the importance of this criticism. Between 40% and 50% of workers holding qualifications at both Levels 2 and 3 regarded themselves as overqualified. The incidence of perceived overqualification appears to have increased for workers who hold Level 2 qualifications but no clear trend was observed for workers with Level 3 qualifications.

Reconciling the evidence

Leaving aside problems with measurement and estimation techniques, the conflicting evidence provided by these two approaches has important implications for labour market performance. On the one hand, the evidence based on returns to qualifications suggests there is a wage premium for obtaining some of them. On the other hand, the evidence on the actual requirements in the labour market suggests there is an excess supply of them. There are at least two economic scenarios where both these observations could coexist.

One possibility is a case of overqualification in the labour market.

Overqualification arises in the presence of an excess supply of qualifications. Workers can be thought of as being picked from a queue where the more qualified workers are first in line. Since there are more workers than jobs, workers with higher qualifications will end up in jobs for which only lower qualifications are required. These workers will be overqualified but they could still earn more than the worker with the appropriate level of qualifications for the job. Thus, some positive return to qualifications will be obtained even if there is an excess supply of qualifications.

Overqualification[6] represents a mismatch between the educational requirements of the job, and the educational attainment of the job holder. The returns to overqualification can therefore be approached from two angles. One possibility is to keep qualifications held by workers constant and to compare the wages of workers with the same qualifications in jobs with different educational requirements. Holding educational attainment constant, overqualified workers have jobs requiring a lower educational level. Hence, compared to having a job matching their qualifications, overqualified workers are worse-off than adequately qualified ones, and therefore their wages are expected to be lower. Following this approach, Green and McIntosh (2002) find that overqualified workers earn less than their adequately qualified counterparts. It has to be noted, however, that this approach holds qualifications possessed by workers constant and looks at returns obtained by the same qualifications in different jobs. It could therefore be interpreted as the return to holding certain jobs given qualifications.

The alternative way to look at returns to overqualification is to hold the educational requirements of the job constant and compare the wages of workers with different educational attainments in the same type of job. Holding job requirements constant, overqualified workers have higher educational attainment than their adequately qualified peers for the same job. Within this framework, the presence of some positive return to overqualification will result in overqualified workers earning more than workers who have qualifications matching the job requirement. Put differently, overqualified workers will get some additional earnings out of holding qualifications even if they are not required for the job. Groot and van den Brink (2000) survey the existing evidence on these two approaches for several countries. The evidence shows that, controlling for educational attainment, returns to over-education are negative, while, controlling for job requirements, returns to over-education are positive.

For the particular case of the UK, we reproduce an analysis similar to the ones mentioned. The database we use is the 2001 Skills Survey in Britain (Felstead et al, 2002) funded by the UK government's Department for Education and Skills (DfES) through the Centre for Skills Knowledge and Organisational Performance (SKOPE). Descriptive statistics of all variables are presented in this chapter's Appendix (for a description of the variables, see Green and McIntosh, 2002). To compare the outcomes of the different approaches, Table 5.3 presents three specifications. All specifications are based on a log-linear equation in the spirit of Mincer (1974).

Specification I replicates Table 10 in Green and McIntosh (2002) without

Table 5.3: Wage effects of over/underqualification, employees only, robust standard errors

Dependent variable: Log of hourly pay	Specification I		Specification II		Specification III	
	Coefficient	SE	Coefficient	SE	Coefficient	SE
Overqualified (yes/no)	−0.172**	0.015	0.090**	0.015		
Underqualified (yes/no)	0.177**	0.018	−0.052**	0.018		
Levels of overqualification					0.072**	0.009
Levels of underqualification					−0.027*	0.010
Qualifications held by worker						
Level 1	0.135**	0.024				
Level 2	0.217**	0.021				
Level 3	0.362**	0.023				
Level 4	0.564**	0.026				
Degree	0.742**	0.028				
Qualifications required for job						
Level 1			0.084**	0.020	0.107**	0.020
Level 2			0.217**	0.020	0.257**	0.019
Level 3			0.343**	0.022	0.389**	0.022
Level 4			0.586**	0.026	0.642**	0.026
Degree			0.765**	0.027	0.823**	0.027
Female	−0.141**	0.014	−0.145**	0.014	−0.144**	0.014
Years of work experience	0.026**	0.002	0.024**	0.002	0.024**	0.002
Experience squared/100	−0.048**	0.005	−0.044**	0.005	−0.044**	0.005
Married	0.072**	0.013	0.068**	0.013	0.068**	0.013
Has children	0.019	0.015	0.017	0.015	0.018	0.015
Permanent job	0.004	0.028	−0.001	0.027	0.003	0.027
Full-time job	0.142**	0.018	0.138**	0.017	0.135**	0.017
Ever do shift work	−0.039**	0.014	−0.032*	0.014	−0.034*	0.014
Workplace size (employees)						
25-99	0.078**	0.017	0.075**	0.017	0.074**	0.017
100-499	0.120**	0.018	0.119**	0.018	0.117**	0.018
500-999	0.147**	0.034	0.139**	0.034	0.139**	0.033
1,000+	0.137**	0.019	0.120**	0.019	0.123**	0.019
Highest math qualification						
Level 2	0.086**	0.015	0.090**	0.014	0.069**	0.014
Level 3	0.165**	0.029	0.175**	0.029	0.149**	0.029
Degree	0.381**	0.145	0.368*	0.145	0.351*	0.145
Constant	1.147**	0.048	1.164**	0.047	1.120**	0.047
Region dummies	Yes		Yes		Yes	
Observations	3,595		3,595		3,595	
R^2	0.49		0.49		0.50	

Notes: * significant at 5% level default category; ** significant at 1% level: employee in the North East without any qualifications in a job that requires no qualifications and workplace with less than 25 employees.

controlling for over/under-skill. The number of observations in our estimations is therefore slightly higher and produces results that do not exactly match, but are very similar to, those presented by Green and McIntosh. The main message of Specification I is that, holding qualifications constant, overqualified workers earn less than their adequately matched counterparts. At the same time, there are positive and increasing premiums for holding higher levels of qualifications while the coefficients for the individual and firm characteristics show expected signs. Specification II does the same as the previous one, holding job requirements constant. Since there is a positive significant effect of over-education on wages, we can conclude that there are positive returns to over-education, holding job requirements constant. At the same time, holding jobs with higher levels of education appears to pay-off as well as holding those qualifications. The remaining individual and firm characteristics do not change much either. Specification III follows Groot and van den Brink (2000) for the estimation of rates of return to over-education (Specification I in Table 5.3). Since we are looking at overqualifications, instead of years of over/under-education, we include Levels of over/underqualification[7]. The variable levels of overqualification takes values 1-5, where value 1 represents workers who have qualifications one level higher than those required for the job while value 5 represents workers with a degree in jobs that require no qualifications. The message in the first column is not much different from that in the third column: there are some positive returns to over-education in the British labour market.

Since there are some positive returns to overqualification, the labour market appears to be attaching some value to qualifications even though they are not required for the job. However, overqualification can also be the result of some failure in the allocation of workers to jobs through the labour market. The wrong match of worker–job qualification could be due to lack of adequate information about one or the other part of the pair. The presence of underqualification lends support to this argument since it is incompatible with the idea that there are too many qualifications and workers compete for the jobs that require their possessed qualifications. The incidence of underqualification is much lower than that of overqualification though (see Felstead et al, 2002, Table 4.6). Furthermore, underqualification appears to be declining over time, whereas overqualification is on the rise, hence suggesting that over time there could be a stronger case for the excess supply hypothesis than for the information asymmetry story.

An excess supply of qualifications could also concur with positive returns to education if qualifications were being used for signalling productivity when employers cannot observe the worker's productivity[8]. Upon recruitment, employers are normally unable to separate candidates between the better or more productive, and the less productive ones. More-productive workers are willing to indicate their value to the employer so that they get the job and the higher wage. Education or qualifications can be used for this purpose provided that the cost of acquiring education is lower for the better workers (Spence, 1973). Better candidates will signal their value through their qualifications while employers will use the signal to select candidates and offer them higher wages. If this were the case, and education were made available to an increasing number of people at lower cost, every worker would sensibly try to reap some of these benefits. Over time, the signalling value of education will be reduced as an increasing proportion of the labour force acquire qualifications independently of their potential productivity. Some, probably lower, returns to qualifications could still remain, provided that better workers continue to obtain qualifications and they unveil their higher productivity through some alternative means. As stated earlier, however, there does not seem to be a clear declining trend in the returns to qualifications in the British labour market. Hence, either education is not used as a signal or the expansion of education has not reduced significantly the average quality of graduates.

An alternative approach to skills demand

There remains a third approach to analyse the extent of skill mismatch in the labour market, and that is directly asking employers about their needs. Unfortunately, it does not seem to be common to ask employers about required qualifications for the posts they have. Understandably though, and particularly in bigger firms, employers could be unaware of the particular needs of every single job in the firm. The Employers Skill Survey (ESS) in the UK tends to ask employers about recruitment difficulties and skills deficiencies of their workforce so that the comparison with qualifications demand and supply is limited. They are asked, however, whether lack of qualifications is a cause of hard-to-fill and skill-shortage vacancies, although this reason is not one of the most important ones causing vacancies (Frogner, 2002).

Recent educational policies and particularly the introduction of key skills as part of the school/college curriculum seem to have followed findings from the ESS. The evidence provided by the survey suggests that apart from 'technical skills'[9], and 'company/job specific skills', the skills most sought after are generic skills like IT, communication, customer handling and team-working skills. Furthermore, the findings also suggest that the most important reason for the presence of recruitment difficulties is the 'low number of applicants with skills', followed by 'low number of applicants in general' and 'lack of work experience'. Lack of work experience and the need for job-specific skills are not easy to deal with through external interventions. By including the sought-after skills in the school/college curriculum, however, the problem of the lack of applicants with the right skills could be tackled provided that the skills are effectively acquired through formal education and are transferable from educational to work contexts.

One of the innovations of the last 16-19 educational reform in the UK, Curriculum 2000, was to include key skills[10] as part of the curriculum. This intervention provides us with a unique natural experiment to assess whether generic skills can be successfully provided within the formal education system.

The immediate effect of providing the opportunity to acquire these units in the post-16 curriculum is to transform key skills into a qualification, which takes us back to our initial discussion about the market for qualifications. As explained before, to the extent that education is an investment, the perceived rewards to key skills become one of the main determinants of their acquisition in the formal education system. Following from the ESS, increasing wages is not the most likely response of employers to the problem of skill shortages and hard-to-fill vacancies (Frogner, 2002). It is too early to obtain evidence on the returns to these qualifications, but even if key skills qualifications had a positive return in the labour market, students face a trade-off between investing their time in taking these qualifications or other qualifications, such as additional AS levels. If further education is a consideration for the student, then the value that HE institutions put on key skills becomes relevant for the choice.

Two forces are at work when analysing the outcomes of this intervention. On the one hand, colleges and schools have to make the new 'subjects' available with limited guidelines about their contents and with limited financial aid for the provision of key skill qualifications. On the other hand, once key skills units are on supply, students have to decide or be attracted into taking these qualifications rather than some alternative qualification.

The Universities and Colleges Admission Service (UCAS) undertook a series of surveys to investigate the implementation of Curriculum 2000 that provides data on the uptake of key skills. In the survey of November 2001 (UCAS, 2002a), approximately 15 months after the implementation of the Curriculum 2000 reforms, only 44% of the institutions that responded reported offering key skill qualifications to their second-year students taking Level 3 courses. The percentage was highest for Sixth Form (80%) and FE (74%) colleges but much lower in Comprehensive (51%), Grammar (29%) and Independent (25%) schools. Responses to the survey suggested that only 38% of second-year students were working towards one or more key skill qualifications, with 14% of learners being entered for one, 6% for two and 15% for three key skill qualifications. Among the six key skills, entry for certification was highest among the so-called 'hard' key skills of Communication (26%), IT (24%) and Application of Number (17%). Entry for the three 'wider' key skills was negligible: Improving Own Learning and Performance (1%), Working with Others (0.7%) and Problem Solving (0.5%). Furthermore, Hayward and Fernández (2004) calculate that in 2000-02, only 12.1% of 16 year olds, and only 9.5% of 17 year olds, who were in education and training, achieved a key skills qualification at any level. Clearly, despite an apparently strong signal from employers that key skills qualifications, and the skills they signified, would be valued in the labour market, uptake of the qualifications was extremely poor.

The explanation of this poor uptake resides in the cost and benefits of providing/ taking these qualifications, and their perceived rate of return, to both students and educational institutions. Both institutions and students suffered high costs associated with the increased assessment and teaching burden represented by the key skills qualifications. These costs were both direct, in terms of entry fees for key skills qualifications, and indirect, in the form of substantial opportunity costs. Given that students enrolled on two-year Level 3 courses are typically aiming for entry into HE as the primary outcome of the 16-19 phase of education, the apparent lack of benefits of the key skills qualifications for HE entry purposes is a strong disincentive to take the qualifications rather than, say, an additional AS subject.

The lack of interest in the key skills in many quarters of higher education remains a problem since this discourages both teachers and students and makes it difficult to devise and explain a clear and coherent national policy on the key skills. In light of this:

> it will be necessary to continue to emphasise the importance of students developing their key skills particularly in the context of the development of the 14-19 phase. (QCA, 2001, p 4)

The huge scale of the lack of interest in key skills as entry qualifications for HE is borne out by an analysis of the provisional offers made to a random sample of 5,473 students applying through UCAS in 2002 for 2003 entry to HE:

> Key skills were specifically included in only a small minority of [offers] (6.1% of offers made by Post-92 universities, 4.5% of offers made by HE colleges, 3.8% of FE colleges and 0% of Pre-92 universities). (UCAS, 2002b, p 19)

This antipathy to key skills on the part of HE admissions tutors also extends to students who were reported to have "a negative attitude towards key skills, and are only doing the qualification because it attracts UCAS points" (QCA, 2001, p 6)[11].

To overcome this weak uptake, the current policy on key skills is based both on inducements, particularly the provision of funds for participation in key skills programmes, even if they do not lead to assessment and certification, and the revision of the testing regime to make it less of a burden. However, the view that moving "as swiftly as possible to a system of on-demand and, eventually, on-line testing holds the key to the future success of these qualifications" (QCA, 2001, p 3) seems to fly in the face of the evidence that the key to making these qualifications more attractive to learners is to convince HE admissions tutors of their worth, at least for those studying at Level 3. The chances of a weak hortatory policy instrument (Schneider and Ingram, 1997), which continues "to emphasise the importance of students developing their key skills particularly in the context of the development of the 14-19 phase" (QCA, 2001, p 4), overcoming the apparent rejection of key skills qualifications by both learners and their teachers seems slim within the current incentive structure. The lack of clear-cut returns to key skills qualifications and in the presence of a trade-off between these and other qualifications, means that the introduction of key skills as part of the post-compulsory curriculum offer is unlikely to achieve the goal of reducing skills-shortages in the labour market.

Conclusions

This chapter seeks to address the issue of balancing the supply and demand side of the skills equation in Britain. The analysis of the supply of intermediate level qualifications reveals an increase in participation, retention and achievement in post-compulsory education, evidence of a fair degree of success of supply side educational policies. The analysis of the balance between supply and demand, however, reveals some fatigue in the allocation of the increasing number of qualifications supplied by the labour force. Furthermore, the increasing incidence of overqualification in the labour market at intermediate levels of education casts doubt on the suitability of supply side education policies based on qualifications, and brings to mind the possibility that a turning point in the ability of the labour market to absorb an increasing number of qualifications may be approaching. This suggests that policy makers need to turn their gaze to the demand side of the skills equation and consider policies for increasing the demand for skills in order to make better use of the enhanced supply of qualified young people graduating from the publicly-funded education and training system.

In addition, the challenge of trying to develop further supply side reform to boost the supply of generic skills (key skills) was also discussed. The failure of the current key skills policy in England was attributed to an imbalance in the costs and benefits of taking these qualifications identified by both learners and their educational institutions. Correcting such an imbalance is problematic using weak inducement and hortatory policy instruments available to policy makers in an essentially voluntarist post-compulsory learning market and a highly deregulated labour market.

Notes

[1] Following devolution in the UK, education and training policy in England, Scotland, Northern Ireland and Wales has begun to diverge sharply. Consequently, we limit our arguments to the English case, although we use data derived from UK surveys in some places.

[2] The major administrative data sets used in this analysis are the annual statistical bulletins produced by the DfES and its forerunners (DfES, 2002a-2002f).

[3] The England and Wales YCS is a long-standing series of surveys tracking young people over their first few years after the end of compulsory schooling.

[4] The estimation of returns to education through wages approximates the private returns to the individual person. It is beyond the scope of this chapter to discuss whether the social returns would be higher due to positive externalities, Temple (2001) and Sianesi and Van Reenen (2002) consider this possibility.

[5] Dearden et al (2000) and Walker and Yu (2001) contain literature reviews as well as recent evidence on the returns to education in the UK.

[6] Over-education and overqualification are identical concepts in this chapter. The term over-education appears to be associated with 'too much education', an implication we would like to avoid using the term overqualification. We describe the analysis for overqualification since this is our main concern. The reverse is true for underqualification.

[7] For the definition of qualification levels in the Skills Survey, see Felstead et al (2002).

[8] The signalling model can also explain the positive returns to overqualification found in the literature.

[9] 'Technical Skills' refer to advanced IT/software skills and other technical/practical skills. See ESS, Table 2.20.

[10] There are six key skills offered at Levels 1-4: Communication, IT, Application of Number, Working with Others, Improving Own Learning and Performance and Problem Solving.

[11] UCAS Tariff points can be used for admission to HE.

Appendix: Descriptive statistics: 2001 Skills Survey, employees only

Number of observations: 3,595	Mean	Standard deviation
Log pay per hour	2.058	0.517
Overqualified (yes/no)	0.374	0.484
Underqualified (yes/no)	0.174	0.379
Levels of overqualification	0.699	1.075
Levels of underqualification	0.271	0.692
Highest qualifications held by worker		
Level 1	0.094	0.292
Level 2	0.225	0.417
Level 3	0.223	0.416
Level 4	0.143	0.350
Degree	0.177	0.382
Highest qualifications required for job		
Level 1	0.119	0.324
Level 2	0.167	0.373
Level 3	0.157	0.363
Level 4	0.118	0.323
Degree	0.169	0.375
Female	0.501	0.500
Years of work experience	22.268	11.139
Experience squared/100	6.199	5.226
Married	0.555	0.497
Has children	0.434	0.496
Permanent job	0.933	0.250
Full-time job	0.777	0.416
Ever do shift work	0.244	0.429
Workplace size (employees)		
25-99	0.237	0.425
100-499	0.221	0.415
500-999	0.052	0.222
1,000+	0.176	0.381
Highest mathematics qualification		
Level 2	0.386	0.487
Level 3	0.110	0.313
Degree	0.007	0.083
South East	0.147	0.354
East of England	0.095	0.293
London	0.094	0.292
South West	0.087	0.282
West Midlands	0.079	0.270
East midlands	0.059	0.236
Yorkshire	0.102	0.302
North West	0.122	0.327
North East	0.048	0.213
Scotland	0.052	0.222
Wales	0.116	0.321

References

Blundell, R., Dearden, L. and Sianesi, B. (2001) *Estimating the returns to education: Models, methods and results*, Centre for the Economics of Education Discussion Paper No 16 (ccc.lse.ac.uk).

CEC (Commission of the European Communities) (2003) *Education and training 2010: The success of the Lisbon strategy hinges on urgent reforms*, Brussels: EU.

Dearden, L., McIntosh, S., Myck, M. and Vignoles, A. (2000) *The returns to academic, vocational and basic skills in Britain*, London: DfEE.

Descy, P. and Tessaring, M. (2002) *Training and learning for competence. Second report on vocational training research in Europe: Executive Summary* (revised edition), Luxembourg: Office for Official Publications of the European Communities.

DfEE (Department for Education and Employment) (1998) *Youth cohort study: The activities and experiences of 18 year olds: England and Wales 1996*, London: DfEE.

DfEE (1999a) *Youth cohort study: The activities and experiences of 16 year olds: England and Wales 1998*, London: DfEE.

DfEE (1999b) *Youth cohort study: The activities and experiences of 18 year olds: England and Wales 1999*, London: DfEE.

DfEE (2000) *Statistics of education: Vocational qualifications in the United Kingdom 1998-99*, London: DfEE.

DfES (Department for Education and Skills) (2001a) *Youth cohort study: The activities and experiences of 16 year olds: England and Wales 2000*, London: DfES.

DfES (2001b) *Youth cohort study: The activities and experiences of 18 year olds: England and Wales 2000*, London: DfES.

DfES (2001c) *Youth cohort study: The activities and experiences of 21 year olds: England and Wales 2000*, London: DfES.

DfES (2001d) *Youth cohort study: The activities and experiences of 17 year olds: England and Wales 2000*, London: DfES.

DfES (2001e) *Youth cohort study: The activities and experiences of 19 year olds: England and Wales 2000*, London: DfES.

DfES (2002a) *Statistics of education: Education and training statistics for the United Kingdom*, London: DfES.

DfES (2002b) *Statistics of education: Vocational qualifications in the UK: 2000-01*, London: DfES.

DfES (2002c) *GCSE/GNVQ results for young people in England, 2001-02. Early statistics*, London: DfES.

DfES (2002d) *Participation in education and training by 16 and 17 year olds in each local area in England, 1998 to 2000*, London: DfES (www.dfes.gov.uk/statistics/DB/SBU/b0368/index.html).

DfES (2002e) *GCSE/GNVQ and GCE A/AS/VCE/Advanced GNVQ examination results 2000/2001 – England*, London: DfES (www.dfes.gov.uk/statistics/DB/SBU/b0334/index.html).

DfES (2002f) *Annual labour force survey* (www.dfes.gov/uk/statistics/DB/vol/0326/index.html).

DfES (2003) *Youth cohort study: The activities and experiences of 16 year olds: England and Wales 2002*, London: DfES.

DfES (2004) *The level of highest qualification held by young people and adults: England 2003*, London, DfES.

Eraut, M. (1997) 'Curriculum frameworks and assumptions in 14-19 education', in *Research in post-compulsory education* (2nd edn), pp 281-97.

Felstead, A., Gallie, D. and Green, F. (2002) *Skills in Britain 1986-2001*, Nottingham: DfES.

Frogner, M.L. (2002) 'Skills shortages', in *Labour market trends*, London: DfES, vol 110, no 1, pp 17-28 January (www.statistics.gov.uk).

Green, F. and McIntosh, S. (2002) *Is there a genuine underutilisation of skills amongst the over-qualified?*, Oxford/Warwick Universities: SKOPE.

Groot, W. and van den Brink, H.M. (2000) 'Overeducation in the labor market: a meta-analysis', *Economics of Education Review*, no 19, pp 149-58.

Hartog, J. (2000) 'Over-education and earnings: where are we, where should we go?', *Economics of Education Review*, vol 19, no 2, pp 131-47.

Hayward, G. and Fernández, R. (2004) 'From core skills to key skills: fast forward or back to the future?', *Oxford Review of Education*, vol 30, no 1, pp 117-46.

Hogarth, T., Shury J., Vivian, D. and Wilson, R. (2001) *Employers skill survey 2001: Statistical report*, London: DfES (www.skillsbase.dfes.gov.uk).

Huddleston, P. (2002) *'Uncertain destinies': Student recruitment and retention on GNVQ Intermediate programmes*, SKOPE Research Paper 37, Warwick: SKOPE.

Keep, E. (2002) 'The English vocational education and training debate – fragile "technologies" or opening the "black box": two competing visions of where we go next', *Journal of Education and Work*, vol 15, no 4, pp 457-79.

Keep, E. and Mayhew, K. (1999) 'The assessment: knowledge, skills and competitiveness', *Oxford Review of Economic Policy*, vol 15, no 1, pp 1-15.

Lafer, G. (2002) *The job training charade*, Ithaca, NY: Cornell University Press.

Machin, S., McIntosh, S., Vignoles, A. and Viitanen, T. (2001) *Basic skills, soft skills and labour market outcomes: Secondary analysis of the National Child Development Study*, DfES Research Report 250, London: DfEE.

Mincer, J. (1974) *Schooling, experience and earnings*, New York, NY: Columbia University Press.

OECD (Organisation for Economic Co-operation and Development) (2002) *Education at a glance*, Paris: OECD.

Payne, J. (2003) *Vocational pathways at age 16-19*, London: DfES.

PIU (Performance and Innovation Unit) (2001) *In demand: Adult skills in the 21st century*, Performance and Innovation Unit Report, Cabinet Office, December.

QCA (Qualifications and Curriculum Authority) (2003) *The National Qualifications Framework* (www.qca.org.uk/nq/framework/).

QCA (2001) *The review of key skills: The final report*, London: QCA.

Raffe, D., Biggart, A., Fairgrieve, J., Howieson, C., Rodger, J. and Burniston, S. (1998) *Thematic review of the transition from initial education to working life: United Kingdom background report*, Paris: OECD.

Raffe, D. and Sturridge, P. (1995), 'More of the same? Participation of 16-18 year olds in education', *National Commission on Education Briefing* (New Series), no 6.

Schneider, A. and Ingram, H. (1997) *Policy design for democracy*, Lawrence, KS: University Press of Kansas.

Sianesi, B. and Van Reenen, J. (2002) *The returns to education: A review of the empirical macroeconomic literature*, IFS Working Paper 05/02 (www.ifs.org.uk).

Spence, M. (1973) 'Job market signalling', *Quarterly Journal of Economics*, no 87, p 355 (www.ifs.org.uk).

Stasz, C. (2001) 'Assessing skills for work: two perspectives', *Oxford Economic Papers*, no 3, pp 385-405.

Temple, J. (2001) *Growth effects of education and social capital in the OECD countries*, OECD Economic Studies no 33, 2001/II.

UCAS (Universities and Colleges Admission Services) (2002a) *UCAS/QCA questionnaire on Curriculum 2000 provision in schools and colleges*, November 2001 (www.ucas.com/candq/curr2000).

UCAS (2002b) *Analysis of offers involving Curriculum 2000 qualifications for 2003 entry* (www.ucas.com/candq/curr2000).

Walker, I. and Yu, Z. (2001) *The returns to education: Evidence from the Labour Force Survey*, DfES Research Report 313, London: DfES.

SIX

Does apprenticeship still have meaning in the UK? The consequences of voluntarism and sectoral change

Alison Fuller and Lorna Unwin

Introduction

In many countries throughout the world, apprenticeship is still regarded as the exemplary model for formation training. In the UK, a layperson's understanding of apprenticeship, probably based on somewhat hazy recollections of the experiences of a male member of their family in the 1950s or 1960s, would probably cohere with the following definition:

> [A]pprenticeship is a method of employment and on-the-job [usually complemented by off-the-job] training which involves a set of reciprocal rights and duties between an employer and trainee. (Gospel, 1995, p 32)

This definition would probably include the belief that apprenticeship takes place over a substantial time period (at least three years); that it leads to recognised qualifications (typically awarded by a body such as City and Guilds); and is predominantly available to young males located in craft, technical and industrial settings. Unlike many other European countries, apprenticeship in the UK still operates at a distance from the national education system. Yet since 1994, successive governments have sought to raise its profile through their funding of the Modern Apprenticeship (MA) programme. This chapter explores the extent to which contemporary apprenticeships retain any semblance to their historical predecessors and whether, as a model for formation training, apprenticeship still has relevance for young people and employers today.

This chapter is organised in four sections. Section One provides a brief historical overview of apprenticeship in the UK. Section Two focuses on aspects of contemporary participation to indicate how the current picture differs from the past in terms of apprentice characteristics and the sectors in which apprenticeship is available. Section Three identifies some of the issues and problems emerging from the MA and uses case studies from the engineering and banking sectors to illustrate the types of provision which currently count as apprenticeship. Finally, in the Conclusion, we suggest that the flexible and weakly regulated model of apprenticeship, which has emerged in the UK, has given rise to provision of widely varying quality. We suggest that there are considerable challenges for the policy makers promoting this approach, the main one being the need to ensure that all apprentices have access to the same high standards of provision currently available only to a minority of participants. It should be noted that the data used in this chapter considers England only; however the MA operates in Scotland, Wales and Northern Ireland where, we would argue, the issues discussed here also apply.

Section One: Historical background

The history of apprenticeship provision in the UK stretches back to medieval times (Lane, 1996). Originally, apprenticeships were offered in a narrow range of artisan trades, for example in building and printing, and were regulated through legally binding indentures, which covered the roles and obligations of the master and apprentice. In 1567, the Statute of Artificers laid down regulations that gave apprenticeship the distinctive features still recognised around the world. Unlike many other countries that still regulate apprenticeship, however, the Elizabethan Statute was repealed as early as 1814. By the late 19th century and first two thirds of the 20th century, and in line with industrial change, apprenticeships were associated with a wider range of industries and large employers, particularly in engineering and shipbuilding. They were still subject to binding agreements, drawn up with the trade unions, which specified the length of time (usually between five and seven years) the apprentice should serve. During this period, there was little intervention or support from the state for apprenticeship. However, the growth of trade union influence extended the unions' involvement in negotiating apprentice wages, the length of the apprenticeship and apprentice numbers (Gospel, 1995; Ryan, 1999). Following the Second World War, it was common for apprentices at technician level to be given day- or block-release to study for formal qualifications at local colleges.

By the early 1960s, the apprenticeship system in the UK was subject to growing criticism. There were three main areas of dissatisfaction (Senker, 1992; Gospel, 1995):

1. Apprenticeships were largely available only to young men and in certain occupations and trades. They were seen, therefore, to exclude young women and all those working in sectors where apprenticeships were not offered.
2. Time-serving was increasingly seen as an inefficient way of conducting skills training so the notion of training to specified standards began to gain support among employers.
3. Apprenticeships were perceived as mechanisms for reinforcing trade demarcations and restrictive practices. Equipping young people with

narrowly defined skills failed to take account of the broader demands brought about by industrial and technological change.

Despite attempts at reform, notably by the Industrial Training Boards, apprenticeships declined in number and as a proportion of all craft and technical employment. Apprentice numbers fell from 243,700 in 1966 to 53,000 by 1990 (Gospel, 1997). Reductions in apprenticeships in engineering, one of the most important sectors providing apprenticeships, were also dramatic with the numbers of apprentices dropping from 171,000 in 1968 to 34,500 by 1990. By 1990, apprenticeship accounted for just two thirds of 1% of total employment, and this has continued to drop so that, in 2001, apprenticeship stocks stood at between one sixth and one ninth of the share of employment (Ryan and Unwin, 2001).

Several factors help explain this decline: demographic trends (there were fewer young people); economic downturns leading to youth unemployment; the public's poor image of youth training programmes; and, perhaps most significantly of all, that in the late 1980s and early 1990s, a rapidly rising proportion of young people were staying in full-time education rather than leaving school at the first opportunity. In 1994, as a reaction to the decline in apprenticeship, the then Conservative government introduced a publicly funded programme called Modern Apprenticeship (MA), open to 16-25 year olds, as an attempt to increase the stocks of intermediate skills (see Unwin and Wellington, 2001)[1]. A decade later, and despite the fact that the MA has some considerable problems (see later in this chapter), the UK government (Labour since 1997) wants to see it expand so that, in 2004, 28% of young people will start on the programme by the age of 22 (DfES, 2003). The latest figures (LSC, 2003) indicate that the proportion is around 25%, giving a shortfall on the target of 3%.

In contrast with the traditional apprenticeship model, the MA is not based on time serving but on the apprentice's attainment of specified qualifications. Following a DfES review of the MA in 2001, sectoral frameworks are now encouraged to state appropriate periods for the apprenticeship to last (see DfES, 2001). However, there is no mechanism in place that enforces apprenticeships to last for the stipulated time. Costs are shared between the employer, who pays the apprentice's wages, and the state which funds training towards the attainment of mandatory qualifications (NVQs, Technical Certificates and key skill units) and any other vocational awards which have been approved as part of the sectoral 'frameworks' which employers and training providers have to abide by[2]. In 2000, the MA programme was split into two: Advanced Modern Apprenticeship (AMA) leading to a Level 3 NVQ; and Foundation Modern Apprenticeship (FMA) leading to a Level 2 NVQ. This enabled the government to bring the remains of the Youth Training Scheme (YTS) within the MA structure, a move that signalled the end of the original intention to launch an apprenticeship programme, which would stand above the existing government-funded training schemes.

By introducing the MA, the Conservative government had wanted to build on the belief that apprenticeship, as a model of formation training for young people, still held a positive image in the minds of the general public and employers (Fuller and Unwin, 2003a). The term 'Modern' was deliberately chosen to show that, unlike apprenticeships in the past, this new version would be available in a range of occupational sectors including those that had not offered apprenticeship before (for example, retailing, health and social care), and be equally open to girls and boys; and, moreover, that it would lead to an NVQ Level 3. The stipulation of the Level 3 qualification is important, for as well as making a break with the time-served element of the old apprenticeships, this indicated that employers would select their recruits from those young people who were capable of studying beyond the Level 2 standard expected at the end of compulsory education. It also distinguished the MA from previous government-supported youth training programmes, which led to an NVQ Level 2.

Given the separation of the MA into AMA and FMA, this chapter now concentrates on the performance of the AMA component in order to examine how the institution of 'apprenticeship' is being constructed and operationalised in the contemporary UK economy.

Section Two: Contemporary patterns of participation and attainment

This section focuses on the characteristics of participants in the AMA programme, the outcomes attained and on the sectors in which apprentices are located. The picture we present shows how apprenticeship take-up is no longer confined to traditional apprenticeship sectors (craft and engineering) or to the group most commonly involved in the years following the Second World War, that is male, 15–16 year old school leavers.

Providing a statistical overview of the AMA is problematic as the responsibility for gathering and reporting data with regard to recruitment, attainment of qualifications, completion of the apprenticeship and dropout rates, has fluctuated over the lifespan of the programme. When MA began, it was organised and funded at the local level by the then Training and Enterprise Councils (TECs) who passed data to the Department for Education and Employment (DfEE). From April 2001, a network of local Learning and Skills Councils (LSCs) replaced the TECs and the national LSC was established as the operational arm of the newly named Department for Education and Skills (DfES). Modern Apprenticeship data is now collated by the LSC whose latest report, at the time of writing, presents annual rather than cumulative figures. The changes to the pattern of data collection have created problems for researchers, as the current style of reporting is different to when the MA began operation. This chapter draws, therefore, on statistical data from both the DfES and LSC.

The AMA is available in over 80 occupational sectors (public and private). Since the MA split into AMA and FMA, the numbers on AMA have been falling (LSC, 2003). In 1999/2000, 132,200 young people were recorded as engaged in the AMA, compared to 59,600 on the FMA. In 2002/03, the AMA cohort had dropped to 113,300, compared to 120,800 on the FMA. The expansion of the FMA at the expense of the AMA is indicative of the failure of the MA as a whole to establish itself as a different animal to previous government-funded youth training schemes associated more with helping the unemployed as opposed to increasing stocks of intermediate skills.

In Table 6.1 we see a range of features, which indicate that the AMA has not broken the mould with regard to establishing itself as a 'modern' version of apprenticeship in terms of gender stereotyping, but that it is significantly different to apprenticeship in the past in terms of its older age profile. In addition, the statistics show that many young people on the AMA are leaving the programme without completing the full framework. With regard to age, the statistics show that older recruits form a large proportion of participants. This is particularly noteworthy in sectors new to apprenticeship such as customer service, retailing and health and social care where the vast majority of recruits are aged over 18. Even in sectors such as engineering manufacture and the electro-technical industry, which have lengthy track records in employing apprentices, the proportion of those aged 16 hovers at around one third.

Table 6.1: AMA participation, July 2002-July 2003 by age, gender and attainment in the 12 largest sectors

Sector	All recruits Number	Female % recruits	Aged 16 % recruits	Aged 17 % recruits	Aged 18 % recruits	Aged 19-24 % recruits	Completed framework % leavers
Engineering manufacture	4,746	2.7	31.6	23.1	19.3	25.7	52
Motor industry	4,572	1.3	44.3	24.5	15.7	14.9	40
Customer service	3,224	68.6	2.3	4.6	11.2	81.9	24
Electrical Institute of Engineering/ electro-technical industry	3,146	0.4	39.0	26.2	15.8	18.9	44
Hospitality	2,913	48.8	3.5	6.7	8.9	81.0	15
Early years care and education	2,569	97.5	4.6	14.3	20.4	60.1	28
Business administration	2,441	79.6	6.7	11.3	17.9	63.3	33
Health and social care	2,079	88.0	4.3	5.5	9.8	80.0	24
Travel services	1,505	90.0	26.6	22.9	20.2	30.0	55
Hairdressing	1,432	93.6	16.2	12.6	20.9	50.1	29
Retailing	1,327	63.9	0.5	3.6	10.7	85.1	12
Construction	1,247	2.1	26.1	20.8	18.4	34.8	25

Source: LSC MA Database based on Individual Learner Record (ILR) returns; LSC, Coventry

Six of the 12 sectors would not have appeared in a list of 'traditional' apprenticeship sectors, and their inclusion illustrates the shift in the UK economy away from manufacturing to the provision of business and personal services. With regard to outcomes, rates of attainment are generally weak. Three out of the four sectors which manage to get above 40% of apprentices through to completion of their frameworks have a long history in apprenticeship: engineering manufacture; electrical installation/electro-technical industry; and the motor industry. In the two worst performing sectors, hospitality and retailing, 15% or less of apprentices are achieving the required AMA outcome. In his 2002 annual report, the chief inspector for the Adult Learning Inspectorate (ALI, the body which inspects government-funded work-based learning) noted that an apprentice's "chance of receiving a good training, a decent preparation for a career, is largely determined by the sector they enter" (ALI, 2002, p13).

Statistics on the destinations of apprentices who leave the AMA before completion indicate that a large proportion (around a half) of them are employed in the same company (their apprenticeship employer). In a study of reasons why apprentices were leaving the AMA before completion, a number of factors were identified:

- some had found new jobs with better pay and prospects;
- some found their workload made it difficult to study for qualifications;
- some were dismissed or made redundant; and
- others had personal problems (DfEE, 2000).

Most strikingly, a large proportion of the leaver-group in all sectors is employed in the same organisation in which they were serving their apprenticeship. This means that the employer, the apprentice, or both parties, have decided that there is no requirement for the apprenticeship to be completed. If an employer chooses this option there is no statutory duty to 'honour' the original agreement and the apprentice has no alternative but to accept the decision or seek a new position.

Section Three: Consequences of a flexible approach

A key issue for the AMA is that all the sectors are struggling to ensure the majority of their apprentices attain the Level 3 qualification. National surveys have shown that there is weak employer demand for intermediate (Level 3) skills and qualifications (Felstead et al, 2002) and this finding, together with other factors, may help explain the disappointing achievement rates. First, some 60% of young people who enter the AMA have not attained five GCSEs at grades A*-C and so may be inadequately prepared to study towards a Level 3 qualification. Second, the numbers of young people remaining in full-time education in the UK after the school-leaving age has now risen to 70%, and 33% of 18 year olds now enter higher education (HE). This means that more young people are delaying their entry to the labour market. As we have shown earlier in this chapter, a phenomenon in the AMA is that many sectors have apprentices who start the programme over the age of 18 and even in their early 20s. This means that some of this group may already be qualified at or above Level 3, and so the requirement for the NVQ Level 3 as the programme's mandatory outcome will not increase their attainment level. In these cases, an employer may decide that the apprentices need to develop middle-level job skills but not necessarily complete the whole NVQ. In this regard, it is important to realise that the voluntaristic nature of the MA programme means that employers can stop their apprentices completing the specified qualification whenever they want and without any penalty.

Equally, employers can turn employees into apprentices in order to fund workforce development activities. In a study of the delivery of key skills units in the MA (Unwin et al, 2000), we visited a large insurance company which, following an approach by a private training provider, had invited employees aged under 24 years old to join the AMA. All the people who took up this offer (17 in number) were already employed in permanent jobs. They were all in their early 20s and had 'good' general educational qualifications including GCSEs at grades A*-C, A-levels, Advanced GNVQs and, in some cases, university degrees. Although their attainment of an NVQ3 via the AMA would be counted towards the proportion of apprentices gaining a Level 3 award, it did not increase these individuals' qualification level. In this case, no *new* Level 3 attainment would be produced by participation in the programme. Put another way, if these candidates were to achieve a full NVQ Level 3 via their participation in the AMA, their attainment would not contribute towards an overall increase in the proportion of the working population with Level 3 qualifications.

It is important to stress that the delivery of qualifications in the UK is mostly unregulated. By this we mean that candidates can pursue the same qualification via different routes and processes; for example, the site and mode of attendance on a course can differ (for example, on the job, off the job, part time, full time, distance learning, self-study, and so on), as can the hours spent in study. Overall, apprentices pursuing AMAs can have very different experiences of the programme including, for example, the range and type of qualifications they are expected to achieve, the hours (if any) they spend studying off the job, the hours they spend training on the job, and post-apprenticeship progression. Some apprentices (particularly those in traditional apprenticeship sectors) will be enrolled on a formal course at a College of Further Education while others, particularly in the service sectors such as retailing or customer service, will complete all their training in the workplace. The following two contrasting examples taken from the engineering and banking sectors illustrate some of these differences.

Engineering

An engineering apprentice will often spend the first year of the apprenticeship studying full time at a College of Further Education. At the end of this year, they will move into the workplace to work four days per week and spend a fifth day at the college continuing their vocational education and pursuing qualifications (typically the Ordinary National Certificate and, in some cases, the Higher National Certificate – HNC – or Diploma). The apprentices' attainment of the NVQ and key skills units will be assessed in the workplace either by an in-house assessor or by a training provider who has been contracted to deliver this service.

The hierarchical nature of technical and engineering knowledge and skills has led to the development of a structured apprenticeship pathway to higher intermediate (technician) or associate professional level employment. It is important to note that, in the AMA, public money is only available to fund the attainment of qualifications up to Level 3. This means that companies employing apprentices on programmes, which go beyond Level 3 do not receive public funding to pay for higher intermediate qualifications such as HNC or NVQ Level 4. In sectors such as engineering, where some companies have a requirement for their apprentices to progress beyond Level 3, the additional costs have to be met by the employers themselves and, hence, these employers are much more likely to be committed to the traditional concept of apprenticeship as a substantive, in-depth programme of training.

Traditionally, engineering has classified apprentices at 'craft' or 'technician' level. Those pursuing craft apprenticeships were training to be skilled 'craftsmen' in areas such as welding, milling and turning. However as computer-aided machinery has been introduced to take over these processes, the skill requirements of craft workers have changed. On the one hand, technological innovation has decreased the level of specialised manual and practical skills that apprentices have to develop. On the other hand, they now have to be trained to operate computerised machines and to work with computer-aided designs and drawings. Engineering apprenticeships have thus adapted over the years to accommodate industrial and commercial change, facilitated and supported by the considerable expertise located in the sector's training and development infrastructure. This contrasts with those sectors where there has been little history of substantive training let alone apprenticeship.

Public funding of the AMA is linked to the apprentice's attainment of the mandatory outcomes specified in the sectoral frameworks, and a significant amount of this is linked to the individual's attainment of the NVQ Level 3. The need to monitor how public funds are spent helps explain why statistics are collected on apprentices' achievement of the NVQ Level 3, however, data on the type and quantity of Level 4 qualifications achieved, such as the HNC, are not collected. This makes it extremely difficult to quantify the extent of apprentice participation and achievement at higher levels. The partial and somewhat arbitrary collection of statistics in relation to the AMA is a real weakness in the UK's apprenticeship system and shows how, in a fragmented institutional system, even an established apprentice sector like engineering is unable to provide specific information on this important area of progression. It is only through our own fieldwork that we have been able to shed light on the way in which the AMA, if delivered by committed and progressive employers, can maximise a young person's potential bringing benefits to them and their employer. The following vignette provides an illustration of one apprentice's progression route[3].

Peter

Peter is in his early 20s and is employed in the steel industry by a medium-sized company (around 700 employees), which manufactures bathroom showers. The first three year's of the company's four-year apprenticeship (to NVQ Level 3) are supported under the AMA and come under the Engineering and Marine Authority's sector framework. Peter successfully completed the AMA and was given a permanent job in the company's special projects department. Engineering apprentices at the company are paid a fixed salary with annual increments. At the end of the programme, apprentices are transferred to a point on the normal company salary structure for the job they have taken.

Successful completion of the company apprenticeship included the achievement of an NVQ Level 3 in Technical Services, an HNC in Mechanical and Manufacturing Engineering and key skills units at Level 3 in Communication, Application of Number, IT, Working with Others, Problem Solving and Improving own Learning and Performance. Peter's current job title is Ancillary Project Engineer. For the past few months, he has been working with five others on a project to redevelop one of the company's 'power shower' models. Peter reports to the project team leader and undergoes a monthly performance review and development session. In addition, he has also been given sole responsibility for reclassifying the parts of the previous power shower model as 'old spares' and for moving these to a 'spares cell'. When showers are superseded by new versions, it is company policy to make spare parts available to customers for a period of ten years after the line has been discontinued.

Peter believes that his career progression in the company and in the wider labour market is linked to gaining increasing work experience and proving his ability at this level, as well as to the attainment of further qualifications. Peter is currently considering which qualifications he should pursue in the coming academic year and how to build on his apprenticeship achievements. He thinks it likely that he will take an HND in Manufacturing but he may decide to pursue management qualifications. Peter will discuss his options with the company's training officer who was responsible for him when he was an apprentice. The company is willing to pay the HND course fees and will allow him to attend college for one day a week, although he will be expected to make up the time he spends at college by working longer hours on other days. There is no written agreement specifying what time he is allowed for study and what time he has to make up but Peter says that there is an unwritten understanding that employees "make up their hours".

In contrast to engineering, a retail or customer services apprentice will typically spend the whole of their apprenticeship in the workplace operating as a standard employee. Virtually from their first day, their employers will regard these apprentices as productive workers rather than 'novices'. They may spend some time following their company's in-house training programme and be visited occasionally (for example, once every six to eight weeks) by an assessor from a training provider who reviews their progress and assesses them for the NVQ and key skills units. Some retailers employ trainers who deliver some off-the-job training in a designated room on the company's premises. In a study of the net costs of MA training to employers, Hogarth and Hasluck (2003) found that in sectors such as retailing, where apprentices were productive from very early in their apprenticeship, apprenticeship could be provided at no net cost to the employer. The diversity in quality and experience available under the MA programme can be further illustrated in the following case study of apprenticeship in the banking sector.

Banking

By way of background, it is important to note that in terms of the MA, banking is not classed as a sector in its own right but is subsumed within the much broader financial services sector. During the 1980s and early 1990s, the UK government legislated to deregulate large parts of the financial services sector leading to: changes in organisational structures including greater automation of procedures and the centralisation of some services; expansion of the range of companies allowed to provide such services (for example, supermarkets); and greater competition. Employment in banking is particularly gendered: over 30% of male employees are employed at managerial and administrative level, whereas the vast majority of female employees are found at clerical and secretarial level (Hasluck, 1999). The banking sector was particularly affected by the UK's economic recession between 1989 and 1992 and suffered more job losses than at any other time in history. The introduction of new technologies has led to the development of e-banking and telephone banking, hence the sector now has significant numbers of employees based in call centres. During the 1990s and currently, the skills and knowledge required to work in retail banking have been changing. There has been a shift away from specialist knowledge to more generic customer-service skills, selling techniques and IT skills. Hasluck (1999) estimates that the demand for qualifications in the sector will be mainly at the intermediate and lower levels (that is NVQ Level 3 and below), reflecting an increase in the number of clerical-type jobs and the corresponding decline in the recruitment of people with higher-level skills (for example, managers and specialist professionals).

For many years, there have been two direct routes into a career in banking. Banks recruited young people aged 16-18 straight from school and also recruited graduates from universities. Once employed, young people would study for a range of banking qualifications, progressing up the ladder to professional or chartered status. The level and number of qualifications studied would depend on the young person's previous educational attainment and the opportunities provided by their employer. Some universities provide degree courses in financial services and related subjects. Training towards banking qualifications is carried out both on and off the job, with the latter being conducted by further education colleges, private training organisations and, in the case of the large banks, by the banks themselves in their own training centres. These qualifications, which are modular in structure, can also be studied through distance learning.

As a reflection of the changes in the skills required in the sector, the most commonly used framework for apprenticeships in banking is that of customer services rather than financial services. This also reflects the complex nature of contemporary businesses, which cross the boundaries of more than one sectoral classification. For our purposes, this boundary crossing poses problems as it means that from the statistics alone we cannot disaggregate banking apprentices from other apprentices in the customer services sector, which is one of the ten most highly populated of the MA sectors. Again, fieldwork is necessary to shed light on the reality of apprenticeship experience. From our conversations with a number of banks and related organisations, it would seem that banking apprentices are following the customer service framework.

One bank in our study is one of the leading all-purpose banks in the UK, with branches in every town and city and an international profile. In 2001, the bank decided to run a pilot AMA programme for 16-18 year olds and recruited 85 young people located mainly in the north east of England. This was the first time that the bank had recruited young people in this age bracket for over ten years. In 2002, the bank recruited a further 250 apprentices. The programme's coordinator explained:

> The bank decided it needed to bring in a pool of young people whom it could develop. We want to grow our own talent here and find young people who are interested in a career in banking. The advantage of recruiting school leavers is that they get the chance to learn about the banking industry and we get the chance to get to know them. The first year of running the Modern Apprenticeship has been very successful and it's given the bank the right programme for our needs.

She added that the bank chose to use the customer service framework because:

> The Customer Service framework meets our needs because the young people we have recruited will be working in the bank's branch offices and will be dealing with retail customers. The bank places a great deal of importance on achieving high levels of customer service and so we need people to be trained in the necessary skills.

To enter the programme, young people are required to have achieved a General Certificate of Education (GCSE) in mathematics and English at grade C or above. The apprentices are employed by the bank and placed in a high street branch office. The apprenticeship programme lasts for 18 months, which is considerably longer than the 39-week average of other apprenticeships using the customer service framework. They work as cashiers handling day-to-day transactions with retail customers, answering the telephone and carrying out some clerical duties. Although they attend the bank's general induction programme for all new staff, the majority of the apprentices' training is carried out on the job. All procedures, such as assessment and evidence collection, related to achieving the NVQ Level 3 and key skills are organised and managed by a private training provider working on behalf of the bank. This latter point is important for it highlights a major difference between apprenticeships today and those in the past, and between the engineering company discussed above and the bank portrayed here. Briefly, the MA has followed the pattern of previous UK youth training schemes over the past 20 years in that training providers act as intermediaries between the government agencies, which fund the programme and employers. In many sectors, employers are curiously detached from the main elements of the apprenticeship programme and treat their apprentices as productive workers rather than as learners on a journey towards becoming a fully rounded employee.

We can also see that in the case of the bank, there is a clear separation between the development of staff with specialist financial skills and knowledge, and the training offered on the MA programme. In terms of progression, successful apprentices can remain as bank cashiers or, if they have shown particular abilities, move into a different area of the bank where they would have the opportunity to take banking qualifications and progress towards professional status. It is not clear, however, how well the customer service NVQ prepares apprentices to cross over into these areas, which the bank itself sees as requiring different skills and knowledge. It is clear from this case study that the majority of banks see apprenticeship as a means of recruiting young people for general customer service duties and not, necessarily, as a career path to professional status.

The age-related statistics for participation in the customer services AMA (as shown in Table 6.1) are interesting in relation to banking for a number of reasons. Unlike banking, the majority of apprentices are over the age of 18 when they start the apprenticeship. It is probable, therefore, that many organisations other than banks are using the AMA as a vehicle to train their existing employees, although some may be deliberately recruiting more mature young people. Banking, of course, is an attractive sector for young people and so banking organisations are able to demand relatively high entrance qualifications. A key question, therefore, is whether the government should be concerned that banks are recruiting reasonably well-qualified school leavers on to AMAs in customer service, which may not utilise or adequately develop their skills and knowledge or offer progression.

Conclusion

Apprenticeship has always had a troubled history and been open to exploitation by employers. In the UK, the problems have been exacerbated by the lack of regulation and an antipathy to substantive training by many employers (see Ryan and Unwin, 2001). The low-skills equilibrium still prevails in too many workplaces. Keep and Mayhew (1999, p 11) argue that:

> Far from seeking an autonomous work-force of polyvalent knowledge workers to whom high levels of discretion have been delegated in order to produce high-spec, customised goods and services, many organisations continue to need workers to perform narrowly specified, closely supervised, repetitive tasks, in an environment where the work has been organised and the job designed in order to allow minimal discretion.

The MA is further hampered by the fact that it has developed as a supply-led rather than a demand-led initiative. Recruitment to the programme is orchestrated by the local LSCs on the one hand, who control the funding, and an army of training providers on the other, who liaise directly with employers. As the livelihood of providers depends heavily on the take-up of government-supported apprenticeships, the resulting patterns of participation probably reflect a distorted picture of actual demand (Fuller and Unwin, 2003a). The high rate of non-completion referred to above suggests that many employers do not feel any particular 'ownership' of the programme. They also suggest that, in many sectors and particularly in those without a tradition of offering apprenticeships, there is not the demand for Level 3 skills. The service industries such as retailing and hospitality appear to have embraced the MA by recruiting many young people. However, these service sectors have so far shown the worst record for completion and achievement, with, at the most, only around one in five leavers completing a full MA framework. We would argue that these findings highlight the problem of implementing apprenticeship in contexts where the relationship between community and apprenticeship is weak, particularly, with regard to its occupational and pedagogical dimensions (see Fuller and Unwin, 2001, for a more detailed discussion of these issues).

Many of the occupational sectors permitted to run the MA are changing in terms of their labour processes, skill requirements and job descriptions. Some are so new that employees may find they are required from the start to be hybrids, their title changing from week to week. Having an occupational identity is very important to young people's sense of worth and carries status in the adult community. We need to be sure that all sectors understand this. If young people are to learn effectively at work, they need some anchors, something to make them feel secure for the time they are training. They need to hear how the sector has developed and, if it is particularly new, where it emerged from and where it might be going. In other words, young people need to learn how to talk about the work they do, to feel part of a skilled occupational community. The analysis presented in this chapter and research in to the MA more generally indicates that those sectors and companies which are best placed to provide a context for apprenticeship-style skill formation:

- have a genuine and distributed requirement for intermediate (Level 3) skills;
- have inherited a tradition of apprenticeship; and
- have an accompanying institutional infrastructure (Gospel and Fuller, 1998) and developed community of practice (including in-house trainers and college lecturers) (see Fuller and Unwin, 2003b).

The UK's policy makers need to consider, therefore, how to intervene in the MA to ensure that all young people have access to as many learning opportunities as possible. On the best MA programmes, this will mean access to a range of traditional, knowledge-based qualifications studied off the job, as well as access to competence-based NVQs assessed in the workplace. It will also mean being employed by a company with trained trainers and workplace personnel accustomed to passing on their expertise, and with managers keen to encourage young people to make the most of their potential. The flexible manner in which the current MA can be configured and implemented across companies and sectors means, however, that many apprentices do not have immediate access to such opportunities.

Notes

[1] As a result of pressure from a number of occupational sectors, which argued that they wanted to address skills shortages by offering apprenticeships to more mature adults, the DfES has announced its intention to remove the age cap on the MA. As a first step, the funding rules now allow young people who start their MA at any point up to their 25th birthday to complete it (see DfES, 2003).

[2] When the MA was introduced in 1994, 'frameworks' were designed by the National Training Organisation (NTO) responsible for each sector. These were abolished in 2002 and responsibility for MA 'frameworks' has passed to the emergent Sector Skills Councils (SSCs).

[3] The research referred to here is titled *The workplace as a site for learning: Opportunities and barriers in small and medium sized enterprises.* This project was part of the research network 'Improving Incentives to Learning in the Workplace' funded under Phase One of the ESRCs Teaching and Learning Research Programme (grant number L 139251005).

References

ALI (Adult Learning Inspectorate) (2002) *Annual Report of the Chief Inspector*, Coventry: ALI.

DfEE (Department for Education and Employment) (2000) *Modern Apprenticeships: Exploring the reasons for non-completion in five sectors*, DfEE Research Report RR 217, Nottingham: DfEE.

DfES (Department for Education and Skills) (2001) *Modern Apprenticeships: The way to work*, The Report of the Modern Apprenticeship Advisory Committee, London: DfES.

DfES (2003) *21st century skills*, Cm 5810, London: The Stationery Office.

Felstead, A., Gaillie, D. and Green, F. (2002) *Work skills in Britain 1986-2001*, London: DfES.

Fuller, A. and Unwin, L. (2001) *From Cordswainers to customer service: The changing relationship between employers, apprentices and communities in England*, SKOPE: Oxford and Warwick Universities.

Fuller, A. and Unwin, L. (2003a) 'Creating a "Modern Apprenticeship": a critique of the UK's multi-sector, social inclusion approach', *Journal of Education and Work*, vol 16, no1, pp 5-25.

Fuller, A. and Unwin L. (2003b) 'Learning as apprentices in the contemporary UK workplace: creating and managing expansive and restrictive participation', *Journal of Education and Work*, vol 16, no4, pp 407-26.

Gospel, H. (1995) 'The decline of apprenticeship in Britain', *Industrial Relations Journal*, vol 26, no 1, pp 32-44.

Gospel, H. (1997) *The revival of apprenticeship training in Britain?*, London: King's College, University of London, mimeo.

Gospel, H. and Fuller, A. (1998) 'The Modern Apprenticeship: new wine in old bottles?', *Human Resource Management Journal*, vol 8, no 1, pp 5-22.

Hasluck, C. (1999) *Employment prospects and skill needs in the banking, finance and insurance sector*, Skills Task Force Research Paper 9, Sudbury: DfEE.

Hogarth, T. and Hasluck, C. (2003) *Net costs of modern apprenticeship training to employers*, Research Report 418, Nottingham: DfES.

LSC (2003) www.maframeworks.lsc.gov.uk/cgi-bin/wms.p1/2

Keep, E. and Mayhew, K. (1999) 'The assessment: knowledge, skills and competitiveness', *Oxford Review of Economic Policy*, vol 15, no 1, pp 1-15.

Lane, J. (1996) *Apprenticeship in England 1600-1914*, London: UCL Press.

Ryan, P. (1999) 'The embedding of apprenticeship in industrial relations: British engineering, 1925-65', in P. Ainley and H. Rainbird (eds) *Apprenticeship: Towards a new paradigm of learning*, London: Kogan Page, pp 41-60.

Ryan, P. and Unwin, L. (2001) 'Apprenticeship in the British "Training market"', *National Institute Economic Review*, no 178, pp 99-114.

Senker, P. (1992) *Industrial training in a cold climate*, Aldershot: Avebury.

Unwin, L., Cole, P., Fuller, A. and Wellington, J. (2000) *The effective delivery of key skills in schools, colleges and workplaces*, London: DfEE.

Unwin, L. and Wellington, J. (2001) *Young people's perspectives on education, employment and training*, London: Kogan Page.

SEVEN

Tradition and reform: modernising the German dual system of vocational education

Hubert Ertl

Introduction: the debate on the dual system of vocational training

In his study, Green (2001) characterised Germany as a 'high-skills society' with national competitiveness primarily based on high productivity in manufacturing a wide range of high-quality goods, relying predominantly on scientific elites and on high-quality intermediate skills. The system of skill formation that serves the "'high skills society' generates wide skills distribution and high levels of social trust, and produces high incomes and relatively high wage equality" (Green, 2001, pp 67-89, 142).

At the heart of the German model of skill formation lies the dual system of vocational education and training (VET). Comparativists have extensively discussed this system for some decades now. The main reasons for the prolonged foreign interest in the dual system are the constantly high participation rates (it prepares about two thirds of German youth for working life), and the comparatively low youth unemployment rates associated with it (the system provides a comparatively smooth transition of young people from initial training to continuous employment). In fact, the German Economic Institute (*Institut der deutschen Wirtschaft*) has pointed out that the dual system has produced "harmonious results" on the training market recently, balancing supply and demand for training places (IDW, 2002, p 2).

However, there are increasingly clear indications that the German model of the high-skills society, and with it the dual system, is at risk (see Culpepper, 1999, pp 44-8; Green, 2001, pp 148-51). In fact, the reoccurring discussions surrounding the 'crisis of the dual system' in the inner-German debate of academics and researchers are almost as old as the system itself (Wüstenbecker, 1997, pp 14-19; Greinert, 1998, pp 93-102; Baethge, 1999, pp 127-36). The future prospects of the system are the subject of great controversy (cf Wilson, 1997, p 437; Deissinger, 2001b; Greinert, 2001). Irrespective of the position one supports in this debate, the need to modernise the dual system seems widely acknowledged by researchers and educationists[1].

In this situation – signs of crisis and the acknowledged need for modernisation – it seems surprising that the decision makers have found it very hard to initiate reforms of the training system. This obvious reluctance to reform the system according to the needs of the modern economy has prompted one observer to complain about the decision makers' complacent 'resting on wilted laurels' (Geissler, 2002).

This chapter argues that there is a broad consensus among the relevant stakeholders on the regulative principles of the dual system and that the prolonged success of the dual system is mainly due to this widespread acceptance of the system. However, the consensus on the system's principles is also at the root of the dragging modernisation process. The system's stakeholders – most importantly employers, trade unions, the federal state and the *Länder* – have such divergent interests that it is immensely difficult to change the status quo. Reform has been attempted at all levels of the dual system. However, the success of these attempts has been limited.

In order to substantiate this line of argument, in this chapter the achievements of the dual system are characterised against the background of its underlying principles. Then, the reasons for the perceived crisis of the system are outlined and different levels of reform and modernisation of training provisions are suggested. In the third part of this chapter, recent examples of reform initiatives are provided. The concluding section describes the reasons for the limited success of some reform approaches and outlines the concept of 'areas of learning'. This concept seems promising since it initiates modernisation at a number of levels while acknowledging the underlying principles of the dual system.

The dual system: achievements and underlying principles

In comparison with exclusively school-based or company-based training systems, the German dual system of VET has the advantages of:

1. connecting experiences derived from the world of work with systematic learning processes at school, both organised in, and regulated by, nationwide training occupations;
2. providing a sufficient supply of training places for school-leavers, and a comparatively smooth transition of trainees into occupation after their training period;
3. establishing cooperation of the state authorities, employers' associations and trade unions on a consensual basis; and
4. transferring the important competences of regulating, supervising and counselling of the partners involved in the system to the chambers, as the self-governing institutions of the economic sector (see Kutscha, 1999, p 106; Greinert, 2000, pp 50-5).

The traditions, legal foundations and structures of the system that provide these advantages have been the extensive focus of international literature (cf Raggatt, 1988; HMI, 1991, 1995; CEDEFOP, 1995; Ertl, 2002b). However, what has been neglected too often in the past is not the structure of the system itself that secures its success but a set of underlying, interdependent principles that make the system work successfully (see Kutscha, 1992, 1995, 1999).

Principle of duality

Vocational training requirements in Germany consist of two basic parts. First, learning processes in training companies focus on learning in the workplace, or instruction in company training departments, with an emphasis on practical elements of the training occupation. Second, the vocational school provides general and vocational education in order to deepen and supplement on-the-job training.

Trainees spend approximately three or four days a week on in-company training, and up to two days a week in vocational schools. Whereas federal law regulates the former, the latter falls under the legislation of the *Länder* (for instance, skeleton curricula – *Rahmenlehrpläne*). Harmonisation processes are in place to integrate both parts of the training and to ensure the comparability of the provisions in the 16 *Länder*. The term 'dual' refers primarily to the division of training into two separate training environments, each regulated by its own distinct legislators.

However, the principle of duality goes beyond the division of training into two training venues. The duality of the structure is also reflected in systematic features such as the role and status of training personnel, the funding regime and the supervision of training processes (Table 7.1).

Table 7.1: The structural duality of the German training system

Systematic features	Dual system components	
Venue of training	Training company	Vocational school
Constitutional and legal authority	Federal government	Federal *Länder* governments
Status of learner	Trainee (based on a training contract with company)	Student (based on compulsory school attendance up to the age of 18)
Training personnel	Trainer (qualified on the basis of the Regulation on the Competence of Trainers)	Teacher (qualified on the basis of higher education Study and Examination Regulations)
Funding	Individual company	Federal *Länder*
General training plan	Training regulations (*Ausbildungsordnungen*)	Framework curricula (*Rahmenlehrpläne*)
Supervision of training	Chambers	*Länder* school supervision authorities

Principle of corporatism

In terms of its regulative structure, the dual system may be best described as a state-controlled market model (Greinert, 1995, Ch 2) in which the state sets the guidelines for the cooperation of employers and trade unions. This model is regarded as an efficient way of limiting the risks of 'market failure' on the one hand, and 'state failure' on the other (Kutscha, 1995, p 10).

In this model, the state delegates regulatory competence for the training system to corporatist bodies. The most important of these bodies are the local, self-governing Chambers of Industry and Commerce, the Crafts Chambers, the Chambers of Agriculture and the Associations of Professions. They have the status of 'competent bodies' (*zuständige Stellen*) and play a crucial role in the organisation, administration and examination of vocational training. More precisely, these bodies act as intermediate organisations between state and companies, and put training laws and regulations into practice. The chambers have the status of public autonomous agencies that oversee the legal and regulatory norms of vocational education and training within their sphere of responsibility according to the legal guidelines set by the state.

Following the 'principle of voluntariness', no employer is obliged to take on trainees. However, all firms have to register with a chamber, and those wishing to provide training must be approved by the chamber as a training company. The approval depends on the equipment and resources of the company, and the qualifications and experience of the trainers working for the company. It has been argued that the Chambers, therefore, not only supervise the outcomes of training (final examinations) but also the quality of the qualification process (resources, trainers' qualifications) by monitoring the observance of legally binding regulations and standards. This is a marked difference from outcome-orientated modular systems, for instance National Vocational Qualifications (NVQs) in England and Wales (Reuling, 1997, pp 64f; Rützel, 1997, p 6). Furthermore, the local chamber supervises the organisation and assessment of intermediate and final examinations and acts as an awarding body for vocational qualifications.

A further example reflecting the principle of corporatism in the training sector is the composition of regulating and executive bodies of the dual system. For instance, supervising and examining bodies are set up by the chambers and consist of equal numbers of employer representatives, employee representatives and vocational schoolteachers. The most important of these bodies at the executive level of the training system are the Vocational Training Committee and the Board of Examiners.

The most prominent body at the legislative and regulative level of the training system is the Federal Institute for Vocational Training (*Bundesinstitut für Berufsbildung* – BIBB). Following the corporatist principle, all the Institute's main boards and committees consist of an equal number of representatives of employers, employees and the federal and *Länder* governments. The most important task of the BIBB is to develop and maintain the list of recognised occupations and all related regulations (duration of training, standards, curricula, and so on). All the groups involved take decisions on this task after mutual consultation. However, it is also the cause of time-consuming negotiations whenever the regulations for a recognised occupation are updated (cf Benner, 1996a, p 3).

'Concept of the vocation'[2]

The concept of 'education by and in work' of training in dual structures is closely bound to the 'concept of the vocation' (*Berufskonzept*). Most importantly, the concept of the vocation places the individual's capability to work and act competently in a vocational environment (*berufliche Handlungsfähigkeit*) as the overarching aim of vocational education and training. Education as part of the learner's personal development has been a constant feature of vocational education in Germany. Furthermore, this concept reflects the need to prepare young people not only for a small number of specific tasks at one company, but to provide a qualification applicable in many employment contexts and responsive to the changing economic and social environments of a whole occupational field.

The 'concept of the vocation' and underlying social standards are reflected in the Vocational Training Act (BBIG) of 1969 and other training regulations. For instance, the first paragraph of the BBIG prescribes a broad basis of vocational education, a well-ordered course of training and the acquisition of sufficient vocational experience for training in a state-recognised training occupation (see Kuda, 1996, p 17). At the moment, there are about 350 training occupations that are designed to prepare for about 30,000 specific jobs in companies (Benner, 1997, p 54). Moreover, the qualification forms the basis for further training and lifelong learning.

Furthermore, the attainment of a skilled worker qualification within a recognised occupation, and subsequent employment in a related vocational sector, are the basis for classification in the wage system (for instance, minimum wages and salaries) and for measures of social security (such as unemployment benefit) in Germany. Some sociological studies have concluded that a person is almost exclusively perceived in relation to her/his vocation and that the vocation is used as a main source of information to form an impression of a person (Kell, 1991, p 300; Bruijn and Howieson, 1995, p 91; Geissler and Orthey, 1998). Therefore, the vocation is a determining factor for a person's status and identity.

The following categorisation of the key features of the 'concept of the vocation' comprises the major elements for what is regarded – in the German context – as the necessary framework for a comprehensive course of training (cf Kloas, 1997a, pp 21-4):

- *qualified work:* professional, methodical and social competences for planning, executing and controlling vocational tasks;

- *broad vocational basis:* multilayered, marketable pattern of competences relevant not only to the training company through a broad knowledge basis but also skills specifically related to the occupation;
- *adaptable skills:* skills are responsive to a changing vocational environment and represent an appropriate basis for further training and lifelong learning;
- *mobility:* national, state-recognised occupations decrease workers' dependence on one employer; labour mobility is enhanced;
- *transparency:* recognised occupations and their value in the educational system are accepted and well known by employers and employees; and
- *social security:* qualification in a recognised occupation ensures a high degree of social security and determines to a large extent the social status.

The past success of the dual system is due to the effective functioning of these underlying principles and, to the same degree, to the broad societal consensus on these principles (Green, 2001). The principle of consensus in Germany on the value of education and training, and strong commitment to it in practice, was expressed by British observers through the term 'training culture' (Brown and Evans, 1994, p 5). In more general terms, the consensus on the concepts and principles of vocational training at all levels of society is regarded as an expression of a living democracy and of a high commitment to training within society (Schmidt, 1996, p 2).

However, the broad acceptance of these principles by all influential social groups in Germany makes the reform of the training system difficult. It seems much easier to preserve an existing consensus than to reach a new one. The complexity of decision-making procedures, in which all the stakeholders have their say, tends to underpin the status quo. The federalist structure of the German state contributes to this tendency. Very similar consequences for the training system result from a characteristic of legislation and administration in Germany known as *Verrechtlichung* (juridification) (Kloss, 1985a, p 9). The far-reaching influence of various layers of bureaucracy and legislation on all aspects of society determines and delays decision making not least in vocational education and training. Advocates of new training models are faced with rigid legal and bureaucratic regulations.

In these circumstances, the reform process regarding the German training system is bound to be slow. It has to take the underlying principles of the dual system into account. Nevertheless, there are indications of a more intense debate on modernisation and of more decisive reform steps. The following sections attempt to trace the direction of the reform debate and provide examples for change introduced into the training sector.

The debate on modernisation and reform initiatives

Many educational researchers have questioned the dual system of VET in Germany, for a variety of reasons. The future prospects of the system are the subject of great controversy. Arguments in favour of a sceptical position are provided by the symptoms of crisis in the training sector: the decreasing appeal of the dual system to potential trainees, the declining willingness of employers to provide training places and drastically dwindling state resources for training (Münk, 1997, p 8). Sloane (1997, p 233) speaks of a double-sided crisis within the system: on the one hand, large training companies are reducing their training places because of the high costs, and on the other hand, small- and medium-sized firms have difficulties finding suitable trainees because their training provisions appear not to be attractive enough to gifted young people in contrast to higher education. The dual system faces significant changes: rising educational standards, increasing heterogeneity of trainees, higher demands on training, higher average age of trainees and changing training conditions in companies (Keune and Zielke, 1992, p 32; Georg, 1997, p 314). Undoubtedly, these changes do not only concern the dual system but are rooted in changing social conditions affecting the main structures of the whole educational system (Reuling, 1998).

Increasingly, the underlying principles of the dual system are questioned too. For instance, during the early 1990s, experts in the field began to question whether the 'concept of the vocation' was still the right basis for the German training system.

Whereas the merits of the concept for reconstruction and development after political and economic crises are unanimously acknowledged, some observers doubt its potential to respond to the modernisation pressures of a rapidly changing economic environment (Geissler, 1994, p 328). The most important consequence of this process of change for VET is the decreasing value of initial qualifications, whereas further training and lifelong learning have become more significant in any worker's career. In their article, 'At the end of the vocation', Geissler and Orthey (1998) argue that vocations will be replaced by quickly adaptable "packages of skills" that are based on "meta-competences" with the ability and willingness to learn constantly being the most important of these.

Irrespective of whether one follows this line of argument or not, it is clear that the debate on the future of the concept of the vocation is still intensifying (cf Deissinger, 1998; Harney and Tenorth, 1999; Georg, 2001; Backes-Haase, 2002; Arnold, 2003). However, there seems to be agreement that the solution to the problems of the dual system of training must include more flexible structures for training. Flexibility in this context means primarily:

1. the responsiveness of training provision to the *changing work environment*. This responsiveness is necessary in order to meet the latest skill demands which emphasise comprehensive skills and knowledge structures; and
2. the responsiveness of training provisions to the *varying degrees of personal potential* of trainees in the form of individualised training pathways. This individualisation is also concerned with increasingly individualised pedagogical approaches and assessment procedures (Sloane, 1997, p 231; Bruijn et al, 1993, p 1).

Most frequently, educational researchers suggest measures of deregulation and differentiation to create flexibility in the two forms mentioned above. More decision-making processes at a regional or local level, and differentiated training paths, both integrated into a national framework, would be needed (Koch and Reuling, 1994).

More specifically, the options of reforms of the dual system can be systematised in a number of different levels:

- *Structural modernisation* (for example, improvements of the transitions between general and vocational educational pathways, integration of initial and further education and extension of the dual system to sectors that have not offered training within the system).
- *Institutional cooperation* (for example, improvements of the cooperation of the partners of the dual system and the integration of other training venues).
- *Reconceptualisation of curricula* (for example, modularisation of training provisions and the implementation of additional qualifications).
- *Didactic innovation* (for example, promotion of activity-oriented and cross-curricular teaching and learning processes) (see Sloane and Hasenbank, 2001, p 224).

In the following, examples of current reform developments concerning these levels are provided, and the debates surrounding a number of reform projects are described in some detail. It is important to note that the identification of different levels and areas of reform is only a means of systematisation: most of the reform developments mentioned not only impinge upon one level or area but also have consequences for other reform levels. In some cases, individual reform projects also go hand in hand with other projects. For instance, the debate on modularisation at the curricula level led to the question of how teacher training provisions need to be developed in order to enable young teachers to work with newly designed curricula guidelines. A further example is projects that combine the introduction of cross-curricular learning, with the improvement of school–company cooperation (Kremer, 1999; Sloane, 2000b).

Structural modernisation

The training occupations offered in the dual system have an 'exclusive status': young people under the age of 18 are only allowed to be trained in one of the recognised occupations (BBIG, para 28). This restrictive regulation requires that the training occupations are continuously developed and updated in line with the vocationally oriented labour markets (*berufsfachliche Arbeitsmärkte*) (Reuling, 1998).

The training regulations are based on common occupational practices. New occupational requirements resulting from new technologies or other innovations can become part of the training regulations only if a sufficient number of companies can offer instruction covering these new requirements. Therefore, training regulations tend to lag behind the latest occupational practices (Koch and Reuling, 1998, p 9).

However, between 1996 and 2001, the regulations of 114 of the total 348 training occupations were updated and 39 new training occupations were established. These numbers are remarkable in the German context as they indicate a stronger commitment for modernising the dual system of the social and administrative groups involved in regulating vocational training in Germany. This becomes clear if the figures for the five-year period (1996-2001) are compared with the corresponding figures for the preceding 15-year period (1980-1995) during which only 14 new training occupations were created and 166 existing ones were updated (BIBB, 2001, p 12). In 2002, 18 existing training regulations were modernised (BIBB, 2001, pp 64f). The newly developed training regulations cover such diverse occupations as stage designer, frontage mechanic, event manager, health manager, automobile dealer and the combination of what used to be the separate occupations of mechanics and electronics engineers (*Mechatroniker*) (see Borch and Weissmann, 1999). It is hoped these new training occupations will raise the attractiveness of the dual system for prospective training companies and trainees (BIBB, 2001, p 5).

Particular hopes in this respect are linked to two fast growing economic sectors that have only started recently to offer training in the dual system: the IT and the media sector (Pütz, 1999). The new training occupations in the IT sector include IT electronics engineering, informatics and IT management and engineering for microelectronics. In the media sector, training regulations were developed for media designers (for audio and visual media/for digital and print media), and specialists for media and information services (BMBF, 2000b, p 6; BIBB, 2001, p 6). The new training occupations in these two sectors seem to be extraordinarily popular with training companies and trainees. The growth rates of training contracts in the newly created training occupations range from 20% to over 50% in the first years of their existence (BIBB, 2001, p 6). In the training year 2001/02, there was an increase of 10% (+28,600) in training contracts in the new IT and media training occupations (IDW, 2002, p 2). This contributes to the structural modernisation of the training sector in so far as training in the crafts sector and in agriculture continues to decline, while training in the services, IT and media sectors increases.

Institutional cooperation

In particular, for start-up companies in the IT sector, in many cases it is impossible to offer all the training contents prescribed in the training regulations. For such companies, three types of cooperation are offered in order to cover all training contents:

1. In a *consortium*, cooperation is initiated between a number of small companies that are specialised in different fields of the same economic sector. The trainees spend time in each participating company in order to cover all the

contents of the respective training regulation. The involved companies form a so-called training association (*Ausbildungsverbund*).

2. A small company can also commission parts of the training process to a larger training company that trains young people in the same training occupation and has spare capacities. In the same way cooperation can be initiated between small companies and external training centres, mostly run by the self-governing bodies of business and industry such as the Chambers of Commerce (Waterkamp, 2002, p 7). In this system of *commissioned training* (*Auftragsausbildung*), administrative matters (including formulation of training contracts, organisation of a training plan, enrolment for intermediate and final exams), as well as responsibility for certain training contents, can be transferred from companies that lack sufficient experience and/or resources to a partner institution.

3. A number of smaller companies can also establish a *training society* (*Ausbildungsverein*) which administers the training of trainees centrally. The individual training companies are members of the society and entrust the overall responsibility for the training process to the society. The training society formally assumes the role of the training institution. It organises the training, including on-the-job training of the trainees with the member companies (see BIBB, 2000, pp 108-15).

There is a certain amount of experience with all three types of cooperation, but they seem of particular relevance for new companies in the IT, media and services sectors that have not offered training places hitherto. Advice and support in setting up and running such cooperations is offered by the responsible federal and Länder ministries as well as by regional chambers and job centres (BMBF, 2000b).

A further field of cooperation of institutions represents the need for coordination of the training processes at the two primary training venues of the dual system: training companies and part-time vocational schools. Due to their independence, there is the danger of a lack of coherence and cooperation between the two venues. This includes the tendency towards insufficient coordination between theoretical and practical training contents (Sloane, 1994, p 205; Pätzold, 1997, pp 124-30). The analysis of current cooperation patterns between vocational schools and training companies has shown that only 30% of institutions are involved in regular cooperation. This means that in over 60% of cases, teachers at schools, and trainers in companies, either have no contact with each other at all, or communication only takes place occasionally. In most of the latter cases, teachers and trainers only start to cooperate when serious problems with a trainee occur[3].

In the light of these results, research has focused on the improvement of the cooperation of the two training venues of the dual system over the last two decades, rather than on calling into question the principle of duality of the training provisions. To do this a number of pilot projects have been initiated[4]. The main aim of these projects, and of the related research, is to overcome the lack of coherence between classroom learning at vocational schools, associated with the acquisition of subject knowledge, and workplace learning in the training companies taking place in an ad hoc style while the trainee is actively engaged in productive work (Walden, 1996). The body of research acknowledges that the learning demands on both training sites are changing. Training at vocational schools and in training companies needs to be developed in ways in which:

> knowledge [can be] situated in specific contexts if it is to become part of the experience of the learner. (Young, 1999, p 19)

The fact that Young has argued for a reconceptualised relationship between training sites in the context of his concept of a 'curriculum of the future' that would unify provisions for academic and vocational provisions in England and Wales (Young, 1998) shows that the problems of coordination between learning at different sites go beyond the context of training in the German dual system. Young (1999, p 18) has identified the following general developments for schools and workplaces as training venues: "Workplaces increasingly require knowledge that cannot be learned 'in practice' and schools are being expected to prepare their students not just to pass exams but to be lifelong learners in contexts where there may not be teachers". With regard to intensified cooperation of the institutions involved in the training process, Kutscha (1993, 1997) advocates the expansion of the dual system into a 'plural system' which would not only integrate learning venues like external training centres and 'polytechnics' (*Fachhochschulen*) into the training structure but also school-based training courses outside the dual system (see Autsch et al, 1993; Hahn, 1997; Rosenau, 1997, p 11).

Reconceptualisation of curricula

The comprehensive nature of state-recognised training occupations, and the complex, and often lengthy, process of developing and updating the regulations and curricula for these training occupations, has been described earlier in this chapter. These complex processes are a main reason for the perceived inadequacies of the dual system for meeting the demands of a rapidly changing economic environment.

Modularisation in VET is one of the main approaches that could increase the aforementioned types of flexibility since modularised structures can potentially be more rapidly updated than conventional training provision. The basic idea of modularisation is to create training arrangements that are composed by a set of self-contained elements or modules. These modules are distinguished from 'conventional' courses by their outcome orientation, their shorter duration and, in some cases, their relevance for more than one course of training (Watkins, 1987; Young, 1995; Lauterbach and Grollman, 1998).

Modularisation is currently applied or introduced in varying conceptual frameworks in several European countries – in most cases with the explicit aim of modernising training structures perceived as too inflexible for matching the demands of an evermore changing economic world (cf Ertl, 2001). Although modularisation is also discussed as a promising way of reforming the dual system, the German debate about modularity seems in many respects to be in the early stages. The assessment by Richardson et al (1995, p 22) that "education and training systems which are relatively stable have shown little interest to date in modularity and credit" applies perfectly to the case of Germany. Moreover, the debate on modularisation in Germany seems to suffer from the fact that it often remains unclear what concept of modularisation is under scrutiny (Wiegand, 1996, p 261). For instance, the comparison of definitions of modules and modularisation (see Ertl, 2000a, appendix II) makes it clear that there is no consensus on the applicability and possible contexts of modularity. In order to overcome this dilemma, a number of conceptualisations have been developed recently, identifying conceivable types of modular structures for the German system of initial training. The following three concepts are a synopsis of different conceptualisations developed in the German context (Deissinger, 1996a, pp 192f).

Expansion concept

Modules supplement initial training qualifications to generate additional competences that are typically the subject of further education and training. The overall functions of initial qualifications are expanded. There are two types of organisational implementation:

- in the *consecutive model*, the contents of initial and further training remain separated; and
- in the *integrative model*, the contents of further training are integrated into the initial qualification.

Differentiation concept

Modules are self-contained and can be assessed and credited individually, but they are only marketable as part of an overall qualification. The framework of the overall qualification regulates the combination of modules. Modules can be the result of restructuring the curricula of existing qualifications. The differentiation concept facilitates the accreditation of prior learning. Modules can be accredited towards different vocational qualifications but also across the academic–vocational divide.

Fragmentation concept

Modules are credited and marketable without the framework of an overall qualification. By combining modules freely, trainees create individualised qualifications that mirror the requirements of a rapidly changing occupational environment. In comparison to the expansion and the differentiation concept, the fragmentation concept offers the greatest opportunities for flexibility and individuality in VET but poses the danger of establishing disintegrated part-qualifications that are not recognised by employers.

The opponents of modular structures in Germany simply put forward the 'concept of the vocation', and describe it as incompatible with any type of modularisation. From conceptualisation, however, it becomes clear that it is only the fragmentation concept that is incompatible with this concept. Therefore, it is only this concept that causes the controversial debate regarding modularisation in Germany (ZDH, 1993, p 128; Zedler, 1996, p 20; 1997, p 42; Schmidt, 1997, p 42).

However, in this politically driven argument, the potential of the other two concepts is neglected. Most importantly, the differentiation concept could be used to create flexible and individualised routes to qualifications which may bridge the gap between vocational and academic careers, and to increase the efficiency in the training sector, particularly with regard to the multiple relevancies of many modules. Further, the traditional, chronological pattern of training comprising vocational orientation and preparation, initial vocational training and further training and education, which has determined the careers of the majority of working people in Germany for decades, is rapidly dissolving. The expansion concept in particular recognises these developments, and integrates initial and further training in a systematic way.

The potential of the two concepts of modularity could be realised by developing the existing elements of occupational profiles (*Berufsbildpositionen*) into self-contained part-qualifications which fulfil the functions of modules (cf Kloas, 1997a, 1997b, 1997c). Currently, occupational profiles are divided into a number of elements regarded as relevant for a vocation. In order to fulfil the functions of modules, these elements of occupational profiles, and the current accreditation procedures, have to be transformed in a number of ways, including the development of:

- *outcome specifications* (as opposed to the current exclusive reliance on the specification of input factors of the training process);
- an adequate *accreditation instrument* for individual modules (as opposed to the 'all-or-nothing' character of the dual system's current assessment regime, which is focused on the all-important final examination);
- flexible *modular assessment systems* (allowing for assessment immediately after a module is completed, and for a greater variety of testing methods); and
- modules with *multiple relevance* (as opposed to the current tendency of developing comprehensive training regulations for each state-recognised occupation in isolation) (see Ertl, 2002a, p 60).

For this strategy to succeed, it is important that these developments take place within the corporative structure of the German regulatory framework to ensure that employers and trade unions of the different occupational areas generally accept the standards of the modules. By developing modules within the framework of existing recognised training occupations, the danger of fragmentation in the VET sector – one of the main criticisms faced by NVQs and GNVQs (Smithers, 1997, p 57) – can be minimised (Deissinger, 1996a, p 200). The combination of self-contained modules (that is, further developed and redesigned elements of occupational profiles) is regulated by an overall qualification, and modules are generally only marketable as part of a comprehensive qualification.

Didactic reform

In order to understand the scope of change didactic innovations have brought to training processes in the German dual system, one has to be aware of the traditional method of teaching that has developed from the beginning of the apprenticeship system, which arose in the Middle Ages in the craft trades. The apprentice adopted the work techniques and skills of his master. He tried to imitate his master as closely as possible and to improve his skills through practise. In the 1920s and 1930s, this basic model was moulded into a linear sequence of steps, when large industrial companies introduced standardised training for a large number of apprentices for the purpose of creating employees skilled for mass production. This process can be seen as the didactic integration of the Taylorist plant regime of labour division into the traditional German 'concept of the vocation'. The result of this integration process at a micro-didactic level was the 'four-step method', which dominated company-based training in Germany for the greater part of the 20th century (cf Kutscha, 1995, p 14).

It is important to note that the four-step method was developed and used in strongly hierarchical and directional company structures. Its effectiveness was dependent on the clearly defined roles of the trainer (who has specialist knowledge and skills and who knows the only possible way of using them) and the trainee (who is willing to accept the dominant role of the trainer and to put aside her or his own interests and aspirations) in the learning process.

With the introduction of new, flexible production processes, primarily as a consequence of the rapid progress of information technology, the Taylorist division of work started to lose its dominance (Kern and Schumann, 1984). Although the identification of a Taylorist and a post-Taylorist era would be simplistic, and in spite of doubts as to the extent to which the new era of production processes has materialised, decentralisation of work in partly autonomous groups, and company-wide quality control measures, did influence training methods. New concepts were developed to take the changed work environment into account (Schumann, 1994). It was concluded that tasks and functions were no longer separate issues and this resulted in the skilled worker having to fulfil the formerly separated functions of planning, executing and controlling work tasks. As a consequence, more complex and integrated training processes had to be developed to enable the trainee to fulfil the new role. The traditional four-step method could not provide such processes.

The following outline represents one example of the introduction of new methods of in-company training, developed in the field of metalwork occupations but analogous to approaches in other fields (see Kutscha, 1995, p 13). The process is organised into six sequences in which trainees solve complex work tasks:

1. The trainees are given the tasks and basic explanations. For this sequence, 'guiding texts' (prepared written materials that support independent learning) and interactive training programmes may be used.
2. The trainees try to find the information they need independently and plan necessary steps and resources.
3. The resulting plan is discussed with trainers who also support decision making.
4. The trainees execute the plan unaided, in most cases in teamwork.
5. The trainees control and assess the final product independently to learn to judge the quality of their work.
6. After this process of self-monitoring, the trainees present their work to the trainers. Together they discuss any problems and draw conclusions for future tasks.

This model is explicitly based on the trainees' actions. Thinking in comprehensive patterns and teamwork are fostered. This implies distinctly different roles for trainees and trainers to those in the four-step method. Kutscha illustrated the concept in Figure 7.1.

Since the mid-1990s, the concept of 'complex and complete tasks', as illustrated by Figure 7.1, has been further developed and extended to training processes at vocational schools. In the school context, the most prominent expression of the ideas of activity-oriented and comprehensive learning is the recently introduced concept of 'areas of learning' as described in the concluding section.

Conclusions: the concept of 'areas of learning'

With regard to the reform measures described in the previous section, it can be said that the modernisation of VET in Germany has only proven to be feasible within the regulatory framework set by the underlying principles of the dual system. The context of the debate at two of the aforementioned levels of reform may illustrate this point of view:

- In the case of projects attempting to improve the cooperation between the dual system's two primary learning sites (institutional level), the debate is based on the acknowledgement that the 'principle of duality' should not be questioned. The assumption that the combination of training at vocational schools and in training companies is the best way of organising VET, not only dominates the respective pilot schemes but it is also, at a closer view, the main reason why the schemes are necessary. Radically different reform models, for instance, the introduction of in-company vocational schools, are hardly ever discussed.

Figure 7.1: New concept for firm-based training: action-oriented learning

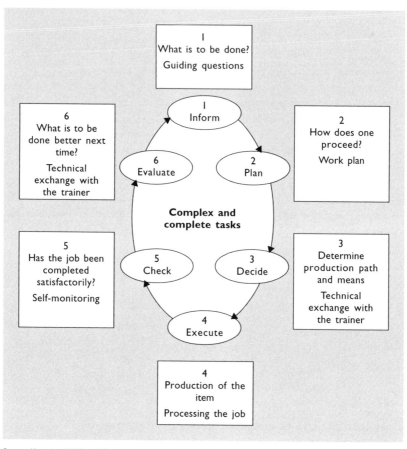

Source: Kutscha (1995, p 15)

- In the case of modularisation in VET (curricular level), the major focus of the debate in Germany seems to be driven by educational policy rather than by arguments concerning pedagogical aspects or the teaching/learning process (Münk, 1995, p 35; Pütz, 1997, p 63). The arguments put forward by supporters of modularisation seem to be unclear and sometimes dubious. On the other hand, the opponents of modular structures simply put forward the 'concept of the vocation' and describe it as incompatible with any type of modularisation. Both positions seem to be inappropriate starting points for an unbiased analysis of the potential advantages modularisation has to offer for the German VET system.

As a result, modular structures can be found only in comparatively small areas of VET, for example in the qualifications of specific target groups, in further training, in retraining schemes, in schemes for initial training of people in work and in schemes for additional qualifications in initial training (Brinke and Rüb, 1995; Davids, 1996, 1998; Kloas, 1996; Reuling and Sauter, 1996, p 6; Zedler, 1996, p 20; Sloane, 1997, p 224; BBJ Servis, 2000). The potential of modular approaches to 'rejuvenate' the 'concept of the vocation' is wasted. Modularisation could be utilised to overcome the static interpretation of the 'concept of the vocation' by introducing measures that allow vocational training to take the rapidly changing economic environment, and the individualised career paths of young people, into account.

For reform attempts that are based on the underlying principles of the dual system, it would seem that those approaches which initiate change at more than one of the levels described have a better chance of becoming reality, and of improving training provisions. As an example for such a 'multi-level' approach, a discussion of the concept of 'areas of learning' (*Lernfelder*) shall conclude this chapter.

The main idea of this concept is the reconstruction and/or simulation of vocational processes at vocational schools. Therefore, self-contained 'areas of learning' are designed against the background of activities and tasks the trainees are confronted with in training companies. Further, the 'areas of learning' draw on the knowledge that is represented in conventional school subjects. However, the traditional subjects are transformed into cross–curricular arrangements in which comprehensive tasks have to be fulfilled and real-life problems have to be solved by the trainees. Ideally, these learning arrangements should be planned and implemented in such a way that the trainees are able to improve their skills by actively engaging in learning arrangements that resemble the structure of the corresponding occupational field (Sloane, 2001, p 198). By completing a specified number of 'areas of learning' the trainee acquires all the knowledge and skills necessary to work effectively in a specific occupational area (cf Kremer and Sloane, 1999, 2000; Bader and Sloane, 2000; Sloane, 2000a).

The concept of 'areas of learning' was introduced formally by a decision of the Conference of Education Ministers (*Kultusministerkonferenz*) in 1999 (KMK, 1999). The concept represents a pragmatic approach for initiating the modernisation of curricula and training processes at vocational schools. Bader (2000, p 41) argues that the concept as a whole has not yet been the subject of sufficient theoretically oriented research. However, main elements of the concept have been investigated in great detail. Indeed the *Lernfeld* concept draws on most of the reform approaches described earlier in this chapter.

The concept applies the notions of didactic innovations such as activity-oriented and comprehensive learning to the school context. It requires and structures the cooperation of the primary training venues of the dual system since it is the task of teachers at vocational schools, and of trainers at training companies, to create the learning arrangements for the 'areas of learning' prescribed for a training occupation. The development of curricula becomes part of their work. This task can only be fulfilled with close cooperation from the training venues. Finally, 'areas of learning' make use of some of the potential of modules in VET, and since they are conceptualised as self-contained entities, they can be relevant for more than one training occupation, and updated individually without revising all the regulations for a training occupation.

Thus, the concept of the 'areas of learning' initiates modernisation processes at all levels of reform identified in this chapter. At the *didactic level*, the emphasis of the concept of 'areas of learning' is on activity-oriented learning (Berger and Diehl, 2000, p 8). At the *curricular level*, the traditional disciplines (reflected in school subjects) are transformed into cross-curricular, self-contained learning areas. This means that the contents of the former curricula are reorganised in structures that resemble the patterns of occupational activity of trainees. Changes at the *institutional level* have to be initiated since teachers at vocational schools have to cooperate with trainers at training companies in order to define 'areas of learning' that address the needs of the world of work. At the *structural level*, 'areas of learning' have the potential to bridge the gap between initial and further training since they are based on a comprehensive notion of occupational competence. Therefore, individual *Lernfelder* will integrate contents that were hitherto scattered in different programmes of initial and further training.

By initiating innovation at different regulatory levels, the concept of 'areas of learning' seems to be well equipped to contribute to the modernisation of the dual system of VET in Germany. The introduction of the concept also proves that far-reaching change in the training sector is possible without leaving the realm of the well-accepted stabilising principles of the dual system. Thus, the dual system could, once more, contribute to the balance of the German "high-skills society" (Green, 2001, p 151).

Notes

[1] An indication for this observation are a number of edited books in which leading educationalists describe the changes the dual system is facing and the ways in which reform and modernisation should lead. The titles of these publications are indicative: Beck and Achtenhagen (eds) (1996) *Berufserziehung im Umbruch* (*Vocational education in upheaval*); Schlaffke and Weiss (1996) *Das Duale System ... Qualität und Reformbedarf* (*The dual system ... Quality and need for reform*); Schmidt et al (1997) *Das Duale System der Berufsausbildung – ein 'Exportschlager' in der Krise?* (*The dual system of vocational training – an export 'best-seller' in crisis?*); Euler and Sloane (1997) *Duales System im Umbruch: Eine Bestandsaufnahme der Modernisierungsdebatte* (*Dual system in upheaval: A stock-taking of the debate on modernisation*); Euler (1998a) *Berufliches Lernen im Wandel* (*Vocational learning in transition*); Flitner et al (1999) *Wege aus der Ausbildungskrise* (*Solutions for the training crisis*); Arnold (2003) *Berufspädagogik ohne Beruf* (*Vocational education without the vocation*).

[2] The translation of the German term *Beruf* poses difficulties. Neither 'vocation' nor 'profession' is congruent with the German term, but the former is used in this chapter because the latter is too closely bound to academic occupations (such as lawyers and doctors).

[3] The evidence for this analysis seems conclusive, that is, research in different economic sectors, in different parts of Germany, and over a longer period of time come to similar results. The evidence also suggests that bigger training companies are more likely to initiate constant and effective cooperation with vocational schools than small and medium-sized companies. Cf for instance Autsch et al (1993), Pätzold and Walden (1995) and Berger (1998).

[4] Cf for instance the approaches developed by the pilot project *Kooperation der Lernorte in der beruflichen Bildung* (*Cooperation of the training venues in vocational education*) (Euler, 1998a, 1998b, 1999) and the project *Fächer- und Lernortübergreifender Unterricht* (*Cross-curricular and cross-venue teaching and learning*) (Kremer, 1999; Sloane, 2000b). For an overview of pilot projects in the area of cooperation of the partners in the dual system see BIBB (1998, pp 109-32).

References

Achtenhagen, F., Tramm, T., Preiss, P., Seemann-Weymar, H., John, E. and Schunck, A. (1992) *Lernhandeln in komplexen Situationen: neue Konzepte der betriebswirtschaftlichen Ausbildung*, Wiesbaden: Gabler.

Arnold, R. (1993) 'Das duale System', *Berufsbildung in Wissenschaft und Praxis*, vol 22, no 1, pp 20-7.

Arnold, R. (ed) (2003) *Berufspädagogik ohne Beruf. Berufspädagogische, bildungspolitische und internationale Perspektiven*, Series: Grundlagen der Berufs- und Erwachsenenbildung, vol 34, Baltmannsweiler: Schneider Verlag.

Aron, R. (1967) *Main currents in sociological thought. Durkheim, Pareto, Weber*, New York, NY: Basic Books.

Autsch, B. (1995) 'Ausgangsbedingungen bei der Umstellung des DDR-Berufsbildungssystems aus der Sicht rechtlicher und organisatorischer Rahmenbedingungen', in U. Degen, G. Walden and K. Berger (eds) *Berufsausbildung in den neuen Bundesländern: Daten, Analysen, Perspektiven*, Berichte zur beruflichen Bildung, vol 180, pp 15-28.

Autsch, B., Berger, K., Brandes, H. and Walden, G. (1993) 'Gestaltungsmerkmale der Kooperation von Betrieben, Berufsschulen und überbetrieblichen Berufsbildungsstätten', *Berufsbildung in Wissenschaft und Praxis*, vol 2, pp 32-40.

Backes-Haase, A. (2002) 'Schnittstelle berufliche Bildung. Der Wandel zur Informationsökonomie und die künftige Ordnung beruflicher Bildung', *Kölner Zeitschrift für Wirtschaft und Pädagogik*, vol 17, no 32, pp 3-27.

Bader, R. (2000) 'Konstruieren von Lernfeldern – eine Handreichung für Rahmenlehrplanausschüsse und Bildungsgangkonferenzen in technischen Berufsfeldern', in R. Bader and P. Sloane (eds) *Lernen in Lernfeldern. Theoretische Analysen und Gestaltungsansätze zum Lernfeldkonzept. Beiträge aus den Modellversuchsverbünden NELE and SELUBA*, Markt Schwaben: Eusl, pp 33-50.

Bader, R. and Sloane, P. (eds) (2000) *Lernen in Lernfeldern. Theoretische Analysen und Gestaltungsansätze zum Lernfeldkonzept. Beiträge aus den Modellversuchsverbünden NELE and SELUBA*, Markt Schwaben: Eusl.

Baethge, M. (1999) 'Strukturwandel in der Berufsbildung und korporatistisches Handlungsmodell: ein Deutungsversuch für die aktuelle Krise des dualen Ausbildungssystems', in T. Tramm, D. Sembill, F. Klauser and E. John (eds) *Professionalisierung kaufmännischer Berufsbildung. Beiträge zur Öffnung der Wirtschaftspädagogik für die Anforderungen des 21. Jahrhunderts. Festschrift zum 60. Geburtstag von Frank Achtenhagen*, Frankfurt a.M.: Lang, pp 106-25.

BBJ Servis (2000) *Modulare Nachqualifizierung: Modellversuch, Differenzierte Wege zum Nachholen von Berufsabschlüssen. Dokumentation und Auswertung*, Berlin: BBJ Servis GmbH.

Beck, K. and Achtenhagen, F. (eds) (1996) *Berufserziehung im Umbruch. Didaktische Herausforderungen und Ansätze zu ihrer Bewältigung*, Weinheim: Beltz.

Beck, U., Brater, H. and Daheim, M. (1980) *Soziologie der Arbeit und der Berufe. Grundlagen, Problemfelder, Forschungsergebnisse*, Reinbek: Rowohlt.

Benner, H. (1996a) 'BIBB-Positionen zu aktuellen Herausforderungen in der beruflichen Bildung: I. Beruf und Berufskonzept', *Berufsbildung in Wissenschaft und Praxis*, vol 25, no 3, pp 3f.

Benner, H. (1996b) *Ordnung der staatlich anerkannten Ausbildungsberufe*, Bielefeld: Bertelsmann.

Benner, H. (1997) 'Entwicklung anerkannter Ausbildungsberufe – Fortschreibung überkommener Regelungen oder Definition zukunftsbezogener Ausbildungsgänge?', in D. Euler and P. Sloane (eds) (1997) *Duales System im Umbruch. Eine Bestandsaufnahme der Modernisierungsdebatte*, Pfaffenweiler: Centaurus-Verl.-Ges, pp 53-69.

Berger, K. (1998) 'Zur Lernortkooperation im Ausbildungsberuf Kaufmann/ Kauffrau im Einzelhandel', in H. Paulini (ed) *Kaufleute im Einzelhandel: Stand der Perspektive eines Berufs*, Materialien zur beruflichen Bildung, vol 100, Bielefeld: BIBB.

Berger, B. and Diehl, T. (2000) 'Theoretische Grundlagen und curriculare Weiterentwicklung des Lernfeldkonzepts – Darstellung der Ergebnisse eines Workshops der Modellversuchsverbünde NELE und SELUBA, vom 25.-26.11.1999 in Magdeburg', in R. Bader and P. Sloane (eds) (2000) *Lernen in Lernfeldern. Theoretische Analysen und Gestaltungsansätze zum Lernfeldkonzept. Beiträge aus den Modellversuchsverbünden NELE and SELUBA*, Markt Schwaben: Eusl, pp 7-29.

BIBB (Bundesinstitut für Berufsbildung) (ed) (1998) *Kooperation der Lernorte im Dualen System der Berufsausbildung. Ergebnisse, Veröffentlichungen und Materialien aus dem BIBB*, Bonn: BIBB.

BIBB (ed) (1999) *Berufsbildung in der Entwicklung. Ergebnisse, Veröffentlichungen und Materialien aus dem BIBB*, Bonn: BIBB.

BIBB (ed) (2000) *Impulse für die Berufsbildung. Agenda 2000 plus*, Bielefeld: Bertelsmann.

BIBB (2001) *Neue und modernisierte Ausbildungsberufe 2001*, Bonn: BIBB.

BMBF (Bundesministerium für Bildung, Wissenschaft, Forschung und Technologie) (ed) (1997) *Modularisierung der Berufsbildung – Gleichwertigkeit von allgemeiner und beruflicher Bildung. Deutsch-Britisches Seminar zur Berufsbildungspolitik 3.-5. Februar 1997 in Berlin*, Bonn: BMBF.

BMBF (ed) (2000a) *Berufsbildungsbericht 2000*, Bonn: BMBF.

BMBF (2000b) *Jetzt selbst ausbilden – die neuen IT-Berufe*, Bonn: BMBF.

BMBF (ed) (2001) *Berufsbildungsbericht 2001*, Bonn: BMBF.

Borch, H. and Weissmann, H. (1999) 'Mechatroniker/Mechatronikerin – Ein neuer staatlich anerkannter Ausbildungsberuf', in BIBB (ed) *Berufsbildung in der Entwicklung. Ergebnisse, Veröffentlichungen und Materialien aus dem BIBB* Bonn: BIBB, pp 89-95.

Brand, W. (1998) 'Change and Consensus in Vocational Education and Training. The Case of the German "Dual System"', in I. Finlay, S. Niven and S. Young (eds) *Changing Vocational Education and Training. An international comparative perspective*, London: Routledge, pp 103-22.

Brinke, A. and Rüb, H. (1995) 'Modularisierte Qualifizierung an verschiedenen Lernorten – Erfahrungen aus dem Modellversuch, Das integrierte Arbeits- und Lernkonzept', in S. Davids, N. Djafari and B. Grote (eds) (1997) *Junge Erwachsene qualifizieren. Nachholen von Berufsabschlüssen im Verbund mit Beschäftigung. Dokumentation der Fachtagung vom 13. und 14. Dezember in Weimar*, Tagungen und Expertengespräche zur Beruflichen Bildung, vol 29, pp 160-70.

Brown, A. and Evans, K. (1994) 'Changing the training culture: lessons from Anglo-German comparisons of vocational education and training', *British Journal of Education and Work*, vol 7, no 2, pp 5-15.

Bruijn, E., Froissart, C., Tirados, R., Howieson, C., Manning, S., Ortega, P., Raffe, D. and Spence, J. (1993) *Current issues in modular training: An interview study with trainers in six European countries*, Edinburgh: Centre for Educational Sociology, University of Edinburgh.

Bruijn, E. and Howieson, C. (1995) 'Modular vocational education and training in Scotland and The Netherlands: between specificity and coherence', *Comparative Education*, vol 31, no 1, pp 83-99.

CEC (Commission of the European Communities) (1997) *Key data on vocational training in the European Union*, Luxembourg: Office for Official Publications of the European Communities.

CEDEFOP (Centre Européen pour le Développement de la Formation Professionnelle) (1995) *Vocational education and training in the Federal Republic of Germany*, Berlin: CEDEFOP.

CEDEFOP (1996) 'Pedagogic innovation: vocational training', *European Journal*, no 7, Thessaloniki: CEDEFOP.

Cleve, B. and Kell, A. (1996) 'Modularisierung der Berufsbildung', *Die berufsbildende Schule*, vol 48, pp 15-22.

Culpepper, P. (1999) 'The future of the high-skill equilibrium in Germany', *Oxford Review of Economic Policy*, vol 15, no 1, pp 43-59.

Davids, S. (1996) 'Berufsbegleitende Nachqualifizierung von Erwachsenen ohne Berufsausbildung – Realisierung eines modularen Konzepts in vier Modellversuchen', in P. Diepold (ed) *Berufliche Aus- und Weiterbildung. Konvergenzen/Divergenzen, neue Anforderungen/alte Strukturen. Dokumentation des 2. Forums Berufsbildungsforschung 1995 an der Humboldt-Universität zu Berlin*, Beiträge zur Arbeitsmarkt- und Berufsforschung, BeitrAB 195, Nürnberg: Institut für Arbeitsmarkt- und Berufsforschung der Bundesanstalt für Arbeit, pp 158-70.

Davids, S. (ed) (1998) *Modul für Modul zum Berufsabschluß. Berufsbegleitende Nachqualifizierung zwischen Flexibilität und Qualitätssicherung*, Berichte zur beruflichen Bildung, vol 216.

Deissinger, T. (1996a) 'Modularisierung der Berufsausbildung. – Eine didaktisch-curriculare Alternative zum "Berufsprinzip"?', in K. Beck and F. Achtenhagen (eds) *Berufserziehung im Umbruch. Didaktische Herausforderungen und Ansätze zu ihrer Bewältigung*, Weinheim: Beltz, pp 189-207.

Deissinger, T. (1996b) 'Germany's vocational training act: its functions as an instrument of quality control within a tradition-based vocational training system', *Oxford Review of Education*, vol 22, no 3, pp 317-36.

Deissinger, T. (1998) *Beruflichkeit als 'organisierendes Prinzip' der deutschen Berufsausbildung*, Markt Schwaben: Eusl.

Deissinger, T. (ed) (2001a) *Berufliche Bildung zwischen nationaler Tradition und globaler Entwicklung*, Baden-Baden: Nomos.

Deissinger, T. (2001b) 'Zum Problem der historisch-kulturellen Bedingtheit von Berufsbildungssystemen – Gibt es eine "Vorbildfunktion" des deutschen Dualen Systems im europäischen Kontext?', in T. Deissinger (ed) *Berufliche Bildung zwischen nationaler Tradition und globaler Entwicklung*, Baden-Baden: Nomos, pp 13-44.

Diepold, P. (ed) (1996) *Berufliche Aus- und Weiterbildung. Konvergenzen/Divergenzen, neue Anforderungen/alte Strukturen. Dokumentation des 2. Forums Berufsbildungsforschung 1995 an der Humboldt-Universität zu Berlin*, Beiträge zur Arbeitsmarkt- und Berufsforschung, BeitrAB 195, Nürnberg: Institut für Arbeitsmarkt- und Berufsforschung der Bundesanstalt für Arbeit.

Dougherty, C. (1987) 'The German dual system: a heretical view', reprinted in D. Phillips (ed) (1995) *Education in Germany: Tradition and reform in historical context*, London and New York, NY: Routledge, pp 171-5.

Ebner, H. (1992) 'Facetten und Elemente didaktischer Handlungsorientierung', in G. Pätzold (ed) *Handlungsorientierung in der beruflichen Bildung*, Frankfurt a.M.: Gesellschaft zur Förderung Arbeitsorientierter Forschung und Bildung, pp 33-53.

Encyclopaedia Britannica (2001) *Millennium edition* (CD-ROM Version).

Ertl, H. (2000a) *Modularisation of vocational education in Europe: NVQs and GNVQs as a model for the reform of initial training provisions in Germany?*, Monographs in International Education, vol 2, Wallingford: Symposium Books.

Ertl, H. (2000b) 'The transitions of vocational education in the eastern part of Germany: some notes on the role of European Union Programmes', *Comparative Education Review*, vol 44, no 4, pp 464-92.

Ertl, H. (2001): *Modularisation in vocational education and training: Conceptualisations and approaches in European Union Countries*, Cadernos PRESTiGE, vol 7, Lisbon: Educa.

Ertl, H. (2002a) 'The concept of modularisation in vocational education and training: the debate in Germany and its implication', *Oxford Review of Education*, vol 28, no 1, pp 53-73.

Ertl, H. (2002b) 'The role of European Union programmes and approaches to modularisation in vocational education: fragmentation or integration?', Doctoral thesis submitted to the University of Munich (currently in print).

Ertl, H. and Phillips, D. (2000) 'The enduring nature of the tripartite system of secondary schooling in Germany: some historical explanations', *British Journal of Educational Studies*, vol 48, no 4, pp 391-412.

Euler, D. (ed) (1998a) *Berufliches Lernen im Wandel – Konsequenzen für die Lernorte? Dokumentation des 3. Forums Berufsbildungsforschung 1997 an der Friedrich-Alexander-Universität Erlangen-Nürnberg*, Beiträge zur Arbeitsmarkt- und Berufsforschung, BeitrAB 214, Nürnberg: Institut für Arbeitsmarkt- und Berufsforschung der Bundesanstalt für Arbeit.

Euler, D. (1998b) *Zwischen Engagement und Exkulpation – Über die (fehlenden) Bedingungen einer Lernortkooperation*, Nürnberg: Lehrstuhl für Pädagogik, insb. Wirtschaftspädagogik an der Universität Erlangen-Nürnberg.

Euler, D. (1999) *Kooperation der Lernorte in der Berufsbildung. Expertise für die Bund-Länder-Kommission für Bildungsplanung und Forschungsförderung im Auftrag des Bundesministeriums für Bildung und Forschung*, Nürnberg: Lehrstuhl für Pädagogik, insb. Wirtschaftspädagogik an der Universität Erlangen-Nürnberg.

Euler, D. and Sloane, P. (eds) (1997) *Duales System im Umbruch. Eine Bestandsaufnahme der Modernisierungsdebatte*, Pfaffenweiler: Centaurus-Verl.-Ges.

Federal Minister for Education and Science (ed) (1992) *Vocational training in the dual system in the Federal Republic of Germany: An investment in the future*, Köln: Kölnische Verlagsdruckerei.

Flitner, A., Petry, C. and Richter, I. (eds) (1999) *Wege aus der Ausbildungskrise. Memorandum des Forums 'Jugend – Bildung – Arbeit' mit Untersuchungsergebnissen des Instituts für Arbeitsmarkt- und Berufsforschung der Bundesanstalt für Arbeit*, Opladen: Leske + Budrich.

Geissler, K. (1994) 'Von der Meisterschaft zur Qualifikations-Collage. Drei Entwicklungen, die die industrielle Berufsausbildung gefährden', in S. Liesering, K. Schober and M. Tessaring (eds) *Die Zukunft der dualen Berufsausbildung. Eine Fachtagung der Bundesanstalt für Arbeit*, Beiträge zur Arbeitsmarkt- und Berufsforschung, BeitrAB 186, Nürnberg: Institut für Arbeitsmarkt- und Berufsforschung der Bundesanstalt für Arbeit, pp 328-34.

Geissler, K. (2002) 'Wege aus der Warteschleife. Auch das Duale System ist in der Krise: In Deutschland fehlen durchlässige Ausbildungsgänge', *Süddeutsche Zeitung*, 2 April.

Geissler, K. and Orthey, F. (1998) 'Am Ende des Berufs', *Süddeutsche Zeitung*, 17 January.

Georg, W. (1997) 'Berufliche Bildung zwischen Internationalisierung und nationaler Identität', in C. Kodron, B. von Kopp, U. Lauterbach, U. Schäfer and G. Schmidt (eds) *Vergleichende Erziehungswissenschaft: Herausforderung, Vermittlung, Praxis. Festschrift für Wolfgang Mitter zum 70. Geburtstag*, Köln: Böhlau Verlag, pp 312-29.

Georg, W. (2001) 'Zur Debatte um das Ende des Berufs und die Zukunft der beruflichen Bildung', *Bildung und Erziehung*, vol 54, no 4, pp 369-82.

Green, A. (with Akiko Sakamoto) (2001) 'Models of high skills in national competition strategies', in P. Brown, A. Green and H. Lauder (eds) *High skills: Globalization, competitiveness and skill formation*, Oxford: Oxford University Press, pp 56-160.

Greinert, W. (1994) *The 'German system' of vocational education. History, organization, prospects*, Studien zur Vergleichenden Berufspädagogik, Baden-Baden: Deutsche Gesellschaft für Technische Zusammenarbeit.

Greinert, W. (1995) *Das duale System der Berufsausbildung in der Bundesrepublik Deutschland*, Stuttgart: Holland + Josenhans.

Greinert, W. (1998) *Das 'deutsche System' der Berufsausbildung. Geschichte, Organisation, Perspektiven*, Studien zur Vergleichenden Berufspädagogik, vol 1.

Greinert, W. (2000) *Organisationsmodelle und Lernkonzepte in der beruflichen Bildung. Analytische Grundlagentexte*, Studien zur Vergleichenden Berufspädagogik, vol 16.

Greinert, W. (2001) 'Die Übertragbarkeit des Dualen Systems in Entwicklungsländer – Möglichkeiten und Begrenzung einer politischen Strategie', in T. Deissinger (ed) *Berufliche Bildung zwischen nationaler Tradition und globaler Entwicklung*, Baden-Baden: Nomos, pp 45-60.

Hagedorn, J. (1997) 'Modulare Ausbildung als Qualifizierungsweg für (gegenwärtig) nicht ausbildbare junge Menschen', *Gewerkschaftliche Bildungspolitik*, vol 11/12-97, pp 16-18.

Hahn, A. (1997) 'Vollzeitschulen und duales System – Alte Konkurrenzdebatte oder gemeinsame Antworten auf dringende Fragen?', in D. Euler and P. Sloane (eds) *Duales System im Umbruch. Eine Bestandsaufnahme der Modernisierungsdebatte*, Pfaffenweiler: Centaurus-Verl.-Ges, pp 27-51.

Harney, K. and Tenorth, H. (eds) (1999) *Beruf und Berufsbildung: Situation, Reformperspektiven, Gestaltungsmöglichkeiten*, Beiheft zur Zeitschrift für Pädagogik, vol 40.

Heimerer, L. (1995) 'Die Berufsschulen – sind besser als ihr Ruf', *Die berufsbildende Schule. Zeitschrift des Bundesverbandes der Lehrer an beruflichen Schulen*, vol 47, no 5, pp 166-70.

HMI (Her Majesty's Inspectorate) (1991) *Aspects of vocational education and training in the Federal Republic of Germany*, London: HSMO.

HMI (1995) *Post-16 vocational education and training in Germany: International report*, London: Further Education Funding Council.

IDW (Institut der deutschen Wirtschaft) (2002) 'Ein harmonisches Ergebnis', *Informationsdienst des Instituts der deutschen Wirtschaft*, vol 28, no 4, p 2.

Kell, A. (1991) 'Berufsbezug in der Kollegschule. Theoretische Begründungen und konzeptionelle Konsequenzen', *Die berufsbildende Schule*, vol 43, no 5, pp 296-319.

Kern, H. and Schumann, M. (1984) *Das Ende der Arbeitsteilung? Rationalisierung in der industriellen Produktion: Bestandsaufnahme, Trendbestimmung*, München: Beck.

Keune, S. and Zielke, D. (1992) 'Individualisierung und Binnendifferenzierung: eine Perspektive für das duale System?', *Berufsbildung in Wissenschaft und Praxis*, vol 21, no 1, pp 32-7.

Kloas, P. (1995) 'Qualifizierung in Beschäftigung – neue Ansätze zur beruflichen Integration von Problemgruppen des Arbeitsmarktes', *Berufsbildung in Wissenschaft und Praxis*, vol 24, no 2, pp 3-10.

Kloas, P. (1996) 'Modulare Weiterbildung im Verbund mit Beschäftigung – Arbeitsmarkt- und bildungspolitische Aspekte eines strittigen Ansatzes', *Berufsbildung in Wissenschaft und Praxis*, vol 25, no 1, pp 39-46.

Kloas, P. (1997a) *Modularisierung in der beruflichen Bildung. Modebegriff, Streitthema oder konstruktiver Ansatz zur Lösung von Zukunftsproblemen*, Berlin und Bonn: Bundesinstitut für Berufsbildung.

Kloas, P. (1997b) 'Modulare Berufsausbildung in Deutschland: Streitthema ohne Wirkung oder Perspektive mit Zukunft?', *Gewerkschaftliche Bildungspolitik*, vol 11/12-97, pp 18-25.

Kloas, P. (1997c) 'Berufskonzept und Modularisierung in der deutschen Berufsbildung', in BMBF (ed) *Modularisierung der Berufsbildung – Gleichwertigkeit von allgemeiner und beruflicher Bildung. Deutsch-Britisches Seminar zur Berufsbildungspolitik 3.-5. Februar 1997 in Berlin*, Bonn: BMBF, pp 15-36.

Kloss, G. (1985a) 'Introduction', in G. Kloss (ed) *Education policy in the Federal Republic of Germany 1969–1984*, Manchester: Department of Language and Linguistics, University of Manchester Institute of Science and Technology, pp 1-12.

Kloss, G. (1985b) 'Vocational education: a success story?', in G. Kloss (ed) *Education policy in the Federal Republic of Germany 1969–1984*, Manchester: Department of Language and Linguistics, University of Manchester Institute of Science and Technology, pp 100-14; [reprinted in D. Phillips (ed) (1995) *Education in Germany: Tradition and reform in historical context*, London and New York, NY: Routledge, pp 161-70].

Kloss, G. (ed) (1985c) *Education policy in the Federal Republic of Germany 1969-1984*, Manchester: Department of Language and Linguistics, University of Manchester Institute of Science and Technology.

KMK (1999) *Handreichung für die Erarbeitung von Rahmenlehrplänen der Kultusministerkonferenz (KMK) für den berufsbezogenen Unterricht in der Berufsschule und ihre Abstimmung mit Ausbildungsordnungen des Bundes für anerkannte Ausbildungsberufe*, Bonn: Ständige Konferenz der Kultusminister der Länder in der Bundesrepublik Deutschland.

Koch, R. and Reuling, J. (eds) (1994) *Modernisierung, Regulierung und Anpassungsfähigkeit des Berufsausbildungssystems der Bundesrepublik Deutschland*, Berichte zur beruflichen Bildung, vol 170.

Koch, R. and Reuling, J. (1998) 'Public quality control of vocational training in Germany, France and the United Kingdom', *Vocational Education European Journal*, vol 15, no 3, pp 7-12.

Kodron, C., von Kopp, B., Lauterbach, U., Schäfer, U., and Schmidt, G. (1997) (eds) *Vergleichende Erziehungswissenschaft: Herausforderung, Vermittlung, Praxis. Festschrift für Wolfgang Mitter zum 70. Geburtstag*, Köln: Böhlau Verlag.

Kremer, H. (1999) *Implementation fächer- und lernortübergreifender Ausbildungskonzepte im Alltag dualer Ausbildung. Konzepte und Erfahrungen*, Lehren und Lernen in Schule und Betrieb, vol 1.

Kremer, H. and Sloane, P. (1999) 'Lernfelder – Motor didaktischer Innovationen?', *Kölner Zeitschrift für Wirtschaft und Pädagogik*, vol 14, no 26, pp 37-60.

Kremer, H. and Sloane, P. (2000) 'Lernfeldkonzept – erste Umsetzungserfahrungen und Konsequenzen für die Implementation', in R. Bader and P. Sloane (eds) *Lernen in Lernfeldern. Theoretische Analysen und Gestaltungsansätze zum Lernfeldkonzept. Beiträge aus den Modellversuchsverbünden NELE and SELUBA*, Markt Schwaben: Eusl, pp 71-83.

Kremer, H. and Sloane, P. (2001) *Konstruktion, Implementation und Evaluation komplexer Lehr-Lernarrangements. Fallbeispiele aus Österreich, den Niederlanden und Deutschland im Vergleich*, Paderborn: Eusl.

Kuda, E. (1996) 'Steigerung der Attraktivität dualer Ausbildung durch "praxisorientierte" Kurzlehrgänge?', *Berufsbildung in Wissenschaft und Praxis*, vol 25, no 1, pp 16-20.

Kutscha, G. (1992) '"Entberuflichung" und "Neue Beruflichkeit" – Thesen und Aspekte zur Modernisierung der Berufsausbildung und ihrer Theorie', *Zeitschrift für Berufs- und Wirtschaftspädagogik*, vol 88, no 7, pp 535-48.

Kutscha, G. (1993) 'Modernisierung der Berufsausbildung im Spannungsfeld von Systemdifferenzierung und Koordination', in F. Buttler, R. Czycholl and H. Pütz (eds) *Modernisierung beruflicher Bildung vor den Ansprüchen von Vereinheitlichung und Differenzierung*, Beiträge zur Arbeitsmarkt- und Berufsforschung, BeitrAB 177, Nürnberg: Institut für Arbeitsmarkt- und Berufsforschung der Bundesanstalt für Arbeit, pp 40-62.

Kutscha, G. (1995) 'General and vocational education and training in Germany – continuity amid change and the need for radical modernization', www.uni-duisburg.de/FB2/BERU/download/vocation.zip

Kutscha, G. (1996) 'Berufsbildungssystem und Berufsbildungspolitik', www.uni-duisburg.de/FB2/BERU/download/berufpol.zip

Kutscha, G. (1997) 'Integriertes Lernen in berufs- und studienbezogenen Bildungsgängen der Sekundarstufe II. Entwicklungen und Konzepte in der Bundesrepublik Deutschland', www.uni-duisburg.de/FB2/BERU/download/integrat.zip

Kutscha, G. (1998) 'Ausbildungsordnungen unter dem Einfluß der Internationalisierung und Pluralisierung von Industrienormen', in D. Euler (ed) *Berufliches Lernen im Wandel – Konsequenzen für die Lernorte? Dokumentation des 3. Forums Berufsbildungsforschung 1997 an der Friedrich-Alexander-Universität Erlangen-Nürnberg*, Beiträge zur Arbeitsmarkt- und Berufsforschung, BeitrAB 214, Nürnberg: Institut für Arbeitsmarkt- und Berufsforschung der Bundesanstalt für Arbeit, pp 265-84.

Kutscha, G. (1999) 'Modernisierung des Dualen Ausbildungssystems durch Entwicklung regionaler Infrastrukturen', in T. Tramm, D. Sembill, F. Klauser and E. John (eds) *Professionalisierung kaufmännischer Berufsbildung. Beiträge zur Öffnung der Wirtschaftspädagogik für die Anforderungen des 21. Jahrhunderts. Festschrift zum 60. Geburtstag von Frank Achtenhagen*, Frankfurt a.M: Lang, pp 106-25.

Lauterbach, U. and Grollman, P. (1998) 'Berufliche Bildung und allgemeine Bildung im Spannungsverhältnis, oder: Die Krise des Dualen Systems', *Vocational education and training in Germany and Sweden: Strategies of control and movements of resistance and opposition*, TNTEE Publications, vol 1, no 1, Osnabrück: Thematic Network on Teacher Education in Europe.

Liesering, S., Schober, K. and Tessaring, M. (eds) (1994) *Die Zukunft der dualen Berufsausbildung. Eine Fachtagung der Bundesanstalt für Arbeit* Beiträge zur Arbeitsmarkt- und Berufsforschung, BeitrAB 186, Nürnberg: Institut für Arbeitsmarkt- und Berufsforschung der Bundesanstalt für Arbeit.

Lipsmeier, A. and Münk, D. (1994) *Die Berufsbildungspolitik der Gemeinschaft für die 90er Jahre. Analyse der Stellungnahmen der EU-Mitgliedstaaten zum Memorandum der Kommission*, Bonn: Bundesministerium für Bildung und Wissenschaft.

MPI (Max-Planck-Institut für Bildungsforschung – Arbeitsgruppe Bildungsbericht) (1994) *Das Bildungswesen in der Bundesrepublik Deutschland. Strukturen und Entwicklungen im Überblick*, Reinbeck: Rowohlt.

Müller, K. and Schaarschuch, A. (1996) 'Das Entwicklungspotential des dualen Systems', *Berufsbildung in Wissenschaft und Praxis*, vol 25, no 3, pp 9-12.

Münk, D. (1995) 'Kein Grund zur Eu(ro)phorie. Anmerkungen zu zentralen berufsbildungspolitischen Kontroversen des "Memorandums der Kommission über die Berufsausbildungspolitik der Gemeinschaft für die 90er Jahre"', *Zeitschrift für Berufs- und Wirtschaftspädagogik*, vol 91, no 1, pp 28-45.

Münk, D. (1997) 'Berufsausbildung in der EU zwischen Dualität und "Monalität" – eine Alternative ohne Alternative?', *Berufsbildung*, vol 45, pp 5-8.

Nijhof, W. and Streumer, J. (1998) *Key qualifications in work and education*, Dordrecht: Kluwer Academic Publishers.

Pätzold, G. (ed) (1992) *Handlungsorientierung in der beruflichen Bildung*, Frankfurt a.M.: Gesellschaft zur Förderung Arbeitsorientierter Forschung und Bildung.

Pätzold, G. (1997) 'Lernortkooperation – wie ließe sich die Zusammenhanglosigkeit der Lernorte überwinden', in D. Euler and P. Sloane (eds) *Duales System im Umbruch. Eine Bestandsaufnahme der Modernisierungsdebatte*, Pfaffenweiler: Centaurus-Verl.-Ges, pp 121-42.

Pätzold, G. and Walden, G. (1995) 'Kooperation zwischen den Lernorten', *Ausbilder-Handbuch*, Köln: Kap. 3.2.6.

Phillips, D. (ed) (1995) *Education in Germany: Tradition and reform in historical context*, London and New York, NY: Routledge.

Pütz, H. (1997) '"Modularisierung" – das falsche Thema, ungenügend bearbeitet, zur ungeeigneten Zeit', in P. Kloas *Modularisierung in der beruflichen Bildung. Modebegriff, Streitthema oder konstruktiver Ansatz zur Lösung von Zukunftsproblemen*, Berlin und Bonn: Bundesinstitut für Berufsbildung, pp 62-75.

Pütz, H. (1999) 'Berufsbildung im Wandel – Die Bedeutung des Berufskonzepts', in BIBB (ed) *Berufsbildung in der Entwicklung. Ergebnisse, Veröffentlichungen und Materialien aus dem BIBB*, Bonn: BIBB, pp 25-37.

Raggatt, P (1988) 'Quality control in the dual system of West Germany', reprinted in D. Phillips (ed) (1995) *Education in Germany: Tradition and reform in historical context*, London and New York, NY: Routledge, pp 176-202.

Reuling, J. (1997) 'Qualitätssicherung in der deutschen Berufsbildung durch kombinierte Verwendung von Input- und Outputkriterien', in BMBF (Bundesministerium für Bildung, Wissenschaft, Forschung und Technologie) (ed) *Modularisierung der Berufsbildung – Gleichwertigkeit von allgemeiner und beruflicher Bildung. Deutsch-Britisches Seminar zur Berufsbildungspolitik 3.-5. Februar 1997 in Berlin*, Bonn: BMBF, pp 64-8.

Reuling, J. (1998) 'The German "Berufsprinzip" as a model for regulating training content and qualification standards', in W. Nijhof and J. Streumer, *Key qualifications in work and education*, Dordrecht: Kluwer Academic Publishers, pp 63-76.

Reuling, J. and Sauter, E. (1996) 'BIBB-Positionen zu aktuellen Herausforderungen in der beruflichen Bildung: V. Modularisierung in der beruflichen Bildung', *Berufsbildung in Wissenschaft und Praxis*, vol 25, no 3, pp 6f.

Richardson, W., Spours, K., Woolhouse, J. and Young, M. (1995) *Learning for the future: Current developments in modularity and credit*, Working Paper 5, London and Warwick: Institute of Education, Post-16 Education Centre, University of London and Centre for Education and Industry, University of Warwick.

Rosenau, R. (1997) 'Berufsausbildung in Schulen', *Berufsbildung*, vol 45, pp 9-11.

Rützel, J. (1997) 'Reform der beruflichen Bildung durch Modularisierung', *Berufsbildung*, vol 43, pp 5-9.

Schlaffke, W. and Weiss, R. (eds) (1996) *Das Duale System der Berufsausbildung. Leistung, Qualität und Reformbedarf*, Kölner Texte and Thesen, vol 27 Köln: Deutscher Instituts-Verlag.

Schmidt, H. (1996) 'Flexibilisierung der Berufsausbildung – Flexibilisierung als Organisationsprinzip?', *Berufsbildung in Wissenschaft und Praxis*, vol 25, no 4, pp 1f.

Schmidt, H. (1997) 'Module in der Berufsbildung – Teufelszeug oder Ausweg aus der Krise?', *Berufsbildung*, vol 43, p 42.

Schmidt, K., Sievering, O. and Wüstenbecker, M. (eds) (1997) *Das Duale System der Berufsausbildung – ein "Exportschlager" in der Krise?*, Arbeitspapiere des Fachbereichs Wirtschaftswissenschaften, vol 48, Paderborn: Universität-Gesamthochschule Paderborn.

Schumann, M. (1994) 'Rationalisierung und Übergang – Neue Befunde der Industriesoziologie zum Wandel der Produktionskonzepte und Arbeitsstrukturen', *WSI Mitteilungen*, vol 47, no 7, pp 405-14.

Sellin, B. (1995) 'Structural conditions for the education, training and employment of young Europeans', in CYRCE (Circle for Youth Research Cooperation in Europe) (ed) *The puzzle of integration, European Yearbook on youth policy and research*, vol 1/1995, pp 187-95.

Sengenberger, W. (1987) *Struktur und Funktionsweise von Arbeitsmärkten. Die Bundesrepublik im internationalen Vergleich*, Frankfurt a.M.: Campus.

Siemon, G. (1991) 'Die kaufmännische Berufsausbildung in der DDR', in M. Twardy (ed) *Duales System zwischen Tradition und Innovation* Köln: Botermann Verlag, pp 269-77.

Sloane, P. (1994) '"Innenansichten" zum Transformationsprozeß der Erziehungswissenschaft', in A. Kell (ed) *Erziehungswissenschaft im Aufbruch. Arbeitsberichte*, Weinheim: Deutscher Studien-Verlag, pp 197-221.

Sloane, P. (1997) 'Modularisierung in der beruflichen Ausbildung – oder: Die Suche nach dem Ganzen', in D. Euler and P. Sloane (eds) *Duales System im Umbruch. Eine Bestandsaufnahme der Modernisierungsdebatte*, Pfaffenweiler: Centaurus-Verl.-Ges, pp 223-45.

Sloane, P. (1999) *Situationen gestalten. Von der Planung des Lehrens zur Ermöglichung des Lernens*, Markt Schwaben: Eusl.

Sloane, P. (2000a) 'Lernfelder und Unterrichtsgestaltung', *Die berufsbildende Schule*, vol 52, no 3, pp 79-85.

Sloane, P. (ed) (2000b) *Fächer-. und Lernortübergreifender Unterricht (FäLoU). Beiträge im Kontext des DFG-Schwerpunktprogrammes, Lehr-Lern-Prozesse in der kaufmännischen Erstausbildung*, Lehren und Lernen in Schule und Betrieb, vol 2, Markt Schwaben: Eusl.

Sloane, P. (2001) 'Lernfelder als curriculare Vorgaben', in B. Bonz (ed) *Didaktik beruflicher Bildung*, Baltmannsweiler: Schneider-Verl, pp 187-203.

Sloane, P. and Hasenbank, T. (2001) 'Lehrermangel und Lehrer(aus)bildung im Blickpunkt: eine wirtschaftspädagogische Positionsbestimmung', in S. Norbert (ed) *Probleme der Lehrerbildung: Analysen, Positionen, Lösungsversuche*, Bad Heilbrunn: Klinkhardt, pp 213-51.

Smithers, A. (1997) 'A critique of NVQs and GNVQs', in S. Tomlinson (ed) *Education 14-19: Critical perspectives*, London: Athlone Press, pp 55-70.

Standing Conference of the Ministers of Education and Cultural Affairs of the Länder in the Federal Republic of Germany (1999) *The education system in the Federal Republic of Germany 1998: A description of responsibilities, structures and developments in education policy for the exchange of information in Europe*, Bonn: Standing Conference and Eurydice.

Tramm, T., Sembill, D., Klauser, F. and John, E. (eds) *Professionalisierung kaufmännischer Berufsbildung. Beiträge zur Öffnung der Wirtschaftspädagogik für die Anforderungen des 21. Jahrhunderts. Festschrift zum 60. Geburtstag von Frank Achtenhagen*, Frankfurt a.M.: Lang.

Wagner, P. (1991) 'Science of society lost: on the failure to establish sociology in Europe during the "Classical" period', in P. Wagner, B. Wittrock and R. Whitley, (eds) *Discourses on society: The shaping of the social science disciplines*, Dordrecht: Kluwer Academic Publishers, pp 219-45.

Walden, G. (1996) 'Gestaltung betrieblicher Lernorte und Zusammenarbeit mit der Berufsschule', in P. Dehnbostel, H. Holz and H. Novak (eds) *Neue Lernorte und Lernortkombinationen – Erfahrungen und Erkenntnisse aus dezentralen Berufsbildungskomzepten*, Berichte zur beruflichen Bildung, vol 195, Berlin: BIBB.

Waterkamp, D. (1987) *Handbuch zum Bildungswesen der DDR*, Berlin: Arno Spitz.

Waterkamp, D. (2002) 'Strengths and weaknesses of the apprenticeship system in central European states', paper given at the Comparative and International Education Society Annual Meeting in Orlando, Florida, March.

Watkins, P. (1987) *Modular approaches to the secondary curriculum*, SCDC Publications, York: Longman.

Wiegand, U. (1996) 'Reform des Ordnungsrahmens: Modulsysteme oder Flexibilisierung der Ausbildungsordnungen?', in W. Schlaffke and R. Weiss (eds) *Das Duale System der Berufsausbildung. Leistung, Qualität und Reformbedarf*, Kölner Texte und Thesen, vol 27, Köln: Deutscher Instituts-Verlag, pp 260-76.

Wilson, D. (1997) 'The German dual system of vocational education and training: a comparative study of influence upon educational policy in other countries', in C. Kodron, B. von Kopp, U. Lauterbach, U. Schäfer and G. Schmidt (eds) *Vergleichende Erziehungswissenschaft: Herausforderung, Vermittlung, Praxis. Festschrift für Wolfgang Mitter zum 70. Geburtstag*, Köln: Böhlau Verlag, pp 437-47.

Wüstenbecker, M. (1997) 'Mangel an Auszubildenden und Mangel an Ausbildungsplätzen – Anmerkungen zu Dualen System der Berufsausbildung', in K. Schmidt, O. Sievering and M. Wüstenbecker (eds) *Das Duale System der Berufsausbildung – ein 'Exportschlager' in der Krise?*, Arbeitspapiere des Fachbereichs Wirtschaftswissenschaften, vol 48, Paderborn: Universität-Gesamthochschule Paderborn, pp 3-24.

Young, M. (1995) 'Modularization and the outcomes approach: towards a strategy for a curriculum of the future', in J. Burke (ed) *Outcomes, learning and the curriculum. Implications for NVQ's, GNVQ's and other qualifications*, London: Falmer Press, pp 169-81.

Young, M. (1998) *The curriculum of the future: From the 'new sociology of education' to a critical theory of learning*, London: Falmer Press.

Young, M. (1999) *Knowledge, learning and the curriculum of the future: An inaugural lecture*, London: Institute of Education, University of London.

ZDH (Zentralverband des Deutschen Handwerks) (1993) 'Beurteilung einer Ausbildung in Modulen aus der Sicht des ZDH', in P. Sloane (ed) *Transnationale Ausbildung im Handwerk*, Köln: Carl, pp 127-30.

Zedler, R. (1996) *Some remarks on modular training in the Federal Republic of Germany*, Thessaloniki: CEDEFOP, pp 20f.

Zedler, R. (1997) 'Modularisierung: keine Perspektive für die Berufsausbildung', *Berufsbildung*, vol 43, p 42.

EIGHT

Learning in the workplace: reappraisals and reconceptions

Stephen Billett

Learning through work

There needs to be both a reappraisal and reconceptualisation of workplaces as learning environments as the learning of vocational practice in workplaces becomes increasingly legitimised through unfolding conceptions of learning, new pragmatics and a growing interest in learning throughout working lives. Further, the growing interest in workplaces and changing conceptions of learning highlights the urgent need for a workplace pedagogy – a science of understanding how vocational practices can be learnt through work and throughout working lives. Yet, workplaces as learning environments or spaces are burdened by discourses and practices engendered in educational institutions that present selective bases for conceptualising these spaces. Drawing on a programme of research conducted over the last decade, this chapter aims to conceptualise workplaces as legitimate learning spaces on their own terms. It proposes how the initial and ongoing development of vocational practice throughout working lives might best proceed. It proposes and discusses a set of salient and interrelated issues about how workplaces should be conceptualised as learning spaces. Informed by recent theory about learning, these discussions advance bases for:

- reconceptualising the discourse of learning through work;
- viewing workplace learning as participation in work practice; and
- the development of a workplace pedagogy that conceptualises learning through work as participatory practices, and the enhancement of workplace participatory practices.

Throughout, and in summary, implications for policy and practice are advanced.

Reconceptualising workplace learning discourses

There is nothing new about learning in workplaces. They have long been valued and acknowledged as important sites for learning vocational practice, and pre-date educational institutions as sites for learning vocational practice. However, some fresh thinking about workplace learning experiences is now warranted as workplaces become of interest as sites for learning to governments, enterprises, industry groups, educators and workers (Boud and Garrick, 1999). These groups' interest in workplaces is probably based on a common concern about their effectiveness as sites to develop individuals' vocational practice for pragmatic reasons associated with cost and accessibility of skill development. Yet, there are other and perhaps more strategic goals to be considered in appraising workplaces as learning environments. These include enhancing the adaptability of individuals' vocational skills to the changing requirements of work throughout their working life and for different applications of the vocational practice (that is, across workplaces), the development of criticality in vocational practice and to understand how these capacities can best be learnt robustly through authentic workplace experiences. These are clear and important pedagogic goals.

It is helpful, therefore, to consider workplaces' contributions to individuals' learning more broadly and strategically than just for pragmatic concerns about the cost and pertinence of what is learnt. Yet, to understand these contributions requires an appraisal that is unencumbered by assumptions, discourses and practices from other sites of learning, particularly those of educational institutions (Billett, 2002a). Understanding workplaces as learning spaces on their own terms is necessary for at least four reasons.

First, contemporary views about learning are placing an increased emphasis on individuals' learning (rather than teaching). Constructivist perspectives, for instance, position learners as active meaning makers, rather than as individuals being taught. Therefore, assumptions premised on strong associations between teaching and learning may not be helpful in understanding how learning proceeds, particularly in those environments where teaching does not occur.

Second, situational contributions to learning are also being accentuated in recent accounts of cognition and learning (such as Brown et al, 1989; Engeström and Middleton, 1996; Resnick et al, 1997). Rather than being neutral, the situations where individuals engage in goal-directed activities, and therefore learning, are held to contribute to how and what is learnt (Billett, 2001a). Therefore, workplace contributions to learning need to be identified and understood more fully and acknowledged on their own terms.

Third, as texts on curriculum practice have long acknowledged, educational institutions are contrived for the promotion of particular kinds of intentional learning. Consequently, their institutional practices and norms, and ultimately assumptions, reflect this contrivance. However, these practices and assumptions may be less useful in understanding learning in other kinds of social spaces, whose goals, norms and practices are different from those of educational institutions.

And fourth, relationships among individuals in workplaces (for example, between those having the knowledge to be learnt and those that wish to learn it), and goals for engagement in workplace activities are founded on different premises than those in educational institutions. Workers often do not see themselves as learners or as learning, and those supporting learning, directly or indirectly, will not see themselves as having primarily a pedagogic role. Learning arising from participation in the workplace is usually directed towards achieving goals associated with products and services, with learning outcomes being a secondary concern.

Consequently, for workplaces to be appraised and conceptualised as learning spaces, it is important to identify and acknowledge their particular qualities and characteristics. Assumptions about learning processes and outcomes from practices in educational institutions have previously shaped appraisals of workplaces as learning environments (for example, Marsick and Watkins, 1990; Evans, 1993; Ericsson and Lehmann, 1996). Given the lack of critical scrutiny of such assumptions, it is perhaps not surprising that workplaces have been, and continue to be, described as being 'informal' and 'unstructured' learning environments (for example, Cseh et al, 2000), often because the structuring of workplace learning experiences fails to reflect the practices of educational institutions. However, far from being without structure or formalisation, learning experiences in workplaces are structured and formalized by their norms and practices (for example, Scribner, 1984; Darrah, 1996) that are present in everyday work activities. Together, these practices serve to shape and distribute opportunities for individuals to engage in workplace activities and interactions through which learning occurs (Scribner, 1997/1988). Moreover, workplace activities are often intentionally directed towards sustaining the work practice through participant learning. Work practices are organised to structure the experiences required for learning to navigate (Hutchins, 1993), weave (Childs and Greenfield, 1980), work in a dairy (Scribner, 1984), become a midwife (Jordan, 1989), a coal miner or hairdresser (Billett, 2001a) and a tailor (Lave, 1990). This learning is often essential for the continuity of the practice that depends on the exercise of those skills. So the goals for and processes supporting learning in workplaces are not ad hoc; they are often directed towards producing, improving or transforming the goods and services the enterprise provides, or maintaining the interests and standing of individuals, or their affiliates within the workplace (Billett, 2002a). The structuring of these experiences is also shaped by deliberate constraints aimed to limit the scope and depth of individuals' learning in order to maintain the division of labour (Billett, 2001b), control of production (Danford, 1998) or service provisions (Hughes and Bernhardt, 1999) or the standing and relations of groups in the workplace (Bernhardt, 1999), or to simply exclude and marginalise some individuals in the workplace (Hull, 1997; Tam, 1997; Bierema, 2001). Therefore, rather than viewing workplaces as 'unstructured' or 'informal' learning environments, it is necessary to understand how the structuring and distribution of individuals' workplace experiences shapes their opportunities for learning.

In sum, persistence in the use of imprecise and negative labels, such as 'unstructured' and 'informal', and describing workplaces by what they are not, does little to assist the effective appraisal and conceptualisation of workplaces as learning spaces. Moreover, the persistence of this labelling makes urgent and necessary the task of identifying and legitimating the workplace's contributions to individuals' learning through work, and how best to enhance workplace learning experiences. To commence building foundations for understanding and improving learning in the workplace, the next section proposes learning in terms of participation in activities and interactions, and the workplace's contributions in terms of participatory practices.

Learning for continuity of the practice: participation and workplace participatory practices

Learning through workplace experience is proposed as being an outcome of participation in workplace activities and interactions. This participation is reciprocal. On the one hand, there is individuals' engagement in workplace activities and interactions, and, on the other hand, how the workplace's norms and practices afford individuals support for that learning – workplace participatory practices (Billett, 2002b).

Learning as participation

Individuals' engagement in workplace activities is not just an end in itself. It also incites cognitive change: learning within individuals (Rogoff, 1995) because there is little or no separation between doing (that is, thinking and acting) and learning. It follows that engagement in different kinds of workplace tasks or activities will result in different kinds of learning. For example, the novice chef chopping vegetables will learn and refine cutting techniques, and come to understand the time required to cook particular cuts of vegetables; and the apprentice electrician planning and installing a household circuit, may refine concepts of electrical flow and control. So different kinds of learning will potentially arise through individuals' engagement in different kinds of activities. Or as Rogoff and Lave (1984) proposed much earlier, activity structures cognition. Moreover, the degree by which work activities are novel to individuals will determine whether reinforcement, refinement or an extension of their knowledge results from their participation. Therefore, the kinds of activities that individuals engage in, and their degree of novelty, shapes what they learn.

However, individuals also mediate how they participate in work and engage with the activities and interactions that the workplace affords them (see Rogoff, 1995). The effort expended by individuals in their engagement is likely to underpin the quality of their learning. The kinds of impasses they seek to overcome and how they engage with what is afforded by the workplace will influence whether rich or superficial learning arises through their engagement in work tasks. The outcome of the former has been described as appropriation (Leontyev, 1981) – learning that is consistent with individuals' beliefs and is taken as 'their own' – and the latter, mastery (Wertsch, 1998) – the learning of behaviours to respond superficially to social demands (for example, witness the unconvincing salutation of service workers). Richer and more demanding forms of learning are usually held to arise from effortful engagement in goal-directed activities. So the degree of congruence or relatedness (Valsiner, 1994) between individuals' interests, and the workplace's norms and values, likely determines the effort they direct to learning through work. All these factors influence how individuals participate in, and what they learn through, engagement in work. For these reasons, learning through work can be understood in terms of individuals' participation in work activities.

Workplace participatory practices

Workplace participatory practices, or how activities and interactions are provided and distributed, are also essential in understanding the pedagogical potential of workplaces (Billett, 2002b). Just as learners' experiences in educational institutions are structured by these institutions' goals, activities and norms, opportunities for learning through work are shaped by the workplace's goals, activities and norms. The structuring of workplace experiences has particular intents and purposes, principally directed to ensuring the continuity of the practice. They also serve to distribute opportunities to access guidance and activities in ways that reflect personal (for example, experts' fear of displacement by those who they assist to learn) or group interests (for example, particular affiliations of personal or occupational interests) (such as, Bernhardt, 1999; Hughes and Bernhardt, 1999). Participation in workplace activities often progresses through engagement in work tasks that are incrementally more accountable, demanding or central to the workplace's goals (for example, Lave, 1990). That is, individuals are invited to proceed from engagement in tasks of relatively low accountability, where mistakes or imprecision can be tolerated, to those tasks where mistakes have significant and perhaps irredeemable consequences. This progression offers the basis for the participatory pathway that Lave (1990) termed the 'learning curriculum' from her analysis of Angolan tailoring apprenticeships.

Different instances of workplace learning curricula have been identified, and associated with the particular requirements for practice. Hairdressing apprentices' progression is determined by the particular salon's practices (Billett, 2001a). In one salon, where clients are serviced by a number of hairdressers, apprentices first learn to keep the salon clean and tidy, and communicate with clients by asking whether and how they want tea or coffee. Through their participation in these activities, apprentices learn about hygiene, cleanliness and how to engage with clients and determine their needs. More than just completing work tasks of low accountability, this participation provides necessary understanding about, and initial participation in, hairdressing activities. The apprentices next engage in and learn to wash clients' hair, and later rinsing out the chemicals used to shape and colour hair. These activities develop new skills through building upon what they already know, such as communicating more intimately and extensively with clients. Later, the apprentices place rods and curlers in clients' hair, working alongside experienced hairdressers, prior to engaging independently in these tasks. Before being permitted to cut women's hair, they commence by cutting men's hair, because it is held to be less difficult and of lower accountability. This pathway of guided engagements in activities continues until the apprentices can style hair independently.

In another salon, where hairdressers conduct the entire hairdressing task, a different pathway exists. The apprentices here need to learn to cut and colour far earlier. Therefore, the structuring of the learning curriculum in this salon includes the early mastery of a set of procedures that permit independent practice. For instance, in the first salon, only the owner-manager ordered and managed the stock, claiming the business would fail if others were allowed access to stock. However, in the second salon, the apprentice has responsibility for this task. Hence, the particular workplace's norms shape the participatory practices, or the kinds of tasks to be undertaken, discretion afforded, and standards of work expected. The apprentices' participation and learning is, in different ways, directed towards the continuity of two distinct practices within the same vocation. Participatory pathways have also been identified in a computer-manufacturing firm (Darrah, 1996), in commercial aviation where a pathway exists from flight engineer, to first officer through to captain (Hutchins and Palen, 1997) and in a food processing plant where workers readily identified the learning curriculum in their areas of work (Billett and Boud, 2001).

However, participation in, and progression along, workplace learning pathways may be contested. Individuals' participation is subject to workplace norms, and cultural and political values that shape how individuals are permitted to engage and learn (Fenwick, 2001). This contestation occurs between 'newcomers' and 'old-timers' (Lave and Wenger, 1991), full- and part-time workers (Hughes and Bernhardt, 1999), among teams with different roles and standing in the workplace (Darrah, 1996), between individuals' personal and vocational goals (Darrah, 1997) and within institutionalised arrangements, such as those representing workers, supervisors or management (Danford, 1998). Beyond, or even instead of, perceptions of personal competence, workplace affiliations (Billett, 2001b), individuals' gender and race (Bierema, 2001), their language (Hull, 1997) and employment status (Darrah, 1996) are all bases that can determine what opportunities they are afforded. Limitations on participation are also associated with practical constraints. A workplace may not be able to develop fully the skills of all individuals, particularly in prized and highly remunerated work, as this would be unsustainable. The workplace may simply lack the capacity to provide the level of practice, or opportunities for the extensive practice required to develop skills. Surveys indicate that there remains an underutilisation of existing skills in workplaces (Livingstone, 2001), which regardless of being deliberate or not, likely leads to worker frustration and their sense of unfulfilled potential. Here resides a key tension in workplaces as learning spaces: the potential for dissonance between the need for sustainable requirements of the workplace, and the individual's desire to realise their aspirations. However, the distribution of workplace opportunities to realise these aspirations is often found to be inequitable. Women, for example, often find workplaces uninviting and resistant of their development (for example, Probert, 1999; Bierema, 2001). A survey of international literature (Smith and Billett, 2003) indicated that those most likely to access intentional workplace support were more likely to be better educated, younger and male, than those denied it. In these ways, workplace participatory practices serve to structure and distribute opportunities for learning and advancement through work, in ways that reflect cultural practices and subjectivities. They are not ad hoc or without intent but, instead, reflect the privileging and structuring of workplace learning experiences by social practices that are both situated and manifested by broader cultural subjectivities.

From these perspectives, a reappraisal of views about workplace learning, curriculum practices and pedagogic bases is clearly warranted. In sum, it is proposed that a consideration of learning as participation, as well as workplace opportunities as participatory practices provides bases to understand the reciprocal process of learning through work. These concepts are held to form the foundations of workplace pedagogy, as they underpin both the processes of learning through work, and the provision of guided learning in workplaces. In the next section of this chapter, these foundations are built upon through a consideration of the goals for workplace learning arrangements and an elaboration of processes that sustain learning through work.

Workplace pedagogy

Beyond the conceptual premises advanced earlier, workplace pedagogy is also now warranted to address a range of important practical or pragmatic concerns. First, for many workers and classes of workers, the workplace provides the only, or most likely, location to develop vocational knowledge because for these individuals courses are unavailable, inappropriate or inaccessible (see Livingstone, 2001). Consequently, the experiences and support workplaces afford these workers often constitute the primary or sole source of their initial and ongoing vocational development. Second, the value of workplaces' contributions to learning vocational practice is acknowledged in the apprenticeship of tradespersons, the internship of doctors and lawyers' experiences as articled clerks. Yet, even in these long-standing arrangements, little attention is given to the intentional structuring of workplace experiences to enhance their potential or to integrate them with those in educational institutions. Third, workplaces are often seen as places where students apply and refine what they have learnt through their participation in educational institutions. Workplace experiences are increasingly valued by educators in promoting students' understanding of the 'world of work', developing specific vocational skills or merely to 'contextualise' what has been learnt in educational institutions. However, again, these experiences are rarely promoted as making legitimate contributions to the learning of vocational skills in their own right. Finally, and perhaps most importantly, workplaces are likely the key learning space for the majority of adults throughout their working lives (OECD, 1998). As provisions of continuing education contract in many countries (for example, Arnaud, 1999), and with enhanced expectations for individuals to maintain the currency of their vocational practice throughout a working life (Forrester et al, 1995), understanding how individuals can best learn through and throughout their working lives has become urgent. Consequently, an empirically and conceptually based pedagogy for the workplace is now warranted. This pedagogy needs to be guided by goals that focus on assisting individuals to develop robust vocational practices and processes aimed to support learning in workplace settings.

Workplace pedagogic goals

There are both situationally specific and strategic goals for workplace pedagogy. There is the development of the capacity to be effective in a particular work practice and the ability for individuals to adapt their vocational practice to changing workplace requirements and to other situations. Although reflecting a culturally derived vocational practice, the goals for learning are likely structured by particular workplace's needs. This was illustrated in the distinct requirements of the two hairdressing salons referred to earlier in this chapter. In one way, these situational goals are appropriate, as the performance requirements for vocational skills can be highly situational (Engeström and Middleton, 1996; Suchman, 1996). What is taken as expertise in one workplace may be deemed as inappropriate or indulgent in another (Billett, 2001c). Unfortunately, the educational intents (such as goals and objectives) of vocational education programmes often ignore the situatedness of vocational performance. National competency standards or key competencies are commonly used to guide vocational education in many western countries. However, such measures may fail to provide the adaptability they seek to secure (see Billett, 2003) – and are even less helpful in addressing – workplaces' particular goals and requirements. Therefore, conceptions of what constitutes vocational practice are unlikely to be represented through national standards and uniform statements of competence. Instead, goals that reflect the diversity of practice are required if adaptability in practice is to be understood and secured.

However, there are legitimate concerns that what is learnt through experiences in workplaces may be reductive and limiting, and constrained to those circumstances (Marsick and Watkins, 1990; Evans, 1993; Ericsson and Lehmann, 1996). Specifically, the learning of particular workplace's practices and goals may result in outcomes not readily adaptable to other workplaces or work tasks. This learning may be so specific as to inhibit the capacity to respond to emerging workplace requirements. These concerns underpin the need for workplace pedagogy to develop individuals' vocational skills in ways that are robust enough to respond to changes in practice and be adaptable to some other instances of practice. However, this is no easy goal and unlikely to be achieved without intention in the organisation of activities and support within workplaces (Boud and Garrick, 1999).

As elaborated later in this chapter, learning through work can result in the development of bad habits, dangerous short cuts and a lack of understanding through workplace experiences. In addition, learning outcomes that have a wider application such as social justice, aesthetics and the environment may be de-emphasised in workplace practices and interactions (Butler, 1999; Solomon, 1999; Bierema, 2001; Fenwick, 2001). This is not to suggest that workplace experiences cannot develop critical views. However, this learning may be limited to only a consideration of issues associated with the particular workplace. For instance, workers are often only too aware of inequalities and injustices in their particular workplace (for example, Danford, 1998). However, opportunities may be lacking to consider and conceptualise this inequality and injustice more broadly, such as how their own actions might be perpetuating inequalities elsewhere (for example, Somerville and Bernoth, 2001). Key limitations of workplace learning experience include inappropriate learning (dangerous, shoddy, inflexible practices), which is available and reinforced in the workplace, and the situational specificity of what is learnt. If these limitations are to be addressed, workplace interventions, such as guided learning (see later in this chapter), will likely be warranted and include opportunities to reflect upon and extend vocational practice. Therefore, interventions that draw on the contribution of the workplace and are enacted as part of everyday activities may be essential to the development of robust vocational practice. These interventions take time, and require support, sponsorship and deliberate organisation. In the following sections of this chapter, some bases for organising learning through work to respond to these concerns are advanced.

Bases of workplace pedagogic practices

Building upon the conceptions of learning as participation and workplace contributions as participatory practices, four interrelated premises are advanced for workplace pedagogy:

- the activities individuals engage in;
- the guidance and support they can access in the workplace;
- how these 'affordances' (activities and interactions) are distributed to individuals and cohorts of workers; and
- how individuals interpret, interact and engage with what the workplace affords them.

These are now briefly elaborated in turn.

Learning through everyday work activities

Participation in everyday work activities has been shown to develop many of the capacities required for effective work practice. Key contributors to this learning include:

- engagement in everyday work tasks;
- the direct or close guidance of co-workers; and
- the indirect guidance provided by the workplace itself and others in the workplace (Billett, 2001a).

As noted, there is little or no distinction between engagement in goal-directed activities, such as workplace tasks, and learning. Participation in work activities variously refines or extends what individuals already know. Whereas familiar tasks assist in refining and reinforcing the knowledge that is learnt, those activities that are novel to individuals can extend their knowledge, as long as they are not too demanding, thereby causing confusion or dissonance.

Direct guidance by more experienced workers is accessible in workplaces, as are more indirect kinds of guidance provided through observing and listening to others, and the contributions provided by the physical context which furnishes artefacts and tools. These indirect forms of guidance can serve as prompts, clues, goals and models for activities, and constitute integrated bases for task completion (Brown et al, 1989). Together, these direct and indirect forms of guidance contribute to making accessible many of the goals for effective workplace performance, and the procedures required to secure that performance. In these ways, participation in everyday work secures access to learning experiences that are authentic in terms of the practice to which the learning is to be applied (Harris et al, 1996; Hamilton and Hamilton, 1997; Billett, 2000). It also supports learning through the provision of opportunities to engage and practice in ways that are simply unavailable elsewhere. Moreover, the requirements for workplace tasks can be made accessible through workplace participation, and pathways of participation often exist that are structured by a concern for participant learning to sustain the work practice.

However, as foreshadowed, learning through work also has limitations and constraints that need to be identified, understood and, where possible, addressed. These limitations include weaknesses in the process of learning, the content of what is learnt and the kinds of learning that might arise through everyday work activities. Concerns about the learning process refer to the:

- contested nature of work practice inhibiting individuals' access to activities and guidance required for rich learning;
- difficulties in learning knowledge not readily accessible in the workplace (for example, conceptual and symbolic knowledge);
- difficulties with accessing appropriate expertise and experiences required to support the development of vocational skills; and

- the reluctance of workers to participate in learning vocational practice through their workplace experiences (Billett, 2001a).

There are also concerns about the situational specificity of what is learnt, as well as the potentially too pragmatic focus of what is learnt, that is, its exclusion of broader social concerns and development of criticality.

In consideration of these concerns, the following sections discuss workplace interventions that aim to address some of these limitations identified above, and also the broader goal of developing adaptable and critical vocational skills.

Intentional guided learning at work

Intentional guided learning arrangements can be deployed to develop aspects of vocational practice that would not otherwise be learnt through everyday work activities. The selective use of intentional guided learning strategies by more experienced co-workers has demonstrated some capacity to make accessible concepts that would be otherwise difficult to access and understand, and to develop procedures that would unlikely be learnt alone (Billett, 2000, 2001a). These strategies aim to develop both specific and strategic procedures (for example, through the use of modelling, coaching and questioning), and make accessible and develop workplace concepts through direct interaction and shared engagement in goal-directed activities between more and less experienced co-workers (for example, through the use of questioning, diagrams, analogies, explanations). The guidance provided by a more experienced co-worker includes engaging in joint problem solving with learners. This comprises the more experienced partner undertaking those parts of the task, that are beyond the existing scope of learners' skills, as well as modelling and elaborating the performance requirements of tasks that are beyond the learners' existing capacity to approximate unaided. In this way, the cognitive load (Sweller, 1989) or demand required to learn new tasks is shared between the learner and the more experienced co-worker. As learners become more competent in making decisions about, and completing larger parts of, the task, the more expert co-worker reduces the level of support.

This process of collaborative learning comprising cycles of modelling, coaching, scaffolding and fading, has become popularly referred to as cognitive apprenticeships (Collins et al, 1989). Significantly, this model of collaborative learning has its origins in the development of apprentices' skills in workplace settings. So, for many in the workplace, these processes of guided learning are familiar and reflect how they learnt their vocational practice. Therefore, through guided participation (Rogoff, 1995) in workplaces, more experienced co-workers can play an important role in guiding the appropriation of proven practices and avoiding some of the kinds of situationally specific and inappropriate learning identified earlier. Furthermore, the use of guided learning strategies (such as questioning dialogues to extend what has been learnt, and group discussion) has demonstrated some potential to extend knowledge (Billett and Boud, 2001).

The provision of intentional guidance in the workplace goes beyond direct pedagogic intervention. It also includes the management, sequencing and monitoring of learners' progression through tasks of increasing complexity and accountability. The role for more experienced co-workers includes making judgments and monitoring learners' readiness to progress, the securing of adequate modelling, practice and providing feedback on progression (Billett, 2000, 2001a). This guidance could extend to providing access to diverse instances of practices and workplace experiences in order to develop adaptable practice. For instance, the rotation of apprentice cooks through different kinds of hotel and restaurant kitchens and cooking tasks, can establish bases for adaptable skills through experiencing different kinds of application of professional cookery. Similarly, the structuring of trainee nurses' experiences through different kinds of hospital wards that have distinct functions also provides access to a diverse range of the application of nursing skills that may engender a robust nursing practice. With some guidance, nurses will likely learn the canonical aspects of patient care that transcend each ward's particular specialisation as well as learning something about that specialisation (that is, maternity, oncology, emergency and trauma). Rather than relying on a purely cognitive basis for adaptable practice, the experience of engaging in variations of the vocational practice develops bases for adaptability, as the novices come to know some variations of what constitutes the vocation. Whether intentional or not, these experiences may extend learners' vocational understanding and procedures. To maximise their benefits, however, there has to be intention and interest within the workplace to organise and support these kinds of interventions.

Whether referring to learning arising through everyday work activities or intentional guided workplace learning, the provision and quality of learning experiences is premised on the kinds of activities and guidance that individuals can access. The relatedness between individuals' interests and workplaces' activities, norms, practices and goals they can access, also shape the kind of learning that arises through workplace participation. These bases are proposed as key pedagogic foundations upon which learning through work can be best understood, and attempts to enhance that learning can be directed. Implications arising from these bases include some reconceptualisation of learning and curriculum. Whereas learning is seen as participation in the social practice of work, the curriculum for workplaces can be viewed as participatory practices at work, in particular work activities, and guided and intentional progression along a pathway of work activities premised on the learner's readiness. These kinds of intentional learning activities are also about enhancing the learner's engagement of the vocational practice. Interestingly, the emphasis of participation along a pathway of experiences is analogous to the original meaning of curriculum – a curée ('a track to follow'). So, although not wholly alien to practices in educational institutions, the provision of learning experiences and intentional efforts to improve learning through work need to be organised in ways that are aligned to particular workplace settings. In sum, four bases for workplace pedagogy have been identified here:

1. Access to workplace activities that provide a progression to tasks of increasing complexity and the monitoring of that progress by more experienced co-workers.
2. Indirect guidance that can be accessed as part of everyday work activities and interventions enacted and guided by more experienced co-workers to assist learning, particularly that learning which will not be secured through discovery alone.
3. How workplaces afford opportunities to participate in work activities and access guidance.
4. How individuals elect to engage with the work practice.

Given their interest, government and industry groups might take a leadership role in illuminating the diversity of vocational practice by establishing and acknowledging broader bases to account for the breadth of vocational activities, rather than its presentation as a unitary practice. Accreditation practices could be reframed to take account of the means by which quality learning can be realised in workplaces and promoted to industry groups and enterprises. Industry groups might seek to capture and represent the diversity of the vocational practice in their sector and develop goals for vocational development programmes that reflect the complexity and breadth of these practices. They may then propose means by which something of the diversity of these practices might be learnt in workplaces. Enterprises, for their part, might seek to identify the goals that reflect their current and emerging needs, and enact workplace participatory practice to best develop these capacities in their workplaces.

The next section of this chapter elaborates this final point through discussing the prospects for enhancing participation and learning through work. The key underpinning propositions refer to the need to enhance individuals' participation, and workplace participatory practices.

Enhancing the workplace 'affordances' and engagement

Given the importance of the reciprocal process of learning in workplaces as participatory, efforts to enhance workplace participation are likely to be worthwhile goals. Over time, workers in a large manufacturing workplace (Billett and Boud, 2001) identified workplace factors that were construed as being highly invitational: encouraging participation and learning. They included:

- access to other workers;
- time to practice and learn;
- inclusion in knowledge sharing;
- discussion groups;
- access to knowledge;

- implementation of training programmes;
- encouragement;
- attitude and skills of co-workers; and
- opportunities to practice.

These factors are similar to work practices identified by Rowden (1995, 1997) in American small- to medium-sized enterprises that have endured over time and remained viable. These work practices included the:

- maintenance and development of the skills and attitudes of the workforce;
- integration of employees into the enterprises' work practice; and
- enhancement of the quality of working life.

The kinds of practices identified in the studies have been proposed by human resource development advocates who, among other things, have argued that, to respond to increasing marketplace competition, enterprises and workers have never needed each other more (Howard, 1995). In other words, workers need to find their workplaces invitational rather than confrontational. To achieve this goal, others (such as Carnevale, 1995) have called for the promotion of positive workplace relationships through the dismantling of hierarchical work management, and their replacement with practice that promotes autonomy, ongoing skilling and the adoption of flexible working practices.

However, this advice has not generally been heeded. There is little evidence that even high-performing enterprises are widely adopting these kinds of practices (Berryman, 1993). Management's desire for control or perceived lack of needs for such arrangements may inhibit enterprises adopting these kinds of practices. Danford (1998) has noted that despite evidence of enhanced levels of productivity, increased worker discretion was curtailed when management feared loosing control of production. There may be limits on opportunities that can be made available to staff, as has been foreshadowed. Learning to perform competently often requires extended practice. It may simply not be feasible for every worker to develop the kinds of skills they want, when they want. Accordingly, the level of skill development required may be lower or slower than workers desire, leading to frustration and reduction in participation (Billett, 2002a).

Nevertheless, engaging workers in ways that address their personal goals may have outcomes that go beyond just securing their energies and talents for the enterprise's purposes. For many, the exercise of their paid vocation has purposes that go beyond just securing remuneration. It also embodies the fulfilment of important personal goals (Noon and Blyton, 1997; Pusey, 2003) and subjectivities (Somerville and Bernoth, 2001). The workers referred to earlier (Billett and Boud, 2001) also identified what influenced how they elected to participate fully in the workplace. They claimed that these included:

1. satisfaction with performance;
2. improving performance;
3. self-interest;
4. self-motivation; and
5. advancement.

While remuneration may motivate, these workers also identified other factors associated with individuals' identities and standing that shapes their engagement in and learning through work. For instance, in two work areas in the manufacturing plant, workers were motivated to be seen as an effective team member and to be doing their work effectively. They proposed, and it was observed, that their engagement and interest was associated with their vocational practice and the sense of pride that they took in that practice. Depending on the kind and status of this work, such sentiments may be dismissed by some commentators as individuals directing their own exploitation or as the legitimate exercise of agency in enacting a vocational practice. Workers who performed tasks that many would view as being low level and relatively unskilled (for example, food packaging, consumer advice) demonstrably engaged effortfully, took their work seriously and reported enjoying satisfaction with its execution (such as the achievement of the days quota, and satisfied customers) (Billet and Boud, 2001). However, it is important to accept that individuals will find meaning in their work that may not be ranked by others as being highly paid or high status. That is, it is what the work means to individuals and their sense of self and identity that is important. As Pusey (2003, p 2) suggests:

> For nearly everyone work is a social protein, a buttress for identity and not a tradeable commodity.

Therefore, a more relative approach to a consideration of the bases by which engagement in, and learning through, work might proceed. Such a view is consistent with what Dewey (1916) argued about individuals' vocations, that it is their course in life and direction that needs to be valued in its own terms rather than in terms of societal status and level of remuneration.

So there is an important dimension of personal and vocational fulfilment in considering engagement in and learning through work. The exercise of one's vocation has long been acknowledged as an important component of meaningful human endeavour (for example, Meade, 1913; Dewey, 1916). What constitutes a worthwhile vocation may be highly individual and subjective, and have particular pertinence and resonance for the individual. The significance here is that individual identities and subjectivities are salient in driving the direction of effort and activities, their agency (for example, Somerville and Bernoth, 2001), and its constitution in diverse ways. Mutual benefits might arise from a concurrence between the kinds of practices occurring in the workplace and individuals' vocations. Enhancing workplace participatory practices and learning may engage individuals in ways that permit them to participate in and appropriate the kinds of knowledge that they wish to learn, because this knowledge is central to their interest to exercise their vocation and sustain their subjectivity. Therefore, beyond pragmatic enterprise goals, important personal outcomes may arise from enhancing participatory practices such as finding ways to be more inclusive in knowledge sharing and discussions with other workers.

Summary: implications for policy and practice

Implications for policy and practice arising from this reappraisal of learning through work have been identified throughout this chapter. A key implication is that promoting learning throughout working life is a responsibility to be shared by government, industry, enterprises, teachers and individuals as learners. Given the salience of the contribution of workplace factors in learning throughout working life, it is not possible, useful or reasonable to expect individuals to be wholly responsible for maintaining the currency of their skills, which seems to be the intent of government policy on lifelong learning (for example, OECD, 1998). Should governments wish to promote and secure positive outcomes from learning throughout working lives, they need to reappraise and reconceptualise learning through work, as much for its pedagogic possibilities as its pragmatic purposes. If employers and employees are to engage effectively in workplace learning arrangements this will include attempts to promote workplace certainty and its invitational qualities. Industry groups, employers and unions need to make a virtue out of the diversity of the practices that constitute the vocations they represent, champion the richness in the breadth of the vocational practice and acknowledge the workplace as a learning space. This requires moving from narrow and unitary competence standards to acknowledge the breadth and richness of the vocational practice. If enterprises want to secure the benefits of their employees' accumulation of working knowledge, including the capacity to respond to novel tasks, then they need to make the workplace invitational and supportive of this kind of learning.

In sum, the implications for policy and practice of the groups interested in promoting learning through work, which have been identified throughout this chapter, are as follows.

Governmental goals and actions should:

- foster a broadened view of learning through work, vocational education, pedagogies for the workplace and assessment and certification practices that reflect diversity;
- foster alternative models of intentional learning such as guided learning in the workplace;
- foster positive relations in workplaces – seek to establish reciprocal relations in the workplace;
- locate an appropriate balance between government agency and voluntary participation;

- develop workplaces' capacities to support learning throughout working life in workplaces;
- establish means for accreditation and certification arrangements that can address the learning undertaken wholly in the workplace.

Goals and practices to be promoted by industry bodies should:

- identify and illustrate the richness and diversity of the vocational practice;
- identify canonical knowledge of the vocation and some of the diversity of practice;
- map the changing requirements of the vocation;
- acknowledge the level of intention and intervention required to develop robust skills in the workplace;
- identify and promote how workplace learning practices might best occur in that industry.

Enterprises that require workers to respond to the changing requirements of the workplace should:

- enhance opportunities to participate in work practice;
- enact a workplace curriculum (sequencing and monitoring of experiences);
- enact and support guided participation for the ongoing development of vocational capacities; and
- engender relations in the workplace that encourage participation.

Vocational educators and others who develop and implement intentional learning arrangements to promote learning in the workplace should consider:

- enacting a workplace, rather than a classroom, pedagogy;
- enacting an approach to learning that draws upon what the workplace affords learners and select strategies to augment and overcome the limitations of these contributions; and
- adopting approaches that seek to extend what is learnt in workplaces to emerging requirements and to other situations.

Conclusion

Participation in work provides opportunities for learning and developing further vocational capacities throughout working life. However, there are barriers and limitations to individuals participating in ways that allow them to develop fully that potential. Consequently, to best realise workplaces' potential as learning spaces requires a reappraisal and broadening of the conceptualisation of what constitutes learning, and enacting the kinds of pedagogic practices that may be utilised to enhance the quality and distribution of workplace affordances. This includes attempts to make workplaces less contested and more affording of individuals' learning. Ultimately, the majority of learning throughout working life will occur in workplaces. It remains for these kinds of practices to be broadly adopted and supported in an attempt to best enhance the quality of learning experiences in workplaces. This would maximise their contributions for the benefits of both individuals and the enterprises where they are employed.

References

Arnaud, N. (1999) 'Obligation of education in the face of globalisation', in M. Singh (ed) *Adult learning and the future of work*, Hamburg: UNESCO Institute for Education.

Bernhardt, A. (1999) *The future of low-wage jobs: Case studies in the retail industry*, New York, NY: Institute on Education and the Economy.

Berryman, S. (1993) 'Learning for the workplace', *Review of Research in Education*, vol 19, pp 343-401.

Bierema, L. (2001) 'Women, work, and learning', in T. Fenwick (ed) *Sociocultural perspectives on learning through work*, (New Directions in Adult and Continuing Education, vol 92), San Francisco, CA: Jossey Bass/Wiley, pp 53-62.

Billett, S. (2000) 'Guided learning at work', *Journal of Workplace Learning*, vol 12, no 7, pp 272-85.

Billett, S. (2001a) *Learning in the workplace: Strategies for effective practice*, Sydney: Allen and Unwin.

Billett, S. (2001b) 'Co-participation at work: affordance and engagement', in T. Fenwick (ed) *Sociocultural perspectives on learning through work*, (New Directions in Adult and Continuing Education, vol 92), San Francisco, CA: Jossey Bass/Wiley, pp 63-72.

Billett, S. (2001c) 'Knowing in practice: re-conceptualising vocational expertise', *Learning and Instruction*, vol 11, no 6, pp 431-52.

Billett, S. (2002a) 'Critiquing workplace learning discourses: participation and continuity at work', *Studies in the Education of Adults*, vol 34, no 1, pp 56-67.

Billett, S. (2002b) 'Workplace pedagogic practices: co-participation and learning', *British Journal of Educational Studies*, vol 50, no 4, pp 457-81.

Billett, S. (2003) 'Vocational curriculum and pedagogy: an activity theory perspective', *European Journal of Educational Research*, vol 2, no 1, pp 6-21.

Billett, S. and Boud, D. (2001) 'Participation in and guided engagement at work: workplace pedagogic practices', Paper presented at 'Researching Work and Learning. Second International Conference', Calgary, Alberta, 26-28 July.

Billett, S., McKavanagh, C., Beven, F., Angus, L., Seddon, T., Gough, J., Hayes, S. and Robertson, I. (1999) *The CBT decade: Teaching for flexibility and adaptability*, Adelaide: National Centre for Vocational Education Research.

Boud, D. and Garrick, J. (eds) (1999) *Understanding learning at work*, London: Routledge.

Brown, J., Collins, A. and Duguid P. (1989) 'Situated cognition and the culture of learning', *Educational Researcher*, vol 18, no 1, pp 32-4.

Butler, E. (1999) 'Technologising equity: the politics and practices of work-related learning', in D. Boud and J. Garrick (eds) *Understanding learning at work*, London: Routledge, pp 132-50.

Carnevale, A. (1995) 'Enhancing skills in the new economy', in A. Howard (ed) *The changing nature of work*, San Francisco, CA: Jossey-Bass Publishers.

Childs, C. and Greenfield, P. (1980) 'Informal modes of learning and teaching: the case of Zinacanteco weaving', in N. Warren (ed) *Advances in cross-cultural psychology: Vol 2*, London: Academic Press, pp 269-316.

Collins, A., Brown J. and Newman, S. (1989) 'Cognitive apprenticeship: teaching the crafts of reading, writing and mathematics', in L. Resnick (ed) *Knowledge, learning and instruction: Essays in honour of Robert Glaser*, Hillsdale, NJ: Erlbaum and Associates, pp 453-94.

Cseh, M., Watkins, K. and Marsick, V. (2000) 'Informal and incidental learning in the workplace', in G. Straka (ed) *Conceptions of self-directed learning*, Munster: LOS, pp 59-74.

Danford, A. (1998) 'Teamworking and labour regulation in the autocomponents industry', *Work, Employment and Society*, vol 12, no 3, pp 409-31.

Darrah, C. (1996) *Learning and work: An exploration in industrial ethnography*, New York, NY: Garland Publishing.

Darrah, C. (1997) 'Complicating the concept of skill requirements: scenes from a workplace', in G. Hull (ed) *Changing work, changing workers: Critical perspectives on language, literacy and skills*, New York, NY: CUNY Press.

Dewey, J. (1916) *Democracy and education*, New York, NY: The Free Press-Macmillan.

Engeström, Y. and Middleton, D. (1996) 'Introduction: studying work as mindful practice', in Y. Engestrom and D. Middleton (eds) *Cognition and communication at work*, Cambridge: Cambridge University Press, pp 1-15.

Ericsson, K. and Lehmann, A. (1996) 'Expert and exceptional performance: evidence of maximal adaptation to task constraints', *Annual Review of Psychology*, vol 47, pp 273-305.

Evans, G. (1993) 'Institutions: formal or informal learning?', Keynote address presented at 'After Competence: the future of post-compulsory education and training Conference', Brisbane, 1-3 December.

Fenwick, T. (2001) 'Tides of change: new times and questions in workplace learning', in T. Fenwick (ed) *Sociocultural perspectives on learning through work*, (New Directions in Adult and Continuing Education, vol 92), San Francisco, CA: Jossey Bass/Wiley, pp 3-18.

Forrester, K., Payne, J. and Ward, K. (1995) 'Lifelong education and the workplace: a critical analysis', *International Journal of Lifelong Education*, vol 14, pp 292-305.

Hamilton, M. and Hamilton, S. (1997) 'When is work a learning experience?', *Phi Delta Kappan*, vol 78, no 9, pp 682-9.

Harris, R., Simons, M., Willis, P. and Underwood, F. (1996) 'Pandora's Box or Aladdin's Cave: what can on and off-job sites contribute to trainees' learning?', in *Learning and work: The challenges*, Proceedings of the 4th Annual International Conference on Post-Compulsory Education and Training, Volume Two, pp 7-19.

Howard, A. (ed) (1995) *The changing nature of work*, San Francisco, CA: Jossey-Bass Publishers.

Hughes, K. and Bernhardt, A. (1999) *Market segmentation and the restructuring of banking jobs*, IEE Brief 24, New York, NY: Institute on Education and the Economy.

Hull, G. (1997) 'Preface' and 'Introduction', in G. Hull (ed) *Changing work, changing workers: Critical perspectives on language, literacy and skills*, New York, NY: State University of New York Press.

Hutchins, E. (1993) 'Learning to navigate', in S. Chaiklin and J. Lave (eds) *Understanding practice: Perspectives on activity and context*, Cambridge: Cambridge University Press.

Hutchins, E. and Palen, L. (1997) 'Constructing meaning from spaces, gesture, and speech', in L. Resnick, Pontecorvo, C. and R. Saljo (eds) *Discourse, tools and reasoning: Essays on situated cognition*, Berlin: Springer, pp 23-40.

Jordan, B. (1989) 'Cosmopolitan obstetrics: some insights from the training of traditional midwives', *Social Science and Medicine*, vol 289, pp 925-44.

Lave, J. (1990) 'The culture of acquisition and the practice of understanding', in J. Stigler, R. Shweder and G. Herdt (eds) *Cultural psychology*, Cambridge: Cambridge University Press, pp 259-86.

Lave, J. and Wenger, E. (1991) *Situated learning – Legitimate peripheral participation*, Cambridge: Cambridge University Press.

Leontyev, A. (1981) *Problems of the developments of mind*, Moscow: Progress.

Livingstone, D. (2001) 'Expanding notions of work and learning: profiles of latent power', in T. Fenwick (ed) *Sociocultural perspectives on learning through work*, (New Directions in Adult and Continuing Education, vol 92), San Francisco, CA: Jossey Bass/Wiley, pp 19-30.

Luria, A. (1976) *Cognitive development: Its cultural and social foundations*, Cambridge: Harvard University Press.

Marsick, V. and Watkins, K. (1990) *Informal and incidental learning in the workplace*, London: Routledge.

Meade, G. (1913) 'A report on vocational training in Chicago and in other cities, by a committee of the City Club', *Elementary School Teacher*, vol 13, pp 248-9.

Noon, M. and Blyton, P. (1997) *The realities of work*, Basingstoke: Macmillan.

OECD (1998) *Lifelong learning: A monitoring framework and trends in participation*, Paris: OECD.

Probert, B. (1999) 'Gendered work and gendered workers', in D. Boud and J. Garrick (eds) *Understanding learning at work*, London: Routledge, pp 90-116.

Pusey, M. (2003) *The experience of middle Australia*, Cambridge: Cambridge University Press.

Resnick, L., Pontecorvo, C., Saljo, R. and Burge, R. (1997) 'Introduction', in L. Resnick, C. Pontecorvo and R. Saljo (eds) *Discourse, tools and reasoning: Essays on situated cognition*, Berlin: Springer, pp 1-20.

Rogoff, B. (1995) 'Observing sociocultural activities on three planes: participatory appropriation, guided appropriation and apprenticeship', in J. Wertsch, J.P. Del Rio and A. Alverez (eds) *Sociocultural studies of the mind*, Cambridge: Cambridge University Press, pp 139-64.

Rogoff, B. and Lave, J. (eds) (1984) *Everyday cognition: Its development in social context*, Cambridge, MA: Harvard University Press.

Rowden, R. (1995) 'The role of human resources development in successful small to mid-sized manufacturing businesses: a comparative case study', *Human Resource Development Quarterly*, vol 6, no 4, pp 335-73.

Rowden, R. (1997) 'How attention to employee satisfaction through training and development helps small business maintain a competitive edge: a comparative case study', *Australian Vocational Education Review*, vol 4, no 2, pp 33-41.

Scribner, S. (1984) 'Studying working intelligence', in B. Rogoff and J. Lave (eds) *Everyday cognition: Its development in social context*, Cambridge, MA: Harvard University Press, pp 9-40.

Scribner, S. (1997/1988) 'Mental and manual work: an activity theory orientation', in E. Tobah, R. Falmagne, M. Parlee, L. Martin and A. Kapelman (eds) *Mind and social practice: Selected writings of Sylvia Scribner*, Cambridge: Cambridge University Press, pp 367-74.

Smith, A. and Billett, S. (2003) *Enhancing employer investment in training*, Adelaide: National Centre for Vocational Education Research.

Solomon, N. (1999) 'Culture and difference in workplace learning', in D. Boud and J. Garrick (eds) *Understanding learning at work*, London: Routledge, pp 119-31.

Suchman, L. (1996) 'Constituting shared workspaces', in Y. Engestrom and D. Middleton (eds) *Cognition and communication at work*, Cambridge: Cambridge University Press, pp 35-60.

Somerville, M. and Bernoth, M. (2001) 'Safe bodies: solving a dilemma in workplace', in *Knowledge demands for the new economy: 9th Annual International Conference on post-compulsory education and training. Volume 2*, Centre for Learning and Work Research, Brisbane, pp 253-60.

Sweller, J. (1989) 'Should problem solving be used as a learning device in mathematics?', *Journal of Research into Mathematics Education*, vol 20, no 3, pp 321-28.

Tam, M. (1997) *Part-time employment: A bridge or a trap?*, Brookfield: Aldershot.

Valsiner, J. (1994) 'Bi-directional cultural transmission and constructive sociogenesis', in W. de Graaf and R. Maier (eds) *Sociogenesis re-examined*, New York, NY: Springer, pp 101-34.

Wertsch, J. (1998) *Mind as action*, New York, NY: Oxford University Press.

NINE

Interests, arguments and ideologies: employers' involvement in education–business partnerships in the US and the UK

Suzanne Greenwald

Introduction

From corporate level political and philanthropic support to ground-level mentoring, tutoring and curriculum design, the education–business relationship reflects a complex amalgam of employment interests, competitiveness arguments and stakeholder ideologies. However, this increasingly powerful collaboration, which appears to have permeated international, national, district and site level education policy, yields questionable results and uncritical examination of school community impact and learning outcomes for all partnership participants. This chapter examines the added value of employers in the context of education–business partnerships by drawing upon the literature, including a comparative study based on survey, interview and observation data gathered in secondary schools within the US and the UK during the 1997-98 academic year.

In search of added value

Ongoing debates on partnerships' added value incorporate arguments of educational purpose and employability of graduates. While some employers view partnerships as a means towards preparing future workers in an increasingly competitive global marketplace (McMullen and Snyder, 1987), educators often look to these collaborations for critical resource and network support. Even though some partnership agendas promote student success as their objectives, the challenge remains to define, operate and substantiate this measure of success in terms which are meaningful to all partnership interests. Negotiating among these different interests poses additional challenges, and reveals inherent conflicts of interests, ideologies and arguments for educational provision. Most likely, the initial reasons for partnership formation are the very ones that should influence and incorporate the ultimate student outcomes that will measure partnership success or failure:

> There are many reasons for developing school, family and community partnerships. They can improve school programs and school climate, provide family services and support, increase parents' skills and leadership, connect families with others in the schools and in the community, and help teachers with their work. However, the main reason to create such partnerships is to help all youngsters succeed in school and in later life. When parents, teachers, students, and others view one another as partners in education, a caring community forms around students and begins to work. (Epstein, 1995, p 707)

The multiple layers of interests that partnerships reveal, in one sense, draw attention to what is missing in publicly supported institutions. Partnerships often provide schools with much needed resources, sometimes alongside controversial, profit-driven agendas. In situations such as these, corporate success, rather than student success, drives private sector partner interests.

Researchers who have studied the value of education–business partnerships have been challenged to isolate benefits and distinguish value added from an otherwise complex movement, which is still evolving. One analytical strategy suggests focusing on trends and patterns in business involvement in education. This longitudinal approach lends itself to typologies by drawing meaning from past partnership models. For example, McLaughlin (1988) delineates three general models:

- Partnership.
- Banking.
- Political.

Since the 1980s, a critical turning point for corporate involvement in public life, McLaughlin argues that these models evolved, revealing a broader cultural change for business at large. Prior to the US federal report, 'A nation at risk', which equated today's underperforming students with the threat of tomorrow's economic under-competitiveness in an increasingly global marketplace, corporate giving could be characterised as 'philanthropic paternalism' or 'enlightened self-interest'. However, following the report, alliances and task forces began to cluster at the national, state and local levels, signalling a rising tide of private sector involvement in education (McLaughlin, 1988).

Unlike McLaughlin's historical typology, Timpane and McNeil (1991) take on a fluctuating theory of corporate involvement in education. They argue that, in the early half of the 20th century, business leaders got involved to shape and influence education content, in this case to promote universal schooling and vocational education. By the mid- to late 1960s, as critical issues of educational equity dominated public policy agendas, business interests began to wane, distancing themselves from primary and secondary schooling issues, and gradually shifting instead towards institutions of higher education (HE). By the late 1970s, and early 1980s, business leaders began to re-establish their public education connections in order to influence a greater and more diverse labour supply which would be able to compete in an increasingly demanding market. Incentives for school improvement, according to these authors, fluctuate according to evolving business objectives:

> The scattered and marginal school/business connections in the early 1980s were thought to be negligible. Yet, these partnerships, seen initially as temporary phenomenon, developed swiftly and surprisingly into strong and widespread business support of school-level projects and help for school district and community enterprises. (Timpane and McNeil, 1991, Introduction, p x)

Partnership typologies and historical modelling, like the ones cited, not only critically analyse this movement, but also suggest a broadening definition for employer involvement in education. From physical support to human capital resources, the goals menu for education–business partnerships offers intangible benefits, such as incentives and role models, as well as targeted, tangible outcomes, such as improved test scores and job placements. In the most classic Partnership Model, schemes such as 'adopt-a-school' in the US (otherwise known as 'twinning' in the UK) often characterise an early stage of collaboration. One distinguishing characteristic of this model is the boundary between schools and businesses, which remains clear, separate and intact. The 'banking model' evolves and expands on this arrangement to a more systemic level, but also maintains clear school and work boundaries. At this stage, channels of corporate support feed school activities of their choosing, but usually on a larger scale, such as the district level. Citywide initiatives, most notably the Boston Compact, remain one of the oldest partnerships in this category.

Unlike the single company Partnership Model, business coalitions begin to challenge the boundaries and practices of the school, moving into the business of school reform, most often found within urban school systems. Sipple et al (1977) emphasise the critical role of this particular interest group, citing a combination of high-level support from coalition and political leaders connecting across different levels of government, and often releasing sizeable financial resources for the purposes of systemic school reform.

At any level of support, partnership critics object to the emergence of the private sector as a parental proxy to state-funded schools. By symbolically transferring responsibility for public education into the hands of private partners, standard school resources become viewed as a gift, rather than as a given (Stone, 1991). Employers themselves worry that their aid may end up replacing, rather than augmenting, state educational budgets.

Furthermore, as partnership models take on more than basic resources and move into global, economic arguments for school partnering, partnership evaluation reports, when they appear, tend to lose their objectivity and gain promotional profiling (CBI, 1988, 1992, 1994, 1999). In this respect, evaluation reports become overextended, undiscerning and otherwise meaningless in yielding recommendations for improving students' instructional outcomes.

Partnerships and policy borrowing: comparing the US and the UK

Comparing certain aspects of the education systems of the US and the UK, one surprisingly discovers occurrences of overlap, imitation and mutual influence. Both systems share some similarities in terms of challenges to prepare students for the world of work and the use of education–business partnerships towards this objective. The formal degree of system centralisation and incentives for students' further education are two critical facets, among others, that distinguish the respective systems from one another. At the same time, the two systems also share an interesting history of policy and programme borrowing, which, in itself, reflects shared goals and purposes, particularly within the area of school partnerships. Education and training policy borrowing was particularly active during Margaret Thatcher's final years as Prime Minister (1986-90), when teams of British government ministers engaged in transatlantic study missions (Finegold, 1993). Education experiments from the US held particular interest to British ministers, ranging from magnet schools, private industry councils, community colleges, student loan programmes, teacher licensing and education–business compacts. Meanwhile, British scholars objected to what was perceived as more than simply an innocent exchange of ideas, but also the adoption of contentious, exclusionary ideology, as defined by some scholars:

> The education politics of Thatcherism have involved a total reworking of the ideological terrain of educational politics and the orientation of policy making is now towards the consumers of education – parents and industrialists; the producer lobbies are almost totally excluded. (Ball, 1990, p 8)

The most classic partnership model during this time, the Compact Model, had originated in Boston in the 1970s, and found its way over to East London by 1987, replicating swiftly into 30 additional models around Britain within two years (Finegold, 1993). Prior to the Compact, Britain had imported America's Junior Achievement model in the 1960s, renaming it Young Enterprise by the late 1980s as the programme serving over 30,000 15- to 19-year-olds across 1,700 of its training programmes. Engaging employers to offer work placements, and skills training while allowing students the opportunity to simulate 'learning by doing', the programme's hallmark pedagogical paradigm, was the main draw behind borrowing policies and programmes such as these from overseas.

Policy borrowing in Britain in the late 1980s evolved into a movement strongly endorsing education–business partnership development nationwide. A 1987 Confederation for British Industry (CBI) conference praised and promoted a generation of school–industry links as short-term interventions for bolstering the British economy in the face of rising international competition (CBI, 1988). Increasing student skills became the focus of school–industry links:

> Given the dramatic fall in the number of school leavers, the existing skill shortages and the increased competition for the more able from higher education and the public sector, businesses which are not closely tied into their local schools will miss out in the recruitment stakes. (CBI, 1988, p 9)

In their examination of policy borrowing patterns between the UK and the US, Halpin and Troyna (1995) observe that decision making tends to decentralise in some areas just as centralising forces begin to intensify in other areas. For example, as Charter Schools, Local School Councils, Local Education Authorities (LEAs), school choice and magnet schools were introduced within their respective, national systems, centralised training and standardisation policies, such as Goals 2000 in America, started to gain momentum. Education reform policies, widely perceived within both cultures as solutions to common economic crises and anxieties, continue to serve as popularly borrowed symbols of solution building. However, some critics argue they are doomed to failure when uprooted from their original institutional and political context (Robertson and Waltman, 1993).

With declining employment and prosperity in both industrialised nations, and high-profile, public criticism for their education and training systems in the late 1970s and early 1980s, both countries shared a sense of urgency to create solutions to destabilising social and economic forces. The political ideologies promoted during this time, for example, demonstrated an intensified support for market solutions over state interventions, and a foray into a sort of entrepreneurial enlightenment.

The educator's perspective: isolationism and exploitation

School isolationism manifests itself in a widening gap between professionals within the school and those from the outer community in terms of exposure and contact. Through surveys and interviews conducted with school principals, teachers and students in the US and head teachers and teachers within the UK, the perception of schools as isolated is widely held to be an obstacle towards forging connections with the 'outside world'. Interestingly, educators tend to draw upon this paradigm when arguing on behalf of allowing business volunteers to enter the classroom.

Among the education community, teachers are ironically most often missing from partnership discussions, designs and evaluations. One could surmise a number of reasons for their conspicuous absence. First, teachers tend to be either overlooked or treated as non-participants in school-based programmes where volunteer business people come in and literally take over teachers' classes. Second, teachers, in general, may have a tendency to be less critical of partnership programmes due to their reported feelings of alleviated isolationism. Third, teachers could be simultaneously criticising the potential threat of commercial infiltration that partnerships pose, but, at the same time, support the presence of partnerships in school communities. And finally, teachers may not consider education–business partnerships directly relevant to the core of instruction, for "it is rare that business becomes involved in foster(ing) the bond of teaching and learning" (Cromarty, 1997, p 36). In the US, as federally promoted corporate involvement with schools increased its presence nationwide, critics dug deeper into the question of partnerships' contributions to educational substance and longitudinal benefits (Levine and Trachtman, 1988; Cuban, 1992; Molnar, 1995).

If not in the enhancement of educational substance, then what is the value added of partnerships for educators? Trachtman's national survey of US teachers in both urban and rural communities confirms the isolationist argument where schools express a growing need to access external professionals (Levine and Trachtman, 1988). As for the methods of involvement that purport to alleviate school isolationism, Trachtman found that teachers preferred more direct contact, rather than the unpredictable, distant handout, particularly between business representatives and students, rather than teachers. The results of these arrangements, according to Trachtman's subjects, became an expansion of teachers' roles, an increase in self-esteem, as well as opportunities for professional growth.

Other scholars have raised more critical objections on behalf of teachers' views of business infiltrations into schools. Student populations can be perceived as a much sought after education market for private sector profits (Cromarty, 1997). In this light, how appropriate is the presence of business given its interests and profit-driven agendas? Conflicts of interest arguments reflect on the fundamental purposes of educating in a protected, rather than isolated, learning environment against student exploitation, school inequities and misappropriated public school funds:

> Are we losing sight of what a school's purpose is – to teach reading, writing, math, science, social studies, etc.? Have our intentions for educating students changed? Do businesses actually improve education and prepare the students for the transition from school to work?... The perks for business are an enhanced public image, increased sales and free advertising. (Cromarty, 1997, pp 32-3)

Further objections point to inequitable distributions of corporate support, targeting, for example, the best schools or the best students, thus perpetuating the divide between the well-funded, from the neediest schools. Timpane and McNeil (1991), in their fluctuating theory of business involvement, as stated earlier in this chapter, highlighted that businesses failed to target support towards the poorest, neediest children. According to these authors, businesses try to avoid getting involved in politically thorny issues, such as school desegregation and racial integration.

The student's perspective: graduation and jobs

Secondary schools, for their relative proximity to entrance into HE and the workforce, tend to gain the most attention in the partnership literature. Employment incentives upon graduation for disadvantaged students represent a particular area of secondary school partnership (Baumol, 1984). In a nationwide survey in the US, researchers found that one of the most effective roles for businesses is as incentive provider for at-risk students to remain in school, graduate, then earn post-secondary degrees or employment with the aid of corporate partners (McMullen and Snyder, 1987).

However, one set of critics argues that the problem of ill-prepared students lies not in the students, nor in the teachers, nor in the institutions of schooling, but rather in the ever-changing nature of the job market. With the replacement of historically low-skilled, highly paid factory jobs with today's low-skilled, low-paid service jobs of the 'secondary labour market' (Hamilton, 1990), today's employment opportunities for secondary school students have changed dramatically, often leading to widespread unemployment. This situation is further intensified for urban youth. A five-year, longitudinal study of America's school-to-work transition revealed the importance of a young person's occupational environment, made up of family, neighbourhood and access to existing opportunities (Bidwell et al, 1996, p 177):

> The environment in which many urban, minority children live often provides few chances to learn or practice jobs that are better or different from what their own parents had. Thus, the replication of social class differences involves not only schools, but also families and neighbourhoods that reproduce differences in knowledge and skills from one generation to another.

Partnership programmes such as the St. Louis Internship Program (Bavly, 1995) appear to address these issues of neighbourhood job opportunities and social class replication. This citywide partnership aimed to alleviate the problem of lack of work exposure and experience in low-income, urban neighbourhoods for secondary students who may be seeking employment immediately upon graduation from high school.

A national survey in the US conducted by Public/Private Ventures classified partnership types and benefits into three main foci – the Student, School and System. Researchers found that disadvantaged students, in particular, tended to reap the most benefits in terms of access to employment, work experience, personal attention, coaching and job-finding skills (McMullen and Snyder, 1987). Similarly, researchers found that for disadvantaged schools, partnerships tended to enhance existing programme resources, upgrade facilities and increase teacher morale. Interestingly, in terms of longitudinal benefits, the intangible benefits of increased attention to and interest in public education carried the greatest impact for education–business partnerships. For the business community itself, researchers found very few benefits except for a more knowledgeable constituency for education. Increased contact with schools influenced business volunteers' knowledge of issues and needs facing today's schools.

Proponents of national apprenticeship systems cite early work exposure for this same population for similar employment advantages. They argue not only on behalf of the benefits of early work introduction, but also work attitudes, work behaviour, even exposure to professional appearances and adult socialisation. For some, apprenticeships are perceived as the missing connective link between schools and workplaces. By modernising students' knowledge of their school subjects, apprenticeships will prepare students for a trade and for the adult world of work (Hamilton, 1990). In some national contexts, apprenticeships serve as critical training and socialisation systems:

> industry-based training system(s) with a contractual employment relationship in which the firm promises to make available a broad and structured, practical and theoretical training of some length in a recognized occupational skill category. (Reubens, 1977, p 55)

In addition to their hands-on transmission of skills and occupational socialisation functions, apprenticeship programmes may serve as a critical mechanism in transmitting rapidly changing industrial and technological tools and methods.

The employers' perspective: approaching the education–training agenda

> This major divide between academic and vocational, between education and training, between thinking and making is deeply rooted in our culture. (Pring, 1995, p 55)

> [P]eople had thought that industry and business required millions and millions of unskilled and semi-skilled people to do the jobs that were required, and therefore on the whole, everybody colluded with a system where a few were educated really well through the public school system or through grammar schools, and simultaneously, the comprehensive schools were being introduced with a greater ambition to educate everybody, by not differentiating, not putting some people down. That coincided, I think, with many people in industry, though not all, beginning to realise and say, 'We have got to dramatically raise standards of education and training'. (Interview with Birmingham schools representative, UK, 21 January 1998)

For many students in the UK, their first real exposure to employers and the world of work occurs through a mandatory work placement scheme in Year 10 or 11. By allowing access to future recruits, the work placement theoretically presents itself as beneficial to both parties promising access and exposure. In some cases, work placements have also launched critical career decision making.

Employers sponsoring these schemes seem to be aware of the variable outcomes that emerge from these placements, despite their best intentions and approaches to early training:

> We try to give them the opportunity to see the entire process of the bank, whether it's retail banking or commercial banking.... What we don't want to do is stick them in a corner and say, 'File this'. We really want to give them an overall view.... What we would really like is some sort of selection process to make sure that the people who come here are the ones who have identified career aspirations, or they're looking at developing their work experience as a method of achievement. (Interview with Birmingham business representative, 14 January 1998)

In addition to giving students potential insights into trades and professions, the value of work experience, as expressed by some employers, lead to a broader understanding of the meaning of work. Work placement schemes offer some a secure and well-informed vantage point from which to witness work and work environments:

> [T]hey see what is work, what people really do when they arrive in the morning. 'I know what happens at school, a bell goes and I go into this room here and I sit and listen. What do people actually do at work?' They have no idea until they've got a real job. And the real jobs that they can get otherwise are on a check-out till at Sainsbury's on a Saturday morning, that sort of thing. That is work, of course, but it's not work in the broader sense. (Interview with Oxfordshire business executive, 8 April 1998).

Programmes designed to recruit students early into a particular trade have also broadened their missions towards business exposure. For example, Understanding Industry, an initiative that began in 1977, originally set out to recruit young people, aged 16-19, for the manufacturing industry (interview with British business coalition representative, 28 January 1998). Since then, its mission has expanded with the objectives to 'inform, involve and inspire young people' to understand industry and commerce. In its delivery, a business volunteer will present a small lecture, management game, business exercise or problem, in order to challenge students' communication, team building and problem solving skills. Part of the impetus behind placing a representative from business into the classroom was to dispel myths, stereotypes or naivety about industry:

> [Y]oungsters actually have a poor understanding of industry and commerce, a very poor understanding of the skills required, and they don't rate it very highly either, which is frightening, really. (Interview with British business coalition representative, 28 January 1998)

What do business volunteers themselves gain from classroom exposure? As far as the particular scheme, Understanding Industry, is concerned, employees note this is an opportunity for personal development and for harnessing a captive, young audience for market research (Interview with British business coalition representative, 28 January 1998). Profit incentives such as these, discussed earlier on, embody the contentious conflicts of interest, which sometimes pit employers against educators. The benefits for schools involved in initiatives such as these, rely heavily on the enthusiasm of the particular volunteer, and the potential for a continued and evolving relationship, incorporating work experience placements, mentoring, site visits and other link activities.

Aside from work exposure, work readiness features prominently in employers' incentives for early contact with students. Work readiness initiatives grew increasingly popular in the UK during the 1980s, heavily endorsed by government. In 1988, the Department for Education and Skills (DfES) and the Department for Trade and Industry (DTI) launched schemes encouraging school–business links for the purposes of improving school leavers' 'work readiness'. To this end, the powerful business watchdog group, CBI, set up a foundation to persuade local industries to work with local education services, otherwise known explicitly as Education Business Partnership (EBP). The goals here were to identify and align national priorities for school–industry liaisons with local plans of action (White Paper, *Better schools*, 1985).

Widespread communication of goals and actions of school–business links showed up in high-profile reports commissioned by the CBI throughout the 1980s and 1990s. Strongly promoting a self-interest argument, the first of these reports extrapolated the school-dropout problem into an ultimate crisis in global competitiveness. This report, as well as many others like it, laid down contractual positions for reducing the gap between school and work, rather than critically evaluating the effectiveness and potential value of school–business links:

> The partnership approach builds on the common interest which schools, companies, and pupils have in reducing the divide between education and the world of work. (CBI, 1988, p 10)

Partnership sustainability, another theme unfortunately missing from these high-profile reports, turns out to be a critical factor in the long-term value of these alliances. Well-coordinated infrastructure, which appears to be more in place in the UK compared with the relatively higher decentralised US, has a stronger chance of connecting the necessary political support with the institutional requirement.

Selected findings from the School–Business Partnership Study, US and UK

From September 1997 through December 1998, state school head teachers in the Birmingham and Oxfordshire District, and principals in the Chicago Public School District, were surveyed regarding their schools' partnership involvement. In addition, business representatives from all three districts were interviewed regarding their perspectives on corporate partnerships and policies with schools. Interviews were also conducted among district government officials, local boards of education and regional education and business coalitions regarding their role in partnership network operations.

The most popular type of resources coming from the business community into schools included student work experience, followed by equipment donation, business representative attendance at career fairs and tutoring and mentoring. In terms of frequency of communication, among those schools reporting the presence of at least one partnership, overall, about half the principals or head teachers (46%) reported that they communicate with business representatives about their partnership initiative, on average, less than once a month. As to what role principals and head teachers play overall, most reported playing the lead negotiator, providing at least the initial contact. In terms of extent of involvement in partnership planning, among the three school districts studied, a stronger existing level of district level networks and support appeared among the British schools. Intermediary organisations, between schools and businesses, appear to contribute to the administrative aid of partnership programmes.

Within the two English school districts studied – Oxfordshire and Birmingham – when comparing state versus independent schools, there appeared to be greater levels of business partnership involvement among the state schools. Due to their relatively greater need for external support, facility and equipment upgrading, as well as professional networks for student work experience, the state schools tend to draw greater partnership activity towards their campuses. However, among the independent schools, 'student work experience' as well as 'business attendance at career fairs' still predominantly characterised the nature of their partnership support as well.

Since 1995, within the Chicago Public School District, an intermediary agent has been introduced to facilitate system-wide partnerships. The Chicago School Partners Program, which runs out of the Chicago Board of Education, now matches and coordinates school site visits, and initiates involvement of businesses in the urban schools. However, once the partnership is formed and operating, this intermediary piece drops out and leaves monitoring and evaluation up to a separate department within the Board of Education, namely the Vocational Education Department. A review of vocational programmes occurred within the city in 1997, and the best practices were selected based on promising programmes, school support and teacher quality and credentials, industry involvement and numbers of students supported. Eleven of the best programmes received the title, Career Academy, and subsequently were entitled to a greater concentration of federal and state funds, along with additional staff development training, increased connections with industry councils, post-secondary institutions and job-shadowing opportunities. The career skill objectives for the students in these academies include computer literacy, communications, résumé writing, interviewing, appropriate dressing for work, job shadowing, internships and summer jobs.

Like Chicago's framework, Birmingham's organisational infrastructure relies on multiple organisations for its partnership development, but with a more complex network of support. Similarly, a cohesive and collectively responsible business community sustains the indigenous education–business links. However, unlike the Chicago framework, merged career service agency and business partnership broker, the Careers and Education Business Partnership (CEBP), ensures partnership services, monitoring school resource equity and programme evaluation through neighbourhood satellite offices. Both state and local business finance fund this intermediary agent (*The Economist*, 8 August 1998), as they deliver career advice, guidance and work opportunities to the neighbourhood's young people. As a result of their unique vantage point, residing neither in schools nor local businesses, the CEBPs can collectively monitor progress within a district, make decisions and form a strategic network of support, including the Training and Enterprise Councils (TECs), the Chamber of Commerce, as well as the Birmingham City Council Education Department. Structural continuity, rather than serendipitous good will, aims to prevent the common pitfall of partnership fragmentation and high professional turnover.

Like Birmingham, Oxfordshire harbours a central EBP brokering organisation, coordinated by leaders of their Technical and Vocational Education Initiatives (TVEI) organisation, which focuses mainly on the development of education–industry activities as well as work-based curricula. The TVEI agent essentially evolved into the organisation of EBPs, inheriting county divisions. Despite the organisational framework in place, local business managers who attend EBPs' meetings express difficulty in keeping track of the sheer numbers of school initiatives being promoted and developed. In turn, when some businesses approach the schools with their partnership proposals, they feel the schools cannot manage the magnitude and variety of interests emerging from the community. The EBP, therefore, acts as a much needed middle managing agent, at the very least simply to keep track of local business resources and opportunities.

One of the unintended benefits of local business involvement in schools is the rise of school, community and company social profile as a result of the publicity. Head teachers and business managers across districts express observations of this nature:

> I think the potential links with business ... it works in all sorts of subtle ways. It raises the profile of the school, the status, because of these business people supporting you. The place buzzes, and that's all over the newspapers. (Interview with Oxfordshire head teacher, 10 December 1997)

There's quite a strong identity…. People think of Birmingham as a very drab place, with a lot of heavy industry. There is a particular mind set about Birmingham, which I admit I had before I came to work here. The people who work here particularly want to prove the point that Birmingham is worth supporting. (Interview with Birmingham business manager, 14 January 1998)

No company does it just because they want to be altruistic, and I don't think that any of them do. They do it because it raises their social profile, or eases the chairman's conscience, or whatever it is. (Interview with Oxfordshire head teacher, 9 January 1998).

Conclusion: implications, reservations and recommendations

Our best attempt, as researchers of this phenomenon, would be to look more closely into patterns of involvement between schools and businesses. In what ways, for what purposes, and for whom do these links between education and industry exist? Aside from preparing students for work readiness, how will partnerships specifically address improving students' overall academic attainment? What sort of business community leadership will be necessary to make informed decisions regarding future partnerships? What type of state, district and neighbourhood network infrastructure will need to be in place for long-term sustainability of these links? What will become of mandatory work experience at the school site level? Through additional, multi-level analyses, the partnership research agenda holds many lessons for improvement from borrowed policies and programmes, both domestic and international.

Partnerships are perceived by most to be inherently good for the future. While most participants in existing partnerships can list what each side has to gain from their contacts with one another – professional development, mentoring, resources or work experience – the majority of participants would like to see a growing interdependence through the exchange of ideas, needs, benefits and positive profiles.

The philosophical debate over the future role of the private sector revolves not only around the aid of business, but the long-term impact this aid may potentially have on state assistance. Some business leaders believe partnership interventions may be deleted from national education budgets, unless intentions to supplement, not supplant, state aid are indicated. Other business sceptics express reservations regarding taking over what is believed to be the state's inherent responsibility to provide education to all:

[W]hether business should pay for education, I personally don't think it should. I think if you have a huge, public education sector as we do in this country, it's taxation … there's sort of a recognised source within society to pay for education…. Because you could shift the burden onto industry directly rather than indirectly, but I think that would be a huge mistake ... you'd say Sanskrit? Ancient Norse? We'd rather talk about engineering and manufacturing and mathematics and business studies ... education to me is a great learning spread ... and that is why primarily it should be a burden directly on the tax payer. (Interview with Oxfordshire business executive, 8 April 1998)

As the public discourse surrounding education continues to allude to a shared social responsibility, implying that partnerships between education and industry are a necessary good, the shifting burden of paying for state education may continue to fall further away from the state.

References

Ball, S. (1990) *Politics and policy making in education: Explorations in policy sociology*, London: Routledge.

Baumol, W. (1984) 'Matching private incentives to public goals', in H. Brooks, L. Liebman and C. Schelling (eds) *Public and private partnership: New opportunities for meeting social needs*, Cambridge, MA: Ballinger, pp 175-93.

Bavly, S. (1995) 'Gateway to the future: an evaluation of the St. Louis Internship Program', Unpublished Report, St Louis, MI: St Louis Public Schools.

Bidwell, C., Csikszentmihalyi, M., Hedges, L. and Shneider, C. (1996) *Youth and work in America*, Chicago, IL: University of Chicago.

CBI (Confederation of British Industry) (1988, 1992, 1994, 1999) *Building a stronger partnership between business and secondary education*, Sussex: CBI.

Cromarty, N. (1997) 'School–business partnerships – at whose expense? Some pros and cons of business involvement', *Education Canada*, Spring, vol 37, no 1, pp 32-7, 52.

Cuban, L. (1992) 'The corporate myth of reforming public schools', *Phi Delta Kappan*, October, pp 157-9.

Epstein, J. (1995) 'School/family/community partnerships: caring for the children we share', *Phi Delta Kappan*, May, pp 701-12.

Finegold, D. (1993) 'The changing international economy and its impact on education and training', in D. Finegold, L. McFarland and W. Richardson (eds) *Something borrowed, something blue? The transatlantic market in education and training reform*, Washington, DC: The Brookings Institute, pp 47-72.

Halpin, D. and Troyna, B. (1995) 'The politics of education policy borrowing', *Comparative Education*, November, vol 31, no 3, pp 303-10.

Hamilton, S. (1990) *Apprenticeship for adulthood: Preparing youth for the future*, New York, NY: Free Press.

Levine, M. and Trachtman, R. (1988) *American business and the public school: Case studies in corporate involvement in public education*, New York, NY: Teachers College Press.

McLaughlin, M. (1988) 'Business and the public schools: new patterns of support', in D. Munk and J. Underwood (eds) *Microlevel school finance: Issues and implications for policy*, Cambridge, MA: Ballinger, pp 63-80.

McMullen, B. and Snyder, P. (1987) *Allies in education: Schools and businesses working together for at-risk youth*, Philadelphia, PA: Public/Private Ventures.

Molnar, A. (1995) 'Schooled for profit', *Education Leadership*, September, pp 70-1.

Pring, R. (1995) *Closing the gap: Liberal education and vocational preparation*, London: Hodder and Stoughton.

Reubens, B. (1977) *Bridges to work: International comparisons of transition services*, New York, NY: Universe Books.

Robertson, D. and Waltman, J. (1993) 'The politics of policy borrowing', in D. Finegold, L. McFarland and W. Richardson (eds) *Something borrowed, something blue? The transatlantic market in education and training reform*, Washington DC: The Brookings Institute, pp 21-44.

Sipple, J., Miskel, C., Matheney, T. and Kearney, P. (1997) 'The creation and development of an interest group: life at the intersection of big business and education reform', *Educational Administration Quarterly*, October, vol 33, no 4, pp 440-73.

Stone, N. (1991) 'Does business have any business in education?', *Harvard Business Review*, March/April, pp 46-62.

Timpane, M. and McNeil, L. (1991) *Business impact on education and child development reform*, Study prepared for the Committee for Economic Development, New York, NY: Committee for Economic Development.

TEN

Compatible higher education systems and the European labour market: Bologna and beyond

Guy Haug[1]

Introduction

European higher education (HE) has entered a major process of structural change related to the determination of its governments and universities to complete the creation of a coherent, compatible and competitive European HE area by the year 2010[2]. This undertaking was first announced in the Sorbonne Declaration signed in May 1998 in Paris by four countries. It was confirmed one year later in the Bologna Declaration, which was signed by 30 countries who took the commitment to initiate national reforms in such a way that overall convergence should emerge at European level. Progress was reviewed, commitments were firmed-up and more specific priorities for action were set at the two follow-up ministerial meetings that took place in Prague in May 2001 (with 33 participating countries), and in Berlin in September 2003 (40 countries, now spanning the whole of Europe, including Turkey and Russia). The so-called 'Bologna Process' aims not only to enhance the cohesion and compatibility of HE systems within Europe and their attractiveness throughout the world, but in the EU it also has a strong link to the common European labour market.

Structural change

A new phase in the process of 'growing together' of European higher education

Modern European HE developed for a long time within the framework of national boundaries. This led to a patchwork of national systems developed in isolation from each other and characterised by marked differences in every respect (types of institutions, degree structure, tuition fees and grants, academic calendar, and so forth). Cooperation was restricted mainly to personal contacts between researchers and to a number of bilateral cultural agreements allowing for the mobility of a small number of students.

From the mid-1980s there came a new phase marked by large-scale mobility. It was triggered by an unexpected player, the EU, which at that time launched within a few years its ERASMUS, COMETT, LINGUA and TEMPUS programmes. With these programmes, which account for the exchange of over 100,000 students per year for recognised periods of study or internships abroad, European universities and other HE institutions and authorities have learnt how to deal with very different systems. However, year after year, the same problems of the basic incompatibility of these systems are encountered.

The Sorbonne and Bologna Declarations built on this experience and signalled the entrance of European HE into a new phase: a phase of structural change, in which mobility and cooperation should become easier thanks to reforms creating more compatibility between the systems. The commitment to carrying out such reforms has been reconfirmed both by universities themselves (at the two European HE conventions held in Salamanca in March 2003 and in Graz in May 2003), and by ministers at their meetings a few months later in Prague and Berlin. The Berlin Communiqué even reflects a determination to speed up the process by setting intermediate targets for 2005.

What is really new in the Bologna Process?

The Bologna Declaration is a key document, which marks a turning point in the development of European HE:

- It is a pledge by all (now 40) participating countries to reform the structures of their HE in a convergent way.
- It is a commitment freely taken by each signatory country to reform its own HE system or systems in order to create overall convergence at European level. The Bologna Declaration is not a reform imposed upon national governments or HE institutions. Any pressure individual countries and HE institutions may feel from the Bologna Process could only result from their ignoring increasingly common features or staying outside the mainstream of change. The Bologna Process aims to create convergence and, thus, is not a path towards the 'standardisation' or 'uniformisation' of European HE. The fundamental principles of university autonomy and educational diversity are respected (and, indeed, promoted).
- The declaration reflects a search for a common European answer to common European problems. The process originates from the recognition that in spite of their valuable differences, European HE systems are facing common internal and external challenges related to the growth and diversification of HE, the employability of graduates, the shortage of skills in key areas, the expansion of private and transnational education, and so on. *The Declaration recognises the value of coordinated reforms, compatible systems and common action.*

- The Bologna Declaration is not just a political statement, but a commitment to an action programme with a set of specified objectives:
  1. the adoption of a common framework of readable and comparable degrees, "also through the implementation of the Diploma Supplement";
  2. the introduction of undergraduate and postgraduate levels in all countries, with first degrees no shorter than three years and relevant to the labour market;
  3. ECTS-compatible credit systems also covering lifelong learning activities;
  4. a European dimension in quality assurance, with comparable criteria and methods; and
  5. the elimination of remaining obstacles to the free mobility of students (as well as trainees and graduates) and teachers (as well as researchers and HE administrators).
- The declaration also reflects fresh concern about the global competitiveness of European HE in the world. Next to the need to "achieve greater compatibility and comparability in the systems of HE" (mainly an intra-European issue), the declaration wants "in particular" to increase "the international competitiveness of the European system of HE". It states that the "vitality and efficiency of any civilisation can be measured by the appeal its culture has for other countries". The signatory countries explicitly express their goal to "ensure that the European HE system acquires a worldwide degree of attractiveness equal to [Europe's] extraordinary cultural and scientific traditions". On these "external" issues, the Bologna Declaration has genuinely opened up new avenues. In stressing so explicitly the need for European HE as a (cohesive) system to become more attractive to students from other world regions, it provides one more reason for moving in the direction of a coherent European system and implicitly invites European institutions to compete more resolutely than in the past for students, influence, prestige and money in the worldwide competition of universities.

The commitment to address this short list of objectives about internal compatibility and external competitiveness stills stays at the core of the Bologna Process. Subsequent meetings of universities or ministers underlined the importance of specific aspects without changing the fundamental objectives; for example, universities' Salamanca Message of 2001 emphasised quality assurance, ministers' Prague Communiqué underlined the lifelong learning perspective and the social dimension of the process and promoted the importance of joint degrees, and their Berlin Communiqué stressed the doctoral level in addition to the Bachelor–Master articulation and introduced a reporting system about progress achieved in the various countries. Two objectives in particular have gained importance and may now have come to the top of the agenda: the need to promote the competitiveness and attractiveness of European universities in the world (in the wake of the growing awareness of the key role of universities in the international competition in the knowledge era) and the need to build up a European-wide mechanism for quality assurance/accreditation as a keystone of the whole attempt to foster compatibility and cross-recognition of qualifications. It is interesting to point out that these two aspects have also become core concerns in recent initiatives taken within the EU context. The Work Programme on the Objectives of Education and Training Systems adopted in 2002 wants to achieve "enough compatibility to allow citizens to take advantage" of the diversity of education/training systems (instead of being constrained by it), and hopes that by 2010 Europe will (once again) "be the most-favoured destination of students, scholars and researchers from other world regions". The growing concern about, and emphasis put on, worldwide competitiveness has also become very clear in other recent EU initiatives, both in HE and in research.

From this, it should be clear that *the process of convergence* towards the European HE area *is both the result of, and a contribution to, broader European integration.*

The Bologna Process did not emerge from HE itself, but from profound changes in its environment

The changes announced in the Bologna Declaration are not an isolated process. They coincide with major changes in the environment, in particular:

- The emergence of a real European labour market, which is bound to shape a good deal of the university offering and functioning in the years ahead – it is unlikely that the combination between a high rate of unemployment of graduates, and a shortage of highly educated young people in key areas will be accepted much longer by society; to really understand the Bologna Process, it is important to point out that it is about 'qualifications' not 'degrees', and that educational agendas are less and less autonomous, and more and more driven by employment aspects.
- The end of the strong numerical expansion at universities, which has already started in some countries and will soon start in several others; the kind of 'natural' growth which universities enjoyed in the last decades is nearing its end and this entails a number of consequences; many universities will have to do something which they are not at all accustomed to do, that is, compete for students, especially since public funding in most countries is, in one way or another, dependent on student enrolment. This is something really new in many HE communities; it can be expected that students' choice will increase and that institutions will have to pay more attention to their needs and satisfaction than in the past.
- The considerable growth of new providers, many of them from overseas; this will add to the choice available to students and for the first time ever we may be in a position to see what they prefer when they have a real possibility to choose from a spectrum of different types of education from inland and abroad. This raises fundamental questions: why do students choose a foreign provider, who may be rather expensive, rather than stay within their own national and often traditional, tuition-fee-free system? As long as there was

no choice, there was no question, and hence no need to provide an answer; in future, universities will need to come up with answers. Concern about strengthening the attractiveness and competitiveness of European HE in the world has grown rapidly since 1988 and has become a major component of the change process in progress.

- Another major change is that the accountability of universities for the use of public funds is likely to increase significantly in future; it seems particularly unlikely that public funding will be available to support institutions and students for studies much beyond the normal duration of the degree. A distinct move in this direction has already started.

These deep changes underpin the opinion already expressed; that is, HE has entered a new phase of internationalisation in which governments and universities will undertake the kind of convergent reforms called for in the Bologna Declaration, not so much because of the declaration, but rather because it encapsulated fundamental trends which most countries need to address for their own interest. This underlines the fact that the declaration's main strength is that it has functioned as a catalyst and has crystallised trends that existed but were not disclosed and shared. To a significant extent, the same could be said of the broader move in progress in education/training in the EU: the main thrust of the Education & Training 2010 work programme is on diversity combined with convergence towards the main EU goals for 2010, on the basis of political cooperation according to the 'open method of coordination'; that is, countries have no legal obligation to change/reform, but accept that it is in their own interest to pursue a list of shared EU objectives important to each of them.

Structural change in action: reforms in HE in Europe

This section is based on a survey of change/reform from Bologna to Prague (Trends 2), and from Prague to Berlin (Trends 3) carried out respectively by Haug and Tauch (2001) and Reichert and Tauch (2003). The major conclusion of both surveys is the large consensus on the core objectives of the process: mobility, employability and competitiveness/attractiveness.

The promotion of the mobility of students and graduates has been unanimously welcomed, while staff mobility still seems to receive insufficient attention. Tools like ECTS and the Diploma Supplement are explicitly welcomed. Trends 3 also notes the clear link established between mobility and employability.

The Bologna Process further increased the awareness that employability is an issue in HE all over Europe. The debate has now taken into account that there are various ways in which first degrees can be "relevant to the European labour market" – as stipulated in the Bologna Declaration – and that all need not be directly geared towards the short-term needs of the labour market. While there are many new 'professional Bachelors' and some new 'professional Masters', especially (but not only) in the college/polytechnic sector across Europe, university Bachelors are mainly seen in some countries as a preparation for further studies and a platform for the choice of postgraduate studies. Better employability of national graduates on the European labour market has been a key issue and a main engine of reforms, as will be shown later in this chapter.

As for competitiveness/attractiveness, most countries now seem to understand 'competitiveness' in a positive sense and to endorse the need for their HE systems to be 'attractive'. Several countries have devised specific plans for informing, attracting and welcoming more non-European students. In EU accession countries, the concern to enhance their attractiveness to students from the EU is in many cases intimately related to their desire to balance their exchanges within the SOCRATES and LEONARDO programmes. Most countries show amazingly little concern about transnational education (that is, education delivered in their country under the control of a university from another country or continent), and about accreditation sought by their universities from non-European accreditation agencies. Conversely, the convergence process unleashed by the Bologna Declaration is attracting interest outside Europe, in particular in Latin America: this confirms one of the objectives of the process, namely to make Europe a more attractive study destination in other world regions by introducing comprehensible and consistent HE structures.

The Bologna Process draws on four main instruments to achieve the desired convergence:

- easily readable and comparable degrees;
- an undergraduate/postgraduate structure of programmes and degrees;
- a credit system; and
- quality assurance.

Regarding the readability of degrees, it has become obvious that the Bologna Declaration did not – and does not – impose any uniformity, as was sometimes feared: on the contrary, it has rather encouraged more diversity and flexibility. In particular, there are now more binary systems (systems with a university sector and a college/polytechnic sector) with more 'bridges' between sub-systems as well as more 'professional' Bachelors and Masters. Several countries are deliberately developing integrated HE systems; that is, a single, comprehensive system combining in an articulated way, different types of institutions linked by bridges. Yet, in many countries, there are still very complex degree structures (for example, in 'trinary' systems with universities, colleges/polytechnics and short post-secondary courses). Furthermore, the Diploma Supplement is seen as all the more important in helping to achieve transparency in degree structures.

The movement of convergence towards a two-tier structure (that is, with a distinction between an undergraduate and a postgraduate phase) continues, both through the implementation of previously adopted reforms, the consolidation of Bachelor–Master structures introduced during the last decade and the initiation of new reforms in several countries. There are now examples of two-tier structures in disciplines such as engineering (although few in medicine). There are, however, also many countries where the Bachelor–Master structure is not applied to curricula in certain professional areas, and, hence, remain organised in the traditional way in long, one-tier courses. The strongest trend is towards three-year Bachelors, but there are also many examples of Bachelors requiring three-and-a-half or four years of study. Many of the most comprehensive reform plans combine the introduction of Bachelor–Master degrees, credits and some kind of accreditation procedure (that is, 'the golden triangle of reforms'), in particular in countries that engaged early in the reform process. A major breakthrough was achieved at the seminar on first degrees (Bachelor-type) in Helsinki, in February 2001, where the format of the European 'Bachelor' degrees (whether they are called Bachelor or any other name in a national language) was defined:

- they should be of diverse profiles (that is, specialised or broadly-based, with a more or less 'professional' or 'academic' profile, geared mainly towards the entrance to the labour market or to the continuation of studies at the postgraduate level); and
- they should require not less than 180 and not more than 240 ECTS credit points.

Similar progress was achieved two years later, again in Helsinki, with respect to Master courses and degrees:

- normally not less than 90 (although the absolute minimum is 60), and not more than 120 ECTS points;
- with diverse approaches (more or less taught, experience-based or research-based), and orientations (more or less academic or professional).

The stress put on joint degrees at the Prague ministerial meeting, and on doctoral studies in Berlin, promises new perspectives concerning the format of European degrees/qualifications at all levels.

The surveys carried out for the Trends 2 and Trends 3 reports show that ECTS has been widely accepted as a multi-purpose tool for the convergence towards the European HE area. There is a strong push for the introduction of ECTS or ECTS-compatible systems, as well as of the Diploma Supplement, in almost all countries, either on a compulsory basis or, more often, following the strong recommendation of the rectors' conference and/or the ministry. The fears that the introduction of credits might deprive universities of the possibility to organise their curricula in coherent sequences, or oblige them to recognise all imported credits, are diminishing. At the same time there is conspicuous need for more determined coordination in the implementation of ECTS, in order to avoid too wide divergence that would defeat the expected advantages of the scheme.

There is also a powerful movement towards more and more 'European' quality assurance (new national agencies, new standards, the ENQA network), but in very different ways and according to a variety of models. The development of 'accreditation' is now more easily recognisable than at the time of the Bologna conference: some countries (in particular among EU accession countries) have had accreditation for a decade or so, and several others have recently introduced, or are considering the possibility of introducing, a new accreditation agency (separate from the national quality assurance agency or combined with it). In some countries, aware of the need to act to increase the international acceptance of their new (as well as old) degrees, accreditation is seen as a sine qua non condition to build up trust and hence demonstrate competitiveness. The decentralised structure of the national accreditation system (sometimes referred to as 'meta-accreditation'), which is being experimented with in Germany, may provide inspiration for a basic European approach based on three main pillars:

- the mutual acceptance of quality assurance decisions;
- the respect of national and subject differences; and
- the need to avoid overloading universities with yet another level of evaluation and control.

Overall, the surveys of recent structural change/reforms show that the convergence process towards the creation of a European HE area has continued and actually accelerated while at the same time gaining breadth since the adoption of the Bologna Declaration in 1999. This was only possible because the Bologna Declaration, far from imposing an artificial set of standards, captured common needs and trends shared by most European countries. In other words, it capitalised on analyses and views that already existed in a number of countries and institutions, but were inhibited because they were not yet expressed and shared at European level.

Structural change to make European HE more attractive to students, scholars and universities of the rest of the world

The growth of the attention given to the various 'external' aspects (that is, those not concerning solely the internal cohesion of Europe's HE systems) is a conspicuous and fundamental feature of the change process in progress. The preparatory report to the Bologna Conference found that both ministerial spheres and HE institutions were largely aware of internal issues (those related to the need for more compatibility, access to the labour market, remaining structural obstacles to mobility), but generally unaware of external issues and challenges. This is in spite of the growth of transnational education and the signals pointing to decreasing attractiveness of European HE in the rest of the world. In the meantime, the issues concerning Europe's place in the world has been acknowledged much more widely and action to address these issues has developed amazingly.

Looking at these issues from the European perspective, it has become ever clearer that the external challenges facing European HE require a change of focus from intra-European (or even intra-EU) activities, to joint European activities able to have an impact elsewhere in the world: European universities have accumulated a tremendous and probably unique experience (know-how, networks/consortia, tools) for cooperation between themselves, but have not done the same to create alliances (both cooperative and competitive) to enhance their external action. Three such developments should be mentioned:

1. *There is a compelling need to close the competitive gap at home.* This would mean in particular that HE institutions in Europe should endeavour to put together, and publicise, the kind of educational opportunities students from the rest of the world would like to find on offer in Europe. Closing the competitive gap at home would also require that the limitations imposed on some of our best non-university institutions, which severely penalise them in the international arena, should be lifted.
2. *It has also become essential to regulate transnational education.* There is currently a legal vacuum in this area, with most countries ignoring this new type of education in their legal system. The aim of legislative action in this area should not be to try and prohibit transnational education – attempts to do so would most likely be doomed anyway; but it has become essential to differentiate between 'legitimate' educational activities and those which do not offer sufficient guarantees, and are not worth the time and money of European students. Quality transnational education, on the contrary, broadens the choice of students and may represent a valuable alternative to traditional education.
3. *Finally, European HE needs to learn to compete better in the world markets for HE.* This is an area of paramount importance, and it seems essential that European universities should mobilise their energies and resources to compete abroad: through the setting up of the type of courses which may suit the needs of overseas students, through increased information and marketing efforts to attract students (including paying students, not only exchange students) from other continents. In order to be able to fully enter this competition, European universities need to become much more present and organised on site. Contrary to what many in continental Europe seem to be thinking, universities from the UK, the US or Australia do not attract foreign students just because they teach in English: they have also invested for years to offer the right type of courses, user-friendly student services (such as accommodation), understandable degrees, and to publicise and explain their offering through permanent representations and recruitment efforts on site. The majority of universities in Europe still lack the mindset and the experience required in the growing competition for students and the related revenues. This is most conspicuous in certain key areas, such as registration procedures, non-educational student services (such as accommodation) and of course, sadly enough, visa policies. The visa policies applied by several European countries

have had a disastrous impact on their image as potential destinations for academic purposes among students and faculty from the majority of the rest of the world. This important issue is now being addressed by a growing number of countries, and at EU level.

Interestingly, the movement towards a more coherent, and hence more compatible, European HE system is increasingly receiving attention from universities outside of Europe. This is hardly surprising, since the completion of an understandable degree structure in Europe would make the continent more attractive for students, teachers and universities from all over the world, and provide a suitable alternative to study destinations in other world regions. This took off first with Latin America, within the framework of the existing Columbus scheme co-sponsored by the Association of Latin-American Universities (AULA) and the European University Association (EUA). The Association of Commonwealth Universities, and the Association of Universities of Asia and the Pacific (AUAP), are also showing a growing interest in the European convergence process.

The key role of employability on the European labour market in the Bologna Process

The Bologna Process has had a strong and positive effect on the debate about the relationship between HE and professional life, in particular concerning the preparation of graduates for 'employability'. It has raised the profile of the issue, and increased the awareness that the employability of graduates has become an increasingly important and shared concern all over Europe.

The aim of the Bologna Declaration is to promote the employability of graduates on the European labour market and increase mobility, and is seen as very important and relevant by the vast majority of signatory countries. The Bologna Process is seen as underpinning national plans promoting employability for four different types of reasons:

1. Several countries stress that employability has been a long-standing guide or baseline in national HE policy and see the Bologna Declaration as reinforcing it. In Sweden, the collaboration of HE institutions, and professional and economic circles, is seen as 'generalised, natural and easy' and responsiveness to the needs of the surrounding society has been made the 'third pillar' of HE, on an equal footing with research and teaching. Similar attitudes exist in other Nordic countries. The Netherlands also sees employability as a major issue for which there is broad support from government and social partners. In France, the shift towards 'professionalisation' has been the backbone of national HE policy for three decades and is strongly reflected in the four-year contracts signed between the ministry and each university.

2. In countries where qualifications, including first degrees, have confirmed acceptance on the labour market (Ireland, UK, Sweden, Malta, Iceland), the main emphasis seems to be not so much on employment in general (graduate unemployment is low), but rather on the adjustments to specific market needs, especially in view of growing skills and labour shortages (for example, in Ireland and some Nordic countries). The introduction of the new two-year Foundation Degrees in the UK was also mainly a response to a shortage of qualified graduates at this level.

3. In countries that are candidates to EU membership, the Bologna Declaration's emphasis on employability has met other convergent calls for reform related to the process of preparation for entrance into the EU. This has been the case in all accession countries in various ways. Some regret the restrictions to access to the European labour market, which will still exist in both directions between the current EU-15 and the new member countries during the transition phase.

4. In several countries, employability is seen as a particularly important national priority as a response to high graduate unemployment. This has been stressed particularly in Italy and Spain. Greece emphasised that necessary change in this direction would require a more intensive dialogue between government, HE institutions, students and employers. In Italy, one of the most innovative aspects of the new architecture of the whole HE system introduced from 1999 is that it is also based on convergence with the labour market.

From the three aims underpinning the Bologna Declaration (mobility, employability and competitiveness), enhanced employability seems to be the most powerful source of change and reform in HE. This has been further significantly reinforced by the European Council of Lisbon in March 2000, which set the EU the ambitious goal to become the "most competitive and dynamic knowledge-based economy in the world, capable of sustainable economic growth with more and better jobs and greater social cohesion" by 2010. This new strategic line of the EU, with a strong (yet not exclusive) emphasis on growth and employment, has also contributed to guiding national agendas in education and training (in particular through the 13 European objectives set out in the work programme Education & Training 2010), as well as in research (in particular, through the development of the European Research Area, the intention to invest 3% of GDP in R&D, and the fresh emphasis put on the role of universities in the Europe of knowledge). All these developments point in the same direction as the Bologna Process, whose impact can be found mainly in three areas:

1. The most visible aspect is that the Declaration created a broad debate about employability after a first degree (Bachelor-type), for example, in Finland, Switzerland, Austria and Flanders. A few countries recall that education is not only for professional purposes (such as Spain and Belgium), and there is still some concern in the university sector that first degrees should not be

geared too narrowly to short-term needs on the labour market. In countries where Bachelor degrees were introduced about a decade ago (in particular Denmark, Finland, Czech and Slovak Republics) there is a renewed debate around the definition (or redefinition) of Bachelor degrees. The general move is clearly towards stronger attention to employment prospects, and the acquisition of core, and transferable, skills. The new qualification frameworks adopted in the UK and Ireland has a strong 'outcomes-based' emphasis, and qualifications are mostly defined in terms of skills/competencies acquired by graduates. Denmark notes that both academic and professional Bachelor degrees needed to be 'relevant' (although in not exactly the same way). Recent legislation in many countries made 'relevance to labour market' a key factor for the authorisation (or 'accreditation') of new programmes, and made the collaboration with professional bodies compulsory in the development of new curricula, such as in Italy (where employability is seen as the major change required in the new system launched in 1999), Germany, Austria, Latvia, France, Flanders and Switzerland. This is often combined with the requirement that all curricula must provide core skills (Italy, Latvia, Netherlands, Bulgaria) or with an encouragement to create shorter curricula (Estonia).

Some countries have also undertaken specific efforts to promote first-degree graduates on the labour market. In Germany, where the Conference of Ministers of Education (KMK) in March 1999, stressed market relevance as a key dimension in the new degree structure, this was reinforced by a similar emphasis in the German Employers' Association's Cologne Declaration (October 1999) on new HE qualifications. Some countries took concrete measures aimed at adjusting the statutes/laws regulating access to civil service (for example, Austria, Italy, Germany) or to regulated professions (such as Slovakia) in order to create opportunities for holders of first degrees.

2. The second impact of the Bologna Declaration's interest in employability is that it provided new impetus for the further development of the college/ polytechnic sector and for its creation in more countries. In nearly all countries with a binary system, the Declaration opened a renewed debate on the respective roles of various types of HE institutions and on the profile of their degrees. This debate has been especially intense in countries where a strong college/polytechnic sector provides a relatively high number of graduates with qualifications geared towards access to the labour market after two, three or four years. In these countries, the need for a shift towards 'employability' in the university sector is clearly not felt in the same way as in those countries where HE is mostly or exclusively found at universities.

The new impetus for professional HE has led to the creation or extension of a binary system in several countries, such as Finland, Malta, Estonia, Slovakia and Italy. Italy introduced in some regions a new sector for advanced professional education and training (FSI) with a view to creating an alternative to university education. The introduction of Foundation Degrees at British universities, although not in direct response to the Bologna Declaration, also points in the direction of the diversification of HE as a means towards broader access and easier employability. The creation of the *licence professionelle* at French universities and the introduction of professional Bachelors in several countries are on the contrary largely a response to the Bologna Declaration. The debate about Master degrees at colleges/polytechnics (see earlier in this chapter) should also be seen in this connection.

3. Finally, the Bologna Declaration has played an important role in drawing attention to the increasingly European dimension of the issue of employability, for example, in France, Malta, Latvia, Iceland and Sweden. According to Sweden, "for a small country, it is natural to develop employability for the national, European and international market in parallel with measures for mobility". In most countries the widening of the European dimension in HE qualifications is seen mainly in conjunction with the development of EU programmes for cooperation and mobility (SOCRATES, LEONARDO). Trends 3 observed a strong link between mobility and employability. In the wake of the Prague Communiqué of Ministers of Education there is also renewed attention given to the setting up of joint, integrated or double-degree courses in several countries, such as Germany and Italy (which have both created special funding possibilities for such courses), Estonia, France, Switzerland, the Czech Republic, Iceland and Denmark. Greece regrets that only a few universities/faculties are engaged in this type of curricular development in the country. A dozen countries mention the development of courses with a 'European' orientation taught in English and designed for national and foreign students alike (there are, for example, some 500 such courses in Sweden). The continuous development of European summer courses in a wide spectrum of disciplines and specialisation areas, run by a single institution or jointly by HE networks (such as UNICA or ECIU), should also be noted in this regard.

Several countries see the EU Directives on professional recognition as an important tool for the implementation of the Bologna Declaration's aims concerning employability in Europe. Accession countries are integrating in their curricula the standards set by the EU for various specific professions (for example, nurses and midwives in Poland, health professionals and teachers in Romania, and so on). These changes, while mainly related to the accession process and the *acquis communautaire*, would have happened anyway in these countries, but at the same time they underpin the objectives of the Bologna Declaration.

The above developments within the Bologna Process may be interpreted as signals of two fundamental changes in European HE:

- education is evermore integrated with economic policies as a key factor of competitiveness – both that of graduates within the European knowledge-based society and that of nations within the framework of the globalisation of technologies and markets; and
- it takes on an ever-growing European dimension, in which relevance, quality and employability are factors that need to be assessed with reference to the European, rather than to the national, space.

Although the Bologna Process now extends to the whole of Europe, these two trends were particularly reinforced within the EU context by the European Council of Lisbon in March 2000, which set the EU the goal to become the leading knowledge-based economy (and society) in the world, and underlined the need for deep changes in the areas of employment and education/training policies. In EU countries, the Bologna Process and the implementation of the Lisbon goals reinforce each other, and their combined impact is likely to bring about change more rapidly than originally expected, particularly in the areas of HE most directly related to employability.

Recent steps at European level: convergent strands of action?

On the university side, the most important document with respect to employability is the Salamanca Message of 2001, which set out a fundamental agenda for change in European universities for the coming decade. It emphasised the European tradition of HE as a 'public good' (that is, a part of public policy for social cohesiveness as well as economic development) rather than as a mere commercial commodity, and stressed the importance of university autonomy as a necessary condition for the successful implementation of the goals of the Bologna Declaration (that is, institutions not in a position to shape their curricula and adjust to the diversity of needs and opportunities will suffer from a competitive disadvantage). Another major statement in the Salamanca Message is that "European HE institutions recognise that their students need and demand qualifications which they can use effectively for the purpose of their studies and careers all over Europe" and that universities "acknowledge their role and responsibility in this regard".

On the government side, the meetings in Prague and Berlin gave ministers an opportunity to put a number of issues in the centre of attention:

- In Prague, ministers formally acknowledged that citizens must be in a position to effectively use their qualifications, competencies and skills throughout the European HE area. They underlined the role of lifelong learning, which needs to be fully acknowledged and reflected in the process, for example, in the common framework of qualifications and in credit transfer schemes. More importantly, for the first time Ministers clearly called for the development of a (single) common framework of qualifications (and for coherent quality assurance and accreditation/certification mechanisms, as a means to build up such a framework); among the tools able to promote both mobility and employability in Europe and attractiveness in the world, ministers in Prague called upon HE to increase the development of modules, courses and curricula which are 'European' by their content, orientation or organisation, in particular those leading to joint degrees.

- In Berlin, little more was added about employability issues, but ministers underlined the importance of improving the understanding and acceptance of the new qualifications, including reinforcing the importance of dialogue between HE and employers, and the need for different orientations and various profiles of qualifications in order to accommodate the diversity of needs, including those in the labour market. At the more operational level they called (again) for a framework of comparable and compatible qualifications, adding that such qualifications should be described in terms of workload, level, learning outcomes, competencies and profile. For the first time, they specifically wondered whether, and how, shorter qualifications "may be linked to the first cycle of qualification"; that is, the Bachelor level. Yet, among the various bodies involved in the follow-up work for the next two years (until the ministerial meeting in Bergen in 2005) there is still no formal representation, or even involvement, of employers or industry.

At the EU level, the Lisbon strategy has entailed significant change in the place of education/training and research/innovation on European agendas. The synergy between the Bologna Process and the 13 shared objectives set out in Education & Training 2010 has already been mentioned earlier in this chapter. It may be further stressed by way of three references:

- The first interim report on the implementation of Education & Training 2010 stresses the role of HE in achieving the Lisbon goals and the need to complement action taken within the (intergovernmental) Bologna Process by other measures falling under the purview of the EU's overall strategy.
- The same document calls for a European framework of reference for qualifications encompassing vocational education and training (in line with the Copenhagen Declaration of November 2002 on enhanced cooperation in vocational education and training (VET) and HE. The two main strands of convergent reforms in progress meet on the need to set in place this crucial instrument: it is a core part of the Bologna agenda (as expressed by ministers in Berlin) and at the same time of the Lisbon strategy, both in accordance with the Copenhagen Declaration on VET and with Objective 3.5 of the work programme Education & Training 2010.
- In a series of recent communications dealing with the Lisbon strategy, the EC put forward the view that a coherent qualification framework was a necessary condition for efficient reforms and investments in education and training, for universities to be able to play their full role in the Europe of knowledge and for the completion of the European Research Area.

The overall conclusion is therefore very clear: the Bologna agenda of convergent structural reforms has every reason to continue all over Europe and to gain acceptance, breadth, depth and speed. It is backed by a determined, if not fully unanimous, political will that was reinforced in 2001 and 2003 in milestone meetings in Salamanca, Prague and Berlin. It is fuelled by core ambitions that are unlikely to vanish or diminish in the months and years to come, in particular the need to better serve home and international students in order not to lose them, and the compelling pressure to enhance the employability of graduates on the single European labour market where they are in competition with those from other European countries and institutions. Last but not least, they are in full synergy with the new agenda on education/training and research/innovation developed in the EU context as part of the Lisbon strategy.

Notes

[1] At the time of first writing this chapter Guy Haug was Principal Advisor to the European University Association (EUA), Geneva/Brussels/Paris. He was closely associated with the preparation of the Bologna Declaration and all subsequent developments until after the ministerial meeting in Prague. This chapter was revised and updated in autumn 2003, when he was working for the EC. The views expressed here are only those of the author.

[2] Documents on the Bologna Process quoted in this chapter, including the Sorbonne Declaration of 1998 and the Bologna Declaration of 1999, the main background reports for the preparation of ministerial meetings (Trends 1 of 1999, Trends 2 of 2001 and Trends 3 of 2003) and the communiqués of the main meetings of European universities (Salamanca in 2001, Graz in 2003) and European ministers in charge of HE (Prague in 2001 and Berlin in 2003) are available at:

- www.bologna-bergen2004.no

Documents on the EU's Lisbon strategy quoted in this chapter are available from the Education/Training or the Research/Development pages of the Europa server:

- europa.eu.int/comm/education/policies/2010/et_2010_en.html
- europa.eu.int/comm/research/era/index_en.html.

ELEVEN

The expansion of higher education: economic necessity or hyperinflation?

Cécile Deer

Introduction

Concern about the expansion of higher education (HE) in western Europe and North America is not a recent phenomenon. Major changes took place in the 19th century that prepared the way for increased participation (Curtis and Boultwood, 1966) and, with the acceleration of the process since the end of the Second World War, HE has become de facto part of the national system of education in most European countries.

Recent growth has raised concerns that are not entirely dissimilar from those expressed when primary and, in particular, secondary schooling expanded during the course of the 19th and 20th centuries. The history of the development of formal education, both in terms of participation rates and the lengthening of study-time, has gone hand in hand with a critical questioning of its real necessity, its usefulness and even its potential drawbacks and dangers. Mandeville's criticisms of charity schools (Mandeville, 1732), Schumpeter's (1943) forecasts of growing dissatisfaction among 'sub-employed' graduates and today's recurrent criticisms of expansionist trends in HE in the form of the 'more means worst', 'dumbing down' or 'over-education' debates share a suspicion of the worth of educational expansion. During the second half of the 20th century, the question of educational expansion attracted much attention and the debate revolved mostly around the evaluation of its socioeconomic benefits and costs. This chapter discusses a number of assumptions, which have underpinned the formulation of this debate.

The modality of expansion of HE

The notion of 'expansion' as applied to HE is an imprecise term, which needs to be examined in terms that go beyond an increase in volume or a greater number of students passing through the system[1].

First, the aggregate level at which the problem is being considered needs to be specified. The subject of expansion has most often been tackled on a national basis without any further justification or explanation, but it may be anticipated that geographical considerations will have implications for the way the question of the modalities of expansion is to be answered. The situation in Britain, for example, shows that the question may be tackled at a cross-national level (OECD, 1998a), a national level (Dearing, 1997), a regional level (Cubie, 2000) or even at a local level (for example, the insistence of certain regional authorities on having their own university). Such differences imply considerable variations in the relative weight of the social and economic factors, which are taken into account in the debate. Defining this level is heuristically fruitful as it helps to understand the range of social, political and economic mechanisms at work behind HE expansion.

Second, past experience shows that the qualitative aspects of the various ways HE can expand are not neutral in terms of their impact on HE input, process and output. For instance, an increase in volume may not be the result of increased participation rates if the size of the relevant population has grown. On the other hand, if the size of the relevant population has decreased and volume increased, this signals increased rates of access which will have qualitative implications for the HE sector given the enduring structure of the social origins of its student intake. During the period 1990-96, in spite of the diminishing size of the relevant population, Britain was among the four OECD countries with the highest increase in tertiary enrolment (OECD, 1998a). Today, a third of all school leavers pass directly into HE and the current government's new target is to have 50% of those less than 30 years of age participating by 2005. This means that growing numbers of young people gaining access to HE now come from an educational, and often social, background with little tradition of university education. In the case of Britain (and the same would be true in many other European countries), the rapid increase in volume due to a rapid increase in participation rates has reinforced a sense of crisis within academia as this evolution has more or less directly called into question its traditional culture and values.

The last remark leads us to reflect on the pedagogical aspects of any expansion. These concern the extent to which expansion has brought about the availability of new qualifications (such as the creation of multidisciplinary courses and the relative demise of single-honour degrees), the setting-up of new degree programmes[2], the formal definition of new levels of study (for example, qualifications at sub-degree level, the development of taught Masters degrees) and/or the reorganisation of syllabuses and examination practice (such as the development of credit accumulation and transfer). For Britain, the problem may also be placed in parallel with a 'rebranding' type of expansion, whereby existing post-secondary institutions have been granted the right to deliver HE qualifications. Crosland's polytechnic initiative may be seen as such a form of expansion. The extent to which these pedagogical changes have become widespread, and even a permanent feature of a HE system, will have a considerable impact on the process and output of the sector. In particular, they are likely to breed a sense of loss and uncertainty among both academics and employers because the meaning of working towards and holding a university degree is no longer what it used to be. In this situation, two attitudes are possible: to resist or to adapt. The rhetoric of resistance tends to embrace the hyperinflationary threat posed by any further expansion of HE, whereas the rhetoric of adaptation tends to appeal to the economic and social necessity of such an evolution (Kerr, 1963; Scott, 1995).

The pedagogical aspects of expansion are influenced by its operational characteristics; that is, the extent to which it is accompanied by an adequate level of investment in general infrastructure (such as buildings, material and facilities) and staff. In this matter, part of the post-Robbins expansion in Britain in the form of newly built universities was distinct from other expansionist steps such as the creation of the Open University at the beginning of the 1970s or the funding rearrangement that preceded and accompanied the decision to bridge the binary divide at the turn of the 1990s. In the British HE system, material and staffing difficulties have been compounded by the fact that academic institutions are publicly funded institutions entrusted with two main tasks: to carry out research and to educate part of the next generation at a higher level. In this context, the qualitative aspect of the expansion of HE has been concerned with the strategic options for economic growth favoured by decision makers. These strategic options have ranged from the priority given to broadening access to undergraduate studies, with an implicit endogenous growth model based on the importance of human capital accumulation, to priority given to research activities, with an implicit exogenous growth model based on the importance of technical innovation as a driving force behind future economic growth.

In the UK, the departure from the University Grants Committee block grant funding procedures, which led to the formal separation of funding for teaching and for research activities, reflected the desire on the part of successive British governments to influence both of the above aspects in the expectation that they would contribute to economic growth. This explains why teaching activities – besides the specific case of Oxford and Cambridge – have been funded on a broadly egalitarian basis. By setting the levels of fees, clawing back funding and ruling out and then monitoring top-up fees, central governments have tried to monitor student intakes while checking unit costs. On the other hand, research money has been allocated on a government-established but academically run competitive basis, harnessing the traditional academic peer-review process to the allocation of research funding. The result has been a steady increase in student–teacher ratios, which has caused a degree of damage to the quality of the traditional university experience. This has been compounded by the fact that academics have had less time to teach and less of a career interest in teaching. In this sense, the view that university experience is being devalued as more graduates are being produced at a diminishing cost per student would contribute to a view of HE expansion as hyperinflation. On the other hand, seeing expansion as an economic necessity would imply that, regardless of the quality of the experience, time spent at university represents in any case a valuable investment for the individual and for society.

One final qualitative aspect of growth in HE is its degree of internationalisation. In the UK, since the introduction of the full-cost fee policy for non-EU students at the end of the 1970s, there has been an increased intake of non-European students on a more or less direct commercial basis (Williams, 1992). The British government's recent expectation that British universities should attract an extra 500,000 foreign students may not be entirely unconnected to this evolution. Offshoot campuses abroad also need to be seen as a form of expansion of HE. The way in which international expansion could be perceived is far removed from the way HE expansion within a strictly national, and now European, context is traditionally considered. Here, the notions of hyperinflation or economic necessity might be debated in a very different manner.

To speak of 'expansion' in relation to HE is to use a term that conveys a broadly quantitative meaning referring to numerous controversial qualitative matters. What is often at stake in the arguments that are used either to justify or question the necessity of HE expansion is not so much expansion as such, but the modality of this expansion. Having said this, we will now turn to the more elaborate arguments that have been developed concerning the likely economic and social impact of growth in HE.

The expansion of HE as an economic necessity

Various studies have claimed to show that economic growth cannot take place without an educated workforce (Solow, 1956; Carré et al, 1972; Matthews and Feinstein, 1982), but the exact nature of the causal link between the two remains undetermined. Economic growth may have taken place because of rising education in certain countries such as Germany, Britain or France, but until a clear methodology can demonstrate that historical events have persistently followed the logic that education precedes any economic development (Kindleberger, 1964), it is equally plausible to suggest that nations which have experienced fast economic growth and increased wealth have consequently been able to invest more in education. In this respect, opponents of educational expansion have perhaps been more insightful in their warnings concerning the potentially disruptive social effects of generalised and prolonged access to formal schooling[3].

Justifying expansion of HE as an economic necessity *stricto sensu* leads more or less directly to an understanding based on cost–benefit analyses of HE provision. These give rise to the well-known methodological difficulties entailed in trying to calculate not only the private but also the social returns to any given stage of formal education (OECD, 1998b; Harmon et al, 2000; Sianesi and Van Reenen, 2000). The economic theory which underpins this exercise and which has informed the debate on the necessity of educational expansion over the last 30 years or so is human capital theory. Proponents of human capital accumulation have emphasised the correlation between education and income to argue that the general training and qualifications of workers play a key role in a country's economic growth (Schultz, 1963, 1971, 1981, 1990). This has been argued from both micro- and macro-economic perspectives.

In micro-economic terms, the understanding has been that individuals can acquire sets of aptitudes, mostly in relation to health and education, such as hygiene or knowledge, which have a direct bearing on their average income throughout their lives. Thus wage differentials between individuals are said to reflect differentials between their own private investments in human capital. The higher salaries that educated entrants are able to command on the job market represent both the interest on the capital they have invested in education and the fact that they have become more productive by having invested, regardless of the type of education they have received. For any individual, accumulating human capital is the equivalent of an investment that builds up his/her initial endowment and in turn increases his/her productivity. The individual's increased earnings may measure an approximate valuation of this increased productivity. These higher earnings are then an incentive for individuals to invest even further and to acquire higher qualifications. In a longer perspective, education has also been presented as a protection against unemployment as it makes individuals more entrepreneurial and adaptable through increased flexibility in the face of change and difficulties. A reverse corollary of this understanding is that when employers are prepared to hire less qualified people, rates of participation in formal education decrease accordingly as the possibility of earning an immediate salary increases the opportunity cost of staying longer in formal education.

From what precedes it should be clear that human capital theory relies on the implicit understanding that, through education, the individual acquires competences and skills, which are essentially transferable and negotiable on the employment market. It presumes that the type of capital accumulated through education comes in the form of a body of knowledge and a set of personal abilities/qualities that cannot only be acquired by anyone, but which also have a transactional value. The difficulty lies in the methodological problems there are in measuring human capital empirically. An approximate value for accumulated human capital has often been reached using the aggregate value of the capacities acquired by individuals, which yield greater income. Human capital has thus been evaluated as a hardly specified accumulation of educational credentials of individuals. The length of their schooling has been used as a proxy to measure the stock of their accumulated competences, which may be exchanged and traded on the job market (Blaug, 1987). However, rapid changes in employment conditions, the future macro-economic environment[1], technical innovation and skills obsolescence are among the variables that throw into question the full validity of the human capital model applied to the individual.

At a macro-level, analysis has focused on the impact of the various factors, which are known to contribute to economic growth. In this matter, it has proved particularly difficult to distinguish and separate the respective contribution of the technological infrastructure and know-how of human capital, understood as the quantitative and qualitative characteristics of the workforce, measured by using the average educational level of the population (OECD, 1998b). In fact, a combination of both is important if higher growth is to be achieved (Fernández, 2001). Furthermore, to calculate the overall rate of return to society of any gains due to extra output found to have been achieved through educational expansion, one needs to offset it with the cost of providing this education. For the period 1960-95, the social rate of return of tertiary education for OECD countries has been estimated at more than 10% (Mingat and Tan, 1996), but whether this estimate provides solid grounds for justifying further expansion at this educational level is another matter.

With the rapid introduction and development of new techniques and technologies, it is reasonable to think that more investment in education in industrialised countries will help boost future rates of economic growth. However, whether this will generate for individuals and society returns on the scale of the two-digit figures that are currently being advanced to justify expansion remains to be seen. In purely economic terms, this may turn out to be a speculative bubble. The main difficulty lies in that the human capital understanding provides little qualitative and quantitative insight regarding the various forms of human capital an educational system should help create in order to secure economic growth. The question that remains to be answered is whether it is possible to assume that greater participation in HE will lead to an optimal return in this matter. Human capital theory offers a one-sided explanation based on the demand for expansion in education, but it is not as helpful when it comes to understanding the role of the supply side (Dearden et al, 2000) for it considers education and training to be like any other goods with supply adjusting to demand. This may be true for certain specific types of short-term training programmes but for various reasons, mostly related to time lag, it does not reflect accurately what is happening in other parts of the HE sector. This suggests numerous sources of market failure, such as uncertainties, asymmetrical information or risk avoidance behaviour. Meanwhile, policy makers eager to match supply to perceived demand are promoting both the vocationalisation and the specialisation of education as well as greater breadth and variety in knowledge transmission (Blunkett, 2001). The perennial question remains, which type of educational investment today – secondary, vocational or higher forms of post-secondary education – would be most likely to generate an adequate rate of growth while securing an equitable redistribution of the wealth created (Dearden et al, 2000)? In OECD countries, we can already see that if, at an individual level, tertiary education brings about greater marginal benefit than upper secondary schooling in the form of higher incomes, the same is not systematically true with regard to social rates of return. This observation has been used to justify greater private contributions to the cost of HE (OECD, 1998b; Greenaway and Haynes, 2000).

International comparative studies have also highlighted the effects of certain educative practices on the world of work (Prais and Wagner, 1985) pointing, in qualitative terms, to types of human capital accumulation that are best promoted by certain ways of organising educational systems. If education and training play a major role in labour productivity in terms of greater flexibility on the job, better machine maintenance, product quality, production and delivery schedules, greater efficiency is achieved not only when the quantitative needs of businesses and enterprises are known but also when certain qualitative aspects of the educational system are recognised or publicised. In particular, the way educational systems are organised can, to a greater or lesser extent, increase the trend for upward credentialism. For instance, in countries such as France where university degrees are recognised nationally and on a strong egalitarian basis, 'inflation' can occur because students continue studying at a HE level using HE qualifications as a signalling device. On the other hand, the absence of a formal national recognition of university degrees in the US may have fed into employers' demands for higher qualifications, which would indicate that HE qualifications have been increasingly used as a screening device. Aggregate corporate strategies at regional and national level can have a large impact on educational structures and strategies (Finegold and Soskice, 1988).

Despite the issues and deficiencies surrounding evidence of the returns to education (Harmon et al, 2000), the strength and visibility of human capital theory has lain in the fact that it shows in theory that there has been a utilitarian type of convergence between the individual and the general interest. Large investments in human capital have repeatedly been presented as a major source of economic strength, of greater efficiency in the use of the workforce and of increased wealth distribution. With education being shown to have a positive effect on labour productivity, which in neoclassical terms is identified with the wage rate in a situation of equilibrium, the conclusion has been that an ever greater accumulation of education stock is fundamental not only for increasing wages but also for equalising them. Education at all levels has therefore been presented not only as a social investment that can contribute to economic growth, but also as a means of achieving greater equity in the distribution of the wealth it helps to create. The fact that the neoclassical understanding is based on a conception of the individual as entrepreneurial and discerning in his/her choice of resource and time allocation is a major assumption that helps to shape this theoretical convergence.

Since the 1960s, human capital theorists have presented education as one of the most productive means of growth investment while at the same time they have upheld it as an equalising social device. It is on this premise that they have met those sociologists who have underlined the correlation between education and status to show education to be an efficient means of opening up professional opportunities and of reducing the impact of family backgrounds on individuals' achievement (Parsons, 1959; Bernbaum, 1977).

The sociological perspective on expansion of HE and the notion of hyperinflation

The sociological debate on education has revolved around the differing degrees of recognition of two aspects of education: on the one hand, the selecting, screening and allocating function and, on the other hand, the potential to help to promote meritocratic social mobility. In the light of these terms of understanding, political discourses – in line with general public expectations – have persistently supported education and access to HE as an effective instrument in the equalisation of life and social chances for individuals. It is notoriously difficult to determine the 'push' and 'pull' factors that have been at work in this matter but the result is that, over the last 30 years, western democracies have effectively been putting into practice the human capital theory which upholds the intrinsic worth of human capital accumulation in the form of increased educational stocks, with HE fitting more and more into this picture.

It has been shown that this general increase in schooling level has been accompanied by a modification of the direct relation between academic titles and their traditionally associated social status (Collins, 1979; Halsey et al, 1980). In Britain, throughout the 1970s, 1980s and 1990s, the time-series pattern of the relative supply of highly educated workers and wage changes shows that there has been a dampening down of wages in response to increased supply (Machin, 1999). Over the years, increasingly qualified staff have filled similar jobs as more people with higher qualifications have emerged from the educational system. In this sense, the case of nurses in Britain or of schoolteachers in France may be considered as symptomatic. Periods of unemployment for graduates or sub-degree level occupations illustrate the growing gap between the nominal value of degrees and their market value in real transactional situations. This goes a long way towards explaining the semantic shift in relation to expansion in HE to terms such as 'hyperinflation' and the 'devaluation of diplomas'.

Various sociological explanations have been put forward to interpret this phenomenon (Boudon, 1969; Bourdieu and Passeron, 1970; Bourdieu, 1973). For the neo-Durkheimian school of thought the rapid expansion of HE has exposed the symbolic dimension that has always been implicitly embedded in university titles through the social and cultural representation of their rarity (Bourdieu, 1973). Academic symbols have multiplied rapidly but this has combined with relative stasis in socio-professional organisations and stratifications, in income distribution, in cultural representations or in social strategies. In the case of Britain, it may be said that the systematic discrepancy that has existed between, on the one hand, the actual state and status of the academic sector and, on the other hand, the cultural representation of academia and the social strategies related to the social representation of academic titles, has helped successive governments to justify their reforms of quantitative expansion and decreasing unit costs.

In the short term, the process of expansion in HE tends to expose variations in the certifying effect of university diplomas as the number of candidates joining the employment market outstrips the number of graduate jobs that are available. This explains the growing use of the notions of 'sub-employed' graduates or an over-educated workforce (Chevalier, 2000). Meanwhile, employers revert to more stringent selectivity in their recruitment practices, which has the paradoxical but understandable effect of reinforcing the role of higher-level diplomas and qualifications as selection criteria. This explains why analysts are able to emphasise repeatedly the perpetuation of the professional advantages conferred by a degree. This remains a broad claim and, in the medium term, the situation in Britain might come to resemble that of the US where HE expanded at an earlier stage. This would mean a reshaping of a job market previously stratified according to educational attainment into 'waiting lists' for available jobs, with each person's place being strongly influenced by the level and the type of diploma held. In this case, the positioning of degree holders remains a relatively strong one but any direct conclusions concerning the impact of an increase in the average qualification of members of the population on the overall productivity of the workforce would be overstretched.

The central assumption of human capital theory – that better qualified workers and employees are more productive than their non-qualified counterparts – has been questioned from an early stage (Berg, 1970). However, more significant for the overall debate is the possibility that the lengthening of average schooling time may lead to a reinforcement of social inequalities, with a decrease in the variance in wage distribution corresponding to each level of education but an increase in the difference between the mean salaries that correspond to these different levels of education (Thurow, 1975). This suggests that by bringing financial rewards not entirely related to productivity, the expansion of HE could bring about greater social stratification.

At this point, we have moved from the human capital interpretation, which, because it was centred on the notion of increased productivity, was implicitly focused on a function of education concerning skills transmission and knowledge acquisition, to an interpretation that puts a premium on the changing relative worth of individual profiles and on the selective social function of education. Likewise, since the end of the Second World War, the sociological debate surrounding expansion in education has revolved around two main notions: democratisation, which has been implicitly rooted in a modern agenda, and reproduction, which has been potentially leading to a 'postmodern' one. In the 1960s, those who sought to justify expansion in HE presented it as a source of personal and social liberation. Thus the Robbins Report (Scott, 1988) endorsed and encouraged HE reforms for socio-economic purposes in the name of an ethical and political ideal. The image of the 'untapped pool of abilities' was used to justify expansion on the basis of the equalisation of social chances and the democratisation of education. What was implicitly expected was that unhindered expansion would eventually bring the sector to a natural state of equilibrium where all those who would have previously been deprived of a HE experience for mere structural reasons would legitimately find a place in the system. The 'untapped pool' image was used to denounce forms of institutional and social resistance and inertia directly linked to the selective educational practice of socially stratified societies. The universities were particularly exposed to such criticisms.

At about the same time, in line with the then prevailing systemic and structural strand of socio-political understanding, the reproduction school of thought developed its influential theory of social mechanisms based on the principle that all societies tend to reproduce their constitutive structures, most notably their social classes. Educational systems, in particular at their final selective stages, figured prominently in the understanding of the causes of these phenomena since it was argued that their main role was to justify social reproduction at work within all modern societies on supposedly objective grounds (Bourdieu and Passeron, 1970; Bourdieu, 1996). The message was clear: whatever the degree of expansion in formal education and whatever its cause and impetus, the dominant groups would always manage to influence and re-stratify the system in the name of objective educational practice in order to preserve their social advantages.

With its polymorphous heuristic apparatus, reproduction theory has proved to be as appealing as it has been self-closing, not to mention self-contradictory (Alexander, 2000). However, there is no denying that an important component of the value of a diploma, represented first and foremost by its transactional value in terms of earnings on the job market, obeys an ensemble of cultural laws which are as much a system of practice in relation to established rules as they are a system of rules which bring about a hierarchy of values and forms of legitimacy (Bernstein, 1975). This interpretation goes some way towards explaining the repeated incidence of 'academic drift' that has accompanied attempts at reforming secondary and tertiary education towards more vocationally-oriented syllabuses in countries such as Britain and France (Prost, 1992).

Repeated failures at trying to regulate educational inflow both quantitatively and qualitatively has spurred empirical forms of research to try to understand the logic of expansion and social stratification in education from the actors' points of view. What these have shown is that, at the level of the individual, the choice to continue into HE remains a rational one in the sense that, as expansion gathers pace, the risk involved in not participating becomes increasingly great. It is generally rational for individuals to try to acquire the highest possible level of qualification. The expansion of HE and its unintended 'hyperinflationary' consequence emerge as the result of an accumulation and combination of individual strategies (Boudon, 1973; Robinson, 1999). These conclusions based on methodological individualism, that is to say on the premise that sociological understanding is best achieved through an analysis of the meaning and actions of its participants, have been shadowed by the understanding based on game theory borrowed from the economic field (Turner, 1992).

Finally, what seems paradoxical when considering the traditional economic model of demand in education, based on the opportunity costs of studying, is that there should be any increased demand for HE qualifications when this increase appears to be concurrent with a devaluation of job opportunities for degree holders. This puts into question the axioms of the rational choice approach. However, it has been suggested that the two phenomena may be reconciled if one takes into account students' control over the use of their time (Eicher and Levy-Garboua, 1979)[5]. University degrees remain broadly attractive because of the certifying structure of a university education. In this context, the modularisation of the time spent studying allows the students to lower the opportunity cost of working towards a degree while contributing to the quantitative expansion of HE (for example, the increasing number of part-time students). On the other hand, the reduction in the cost of study may be said to compensate for the perceived decrease in the rate of return on diplomas; this is often obtained at the expense of the probability of success in examinations, hence the rise in student dropout rates. A direct implication of the latter explanation is that any increase in the direct costs of studying in the form of increased fees or cuts in public subsidies to students, as has occurred in Britain, will have the greatest impact on those from poorer social backgrounds because they react in priority to the worsening of their immediate circumstances. In the long run, the development of part-time jobs for students combined with increased dropout rates could worsen the job market positioning of non-graduates and play in favour of renewed individual educational investment. The problem here is that in the context of an open economy with significant wage differentials, as is the case in Britain (Machin, 1999), economic models suggest that the possibility of this happening on a basis of equal opportunity is becoming increasingly remote (Turrini, 1997).

The expansion of HE: a complex logic

The overall expansion of HE has increased uncertainty and the chances of downward mobility for traditional users of the system without significantly increasing upward mobility opportunities for newcomers, thereby providing more demand for HE (Archer, 1982). Rapid skills obsolescence due to accelerating technological innovations has reinforced this phenomenon. At the same time, the relative importance of elements other than merit, as measured by educational achievement, has increased in social selection (Brown, 1990), illustrating how expansion of education can occur without a significant reduction in social inequalities.

The result is that, today, expansion of HE in its traditional form appears to be:

1. a socio-political necessity in terms of input (that is, who gets access). In the case of Britain, it is interesting to note that rapid expansion in HE has coincided with the end of the long-standing debate concerning the legitimacy of private schooling at secondary level;
2. an economic necessity in terms of process (that is, local job creation and demographic vitality, invisible exports); and

3. a qualitative question mark in terms of output and, by implication, in terms of process.

In this context, the rise of the use of terms such as 'devaluation of diplomas', 'hyperinflation' or 'over-education' points essentially to the loosening of the direct relation, which formerly existed, between university degrees and their social recognition. The expansion process has laid bare the fact that what has been at stake in gaining a university experience are the social benefits that such an experience is expected to confer. In England, this has provided an acid test for the liberal academic ethos as few have hailed expansion and the conditions in which it has taken place as a success for the disinterested pursuit of knowledge. Today, few are those who see the bottle as half-full rather than half-empty or, in other words, who still champion what was strongly argued for previously: the development of education and knowledge in society regardless of graduate job opportunities. It was thought the democratisation of HE would be achieved through equal opportunities for access to a university education. Today, the focus has shifted to other aspects of expansion. Decreasing unit costs in universities, increasing government intervention in academic affairs, higher average private returns than social returns from HE and now also the realisation that it is possible on an individual basis to gain a university degree without getting access to a graduate job, have figured among the reasons advanced in order to try to go beyond the human capital and democratisation approaches that have underpinned expansion of HE. These have formed the basis of current reforms proposed by certain economists, think tanks, UK university representatives and political leaders, the long-term implications of which will need a thorough assessment.

Notes

[1] In the UK, this kind of expansion has been particularly rapid in recent years.

[2] The debate and objections triggered by the setting up of degrees in golf course management or football coaching is an interesting case in point.

[3] Mandeville's remarks for instance, are interesting in the light of Alexis de Tocqueville's interpretations of the causes of the French Revolution. Schumpeter's forecast combined with sociological interpretations such as those developed by Pierre Bourdieu raise interesting questions concerning the 1968 student riots in western democracies.

[4] The economic redistribution of productivity gains is also a matter for social bargaining. One can argue that, in normal circumstances, the need to provide pensions to larger cohorts of retired generations combined with competitive pressures arising from increasingly globalised and integrated economies will help keep salaries down. This calls into question the direct link salaries are believed to entertain with workers' productivity.

[5] This is influenced by: (1) their current incomes (parental and public subsidies, small jobs, etc); (2) their current quality of life (entertainment, food, accommodation, etc); and (3) the likelihood of future benefits arising from graduate job opportunities.

References

Alexander, J. (2000) *La réduction: Critique de Bourdieu*, Paris: Edition du Cerf.

Archer, M. (1982) *The sociology of educational expansion: Take-off, growth and inflation in educational systems*, London: Sage Publications.

Berg, I. (1970) *Education and jobs: The great training robbery*, New York, NY: Praeger Publishers.

Bernbaum, G. (1977) *Knowledge and ideology in the sociology of education*, London: Macmillan.

Bernstein, B. (1975) *Langage et classes sociales*, Paris: Editions de Minuit.

Blaug, M. (1987) *Where are we now in the economics of education?*, Aldershot: Edward Elgar.

Blunkett, D. (2001) *Education into employability: The role of the DfEE in the economy*, London: DfEE.

Boudon, R. (1969) 'La crise universitaire française: essai de description sociologique', *Annales*, vol 3, p 24.

Boudon, R. (1973) *L'inégalité des chances*, Paris: Colin.

Bourdieu, P. (1973) *L'inflation des titres scolaires*, Montreal: Université de Montréal.

Bourdieu, P. (1996) *The state nobility: Elite schools in the field of power*, Cambridge: Polity Press.

Bourdieu, P. and Passeron, J.-C. (1970) *La reproduction: Éléments pour une théorie du système d'enseignement*, Paris: Editions de Minuit.

Brown, P. (1990) 'The "Third Wave": education and the ideology of parentocracy', *British Journal of Sociology of Education*, vol 11, pp 65-85.

Carré J.J., DuBois, P. and Malimvaude, E. (1972) *La croissance française: Un essai d'analyse économique causale de l'après-guerre*, Paris: Seuil.

Chevalier, A. (2000) *Graduate over-education in the UK*, London: Centre for the Economics of Education, London School of Economics and Political Science.

Collins, R. (1979) *The credential society: An historical sociology of education and stratification*, New York, NY: Academic Press.

Cubie, A. (2000) *Higher education: Student finance: Minutes of evidence fairness for the future*, London: The Stationery Office.

Curtis, S. and Boultwood, M. (1966) *An introductory history of English education since 1800*, London: University Tutorial Press.

Dearden, L., McIntosh, S., Myck, M. and Vignoles, A. (2000) *The returns to academic and vocational qualifications in Britain*, London: Centre for the Economics of Education, London School of Economics and Political Science.

Dearing, R. (1997) *Higher education in the learning society – Report of the national committee of inquiry into higher education: Main report*, London: NCIHE.

Eicher, J.C. and Levy-Garboua, J. (1979) *Economique de l'education. Travaux français*, Paris: Economica.

Fernández, R. (2001) *Workforce flexibility in the presence of technological change*, Oxford: ESRC-funded Centre on Skills, Knowledge and Organisational Performance.

Finegold, D. and Soskice, D. (1988) 'The failure of training in Britain: analysis and prescription', *Oxford Review of Economic Policy*, vol 4, pp 21-53.

Greenaway, D. and Haynes, M. (2000) *Funding universities to meet national and international challenges*, Nottingham: University of Nottingham.

Halsey, A., Heath, A. and Ridge, J. (1980) *Origins and destinations. Family, class, and education in modern Britain*, Oxford: Clarendon Press.

Harmon, C., Oosterbeek, H. and Walker, I. (2000) *The returns to education: A review of evidence, issues and deficiencies in the literature*, London: Centre for the Economics of Education, London School of Economics and Political Science.

Kerr, C. (1963) *The uses of the university*, Cambridge, MA: Harvard University Press.

Kindleberger, C. (1964) *Economic growth in France and Britain: 1851-1950*, Cambridge, MA: Harvard University Press.

Machin, S. (1999) 'Wage inequality in the 1970s, 1980s and 1990s', in P. Gregg and J. Wadsworth (eds) *The state of working Britain*, Manchester and New York, NY: Manchester University Press, pp 185-204.

Mandeville, B. (1732) *The fable of the bees; Or, private vices, public benefits*, London: J. Tonson.

Matthews, R. and Feinstein, C.H. (1982) *British economic growth, 1856-1973*, Oxford: Clarendon Press.

Mingat, A. and Tan, J. (1996) *The full social returns to education: Estimates based on countries' economic growth performance*, Washington DC: World Bank.

OECD (1998a) *Education at a glance: OECD indicators 1998*, Paris: OECD Centre for Educational Research and Innovation.

OECD (1998b) *Human capital investment: An international comparison*, Paris: OECD Centre for Education Research and Innovation.

Parsons, T. (1959) 'The school class as a social system: some of its function in American society', *Harvard Educational Review*, vol 29, no 4, pp 297-378.

Prais, S. and Wagner, K. (1985) 'Schooling standards in England and Germany: some summary comparisons bearing on economic performance', *National Institute Economic Review*, no 112, pp 53-76.

Prost, A. (1992) *Education, société et politiques: Une histoire de l'enseignement en France de 1945 à nos jours*, Paris: Seuil.

Robinson, P. (1999) 'Education, training and the youth labour market', in P. Gregg and J. Wadsworth (eds) *The state of working Britain*, Manchester and New York, NY: Manchester University Press, pp 147-67.

Schultz, T. (1963) *The economic value of education*, New York, NY and London: Columbia University Press.

Schultz, T. (1971) *Investment in human capital: The role of education and research*, New York and London: Free Press and Collier-Macmillan.

Schultz, T. (1981) *Investing in people: The economics of population quality*, Berkeley, CA and London: University of California Press.

Schultz, T. (1990) *Restoring economic equilibrium: Human capital in the modernizing economy*, Oxford: Blackwell.

Schumpeter, J. (1943) *Capitalism, socialism and democracy*, London: Allen & Unwin.

Scott, P. (1988) 'Blueprint or blue remembered hills? The relevance of the Robbins Report to the present reforms of HE', *Oxford Review of Education*, vol 14, no 1, pp 33-48.

Scott, P. (1995) *The meaning of mass higher education*, Buckingham: Society for Research into Higher Education and Open University Press.

Sianesi, B. and Van Reenen, J. (2000) *The returns to education: A review of the macro-economic literature*, London: Centre for the Economics of Education, London School of Economics and Political Science.

Solow, R. (1956) 'A contribution to the theory of economic growth', *The Quarterly Journal of Economics*, vol 70, no 1, pp 65-94.

Thurow, L. (1975) *Generating inequality, mechanism of distribution in the US economy*, New York, NY: Basic Books.

Turner, D. (1992) 'Game theory in comparative education: prospects and propositions', in J. Schriewer and B. Holmes (eds) *Theories and methods in comparative education*, Berne: Peter Lang, pp 143-64.

Turrini, A. (1997) *Human capital formation in an open economy with increasing wage differentials*, Torino and Oxford: Centro Studi Luca d'Agliano and University of Oxford, Queen Elizabeth House.

Williams, G. (1992) *Changing patterns of finance in HE*, Buckingham: Society for Research into Higher Education and Open University Press.

TWELVE

Becoming a chef: the politics and culture of learning

Susan James and Geoff Hayward

Introduction

A recurrent theme through the chapters in this book is the desire on the part of policy makers to reform their nation's education and training systems. A clear objective is to bring education and training systems into closer alignment with perceived labour market needs. To achieve this, a leitmotif in the political rhetoric of education and training reform is the implementation of new technologies of outcomes-based assessment. For example, the discussions of the EC's Technical Working Group (cedefop.communityzero.com/credit-transfer) on credit transfer in vocational education and training (VET) have indicated that:

> in addition to measuring the duration of training or equivalent work load there must also be a basic understanding about qualitative elements describing the outcomes in terms of knowledge, skills and competences which are necessary to perform in different job roles and work situations within a sector, labour market segment or an occupational family [and] that learning performance it was agreed thus far should be measured towards outcomes.

Identifying and measuring such outcomes and competences, it is believed, will enable a transparent system of qualifications to be developed at both national and international levels. This may be a desirable aim but achieving it, once a technology for describing and assessing outcomes has been developed, is too often seen as a mere matter of changing systems and producing new qualifications that will then be adopted by both the supply and demand side of the skills equation. However, the chapters by Stanton and Bailey (Chapter Two), Ertl (Chapter Seven), Haug (Chapter Ten) and Deer (Chapter Eleven) speak to the social, political and economic challenges inherent in implementing such reform.

The rather naive techno-rationalistic view of reform alluded to earlier is embedded within a wider politics of learning that largely ignores the cultures of learning embedded in the social practices of workplaces. This politics is mobilized within a discourse that:

- creates unitary constructs of 'employer' and 'worker' necessary to construct national systems of qualifications;
- emphasises deregulation of labour markets in order to increase labour flexibility; and
- redefines concepts such as skill in ways that emphasize the responsibility of individuals to maintain their employability in a globalised economy, rather than the role of the political collective in maintaining opportunities for people to live fulfilling lives.

In this chapter, we wish to reflect on how the politics of learning can clash with established cultures of learning within which the meaning of key terms, such as competence and outcomes, take on quite different meanings from those in official policy discourses. We illustrate such a clash by focusing on one occupation – chefs – in England. This allows us to explore the development over the last 25 years of a competence-based approach to certification of skills in this occupation via National Vocational Qualifications (NVQs) which, we will argue, has been largely ineffectual in making headway against a culture of learning that is long established, favours an alternative conception of competence to that promoted within the NVQ system and places great value on a particular process of learning.

The origin of NVQs – the politics of learning

The repeal of the Statute of Artificers in 1814 represented the end of almost 250 years of state regulation of apprenticeship in England. For some authors (for example, Ryan and Unwin, 2001), the repeal represents the point at which the importance of apprenticeship as a mode of skill formation began to decline in England. Despite successive investigations of the state of Technical and Vocational Education and Training (TVET) from the 1850s onwards, the English state's involvement in TVET remained minimal until the late 1970s (see Chapter Two). There was, for example, no concerted attempt by the state to develop its role as the holder of an arena in which social partners could discuss the structure of professions and occupations, and the training appropriate to enter into them, as in Germany (Chapter Seven).

However, by the late 1970s to early 1980s, with increasing levels of youth unemployment, and civil unrest in the English inner cities, there was a feeling of widespread concern about the adequacy of the English VET system in preparing young people for and in work. For example, the plethora of unrelated vocational education and training initiatives developed from 1960 onwards were strongly criticised for failing to add up to an overall national strategy or system of vocational education (Ainley, 1990), and for lacking an effective interface with formal schooling and higher education (HE). In policy terms, part of the solution to this concern was a turn to outcomes-based assessment in the form of NVQs.

The history of these qualifications, and the notion of competence embedded in them, is well known (for example, see Hyland, 1994) and will only briefly be reviewed here. The DeVille Committee's report led to the publication of the 1986 White Paper *Working together – Education and training*. This paper "reinforced the need to have established standards of competence" (Debling, 1991, p 6). Subsequently, the National Council for Vocational Qualifications (NCVQ) was established "with the remit to take the lead in the reform of vocational qualifications. A target date of 1991 was set for an operational system of competence-based vocational qualifications, which fully reflects the foreseeable needs of modern day employment" (Debling, 1991, p 6). After the publication of the 1986 White Paper, developments began almost immediately and gained momentum. The New Occupational Standards Branch was set up at the Manpower Services Commission (MSC), and the Standards Programme was instigated, both leading to the development of occupational standards – "standards which spelt out exactly what someone doing a particular job had to be able to do" (Hayward, 1997, p 19). These standards became the basis for constructing NVQs.

The new framework for vocational education and training was described in the White Paper 'Employment for the 1990s' (Department of Education, 1988). This White Paper was arguably the most prescriptive and centralised example of VET reform in England since the Statute of Artificers in 1563. Developing a new system needed to take account of and address at least four desirable political ends:

- constructing a VET system that was coherent and responsive to the needs of employers and so increase their demand for, and investment in, training. This, it was envisaged, would raise productivity thereby stimulating economic growth and employment;
- developing a demand-led system would also overcome the perceived problems of 'supplier capture' in the provision of VET by prioritising the certification of on-the-job learning, thereby freeing learning from the tyranny of inputs and time serving, while also overcoming barriers to access erected by training providers;
- improving the quality of existing training programmes, especially the youth training scheme, by forcing employers to train to agreed standards; and
- making the training system more accountable for its expenditure of public money by linking funding to the production of outcomes.

To some extent at least, the design of the new VET system, based upon qualifications awarded through an outcomes-based assessment process that certified competence in a job role, needed to meet these political demands. However, in so doing it had to be a national system of qualifications which, as

Eraut (2001, p 94; emphasis in original) notes led to some important design problems:

> The most novel aspect of NVQs was to prioritise on-the-job learning and make it the central spine of the qualification. Previously, work-related learning in college classes had been accorded priority in assessment and sometimes also in learning effort; but now its role was reduced to subsidiary support for on-the-job learning; and learning was 'liberated' from having to be based in education settings. The term 'competence' was selected as appropriate for its declared purpose of accrediting only effective performance in the workplace; but NVQs also had to be *national* qualifications. So what might have been a bottom-up, evidence-based approach to the specification of competence became a committee-driven project, supported by consultants, to develop a set of National Occupational Standards.

Underpinning the utility of this approach to up-skilling the workforce are a set of assumptions, three of which are examined in the remainder of this chapter in the context of learning to be a chef. First, that the National Occupational Standards developed through the top-down process described by Eraut would be readily adopted and valued by employers. Second, that the version of competence adopted by the NVQ model would supersede existing conceptions of competence already being used to judge effective performance in the workplace. Third, NVQs would be valued as signals of occupational competence by employers regardless of the learning processes through which the knowledge and skill underpinning competence had been constructed.

In order to test these assumptions, we draw upon two sources of evidence. First, the development and evaluation of the CATERBASE project and, second, the results of an intensive ethnographic study of apprentice chefs undertaken by one of the authors (James) and supervised by the other (Hayward).

The CATERBASE project

The first formal attempt to develop an NVQ-like qualification occurred in 1985 when the MSC, in contractual agreement with what was then the Hotel and Catering Board (now the Hospitality Training Foundation [HTF]), developed CATERBASE. A little-known report produced for the MSC in 1988, *The CATERBASE project: Workplace assessment and accreditation for the hotel and catering industry. Report on the first two years to the MSC*, provides details of the background to the project (HCTB, 1988, p 5):

> During the period described [the early 1980s], the Government was detailing its own priorities for education and training provision. The 1981 White Paper, "A New Training Initiative", set out three major national objectives for the future of training. These were subsequently reaffirmed in the 1984 White Paper "Training for Jobs" as:

1 better preparation in schools and colleges for working life and better arrangements for the transition from full time education to work;

2 modernisation of training in occupational skills (including apprenticeships) particularly to replace outdated age limits and time serving with training to agreed standards of skill appropriate to the jobs available;

3 wider opportunities for adults to acquire and improve their skills.

In order to progress these objectives, the Manpower Services Commission agreed to finance a project, subsequently called CATERBASE, to develop work-based assessment and accreditation within the hotel and catering industry. The project, while advancing the objectives of the government's New Training Initiative, was very much in accord with the needs identified by the hotel and catering industry itself. It began on May 1st 1985.

In July 1986, the government published the White Paper 'Working Together – Education and Training', in which it accepted the recommendations of a Review of Vocational Qualifications and announced:

> the creation of a new framework of National Vocational Qualifications in England, Wales and Northern Ireland, to be developed and supervised by a new National Council for Vocational Qualifications. This will allow people to demonstrate clearly what they can do as well as what they know; and to progress with ease to learning and acquiring more skills without going back over ground already covered.

This development served to reinforce the philosophy and intentions underlying the Caterbase project.

The competences to be assessed were identified using a 'hierarchical task analysis approach', and 'a standard format' was devised for presenting competences in a modular format. The elements within this standard format were (HCTB, 1988, p 20):

1. TITLE A short statement of the activity covered by the module.
2. NUMBER A unique reference number which identified the module and located it within the overall structure.
3. AIM An expansion of the module title which concisely described the activity covered by the module in an unambiguous way.
4. COMPETENCE OBJECTIVE(S) The major component activities or tasks of the module identifying
5. PERFORMANCE CRITERIA The critical outcomes of the activity identified for the purposes of assessment.
6. NOTES Points of clarification, expansion or explanation to the performance criteria, but not in themselves performance criteria.

The resemblance of NVQs to the CATERBASE modules in terms of development, methodology and particularly in module design and assessment, is striking. This accreditation approach, based on assessing competence in the workplace, had not been used previously in the vocational education sector in the UK (HCTB, 1988).

The CATERBASE project was evaluated by Psychometric Research and Development (PRD) in two areas, the north east and north west of England, between January and May 1987. Their report, *The PRD evaluation of CATERBASE: Early delivery in hotel and catering YTS schemes* (PRD, 1988), is used as an additional source of evidence about the effectiveness of the move to an outcomes-based approach to the training of apprentice chefs.

An ethnographic study

This involved one of the authors of this chapter (Susan James) working as a participant observer alongside four first-year apprentice chefs in three different kitchens. Each of these apprentices was male and aged 16 years. The kitchens ranged from a large institutional catering facility producing hundreds of meals a day on a fixed budget, to a small, top of the range restaurant producing 100–200 meals per day in order to make a profit. Data collected included detailed field notes constructed over one month of participant observation in each kitchen, and interviews with the apprentices and experienced chefs. These data were used to construct thick descriptions of the activity within the kitchen and to develop models of learning for the apprentices as they moved on their trajectories from peripheral to full participants in the kitchen 'community of practice' (see James, 2004, for further methodological details).

The apprentice chefs in this study were working towards completing a Foundation Modern Apprenticeship (FMA), with a Level 2 NVQ as the main qualification they were seeking to attain. Such an NVQ is set out with three components: NVQ title, units of competence and elements of competence, with their associated performance criteria. Table 12.1 provides an example of an NVQ element with its performance criteria, range and relevant underpinning knowledge taken from the Level 2 BTEC NVQ Catering & Hospitality Food Preparation and Cooking Candidate Guidance and Log Book (Edexcel, 1999).

The apprentices in this study supplemented their on-the-job learning through engagement in the normal work of a kitchen either, in the case of two of the apprentices, through off-the-job learning at a local further education (FE) college or, in the case of the other two apprentices, through work with a Private Training Provider (PTP). In the case of the latter this involved little more than the PTP visiting the workplace to act as an assessor and signing off the apprentice's portfolio in which they recorded the evidence needed to demonstrate they were achieving the various performance criteria for the NVQ elements.

Table 12.1: Mandatory Unit 1FPC1 from Level 2 BTEC NVQ

Unit: 1FPC1 Clean food production areas, equipment and utensils

Element: 1FPC1.1 Clean food production areas

Performance criteria:

1. Clean sinks and hand basins then check that they are clean and free flowing.
2. Clean floors and walls in line with service operations.
3. Clean drains, gullies traps and overflows and check they are free flowing.
4. Check that surfaces, shelving, cupboards and drawers are hygienic and ready for use.
5. Use suitable cleaning equipment and materials and store them correctly after use.
6. Dispose of rubbish and waste food correctly and leave containers hygienic and ready for use.
7. Deal with unexpected situations effectively and inform the proper person where necessary.
8. Prioritise work and carry it out in an efficient manner in line with legal requirements and suitable workplace procedures.

Range:

A Surfaces relates to PC4

Four from the range of A

- metal
- wall tiles
- painted
- glass
- floor tiles
- vinyl
- laminated surfaces

B Unexpected situations relates to PC7

- problems with cleaning materials
- problems with waste containers
- problems with maintenance

C Legal requirements relates to PC8

- current relevant legislation relating to safe and hygienic working practices when cleaning food production areas

Underpinning Knowledge Log

A Health and safety

1. Why separate cleaning equipment should be used for floors and work surfaces.
2. What protective clothing should be used for cleaning tasks.
3. Why areas which are being cleaned should be carefully marked.

B Food Hygiene

1. Why cleaning of food production areas should be carried out as soon as possible after use.
2. Why waste must be handled and disposed of correctly.
3. Why cleaning equipment should be stored separately from food items.

C Food allergies

1. What foods can commonly present problems for those who suffer from severe allergic reactions.
2. What action can you take to prevent allergic reactions.

Adopting and valuing the occupational standards

The 1998 White Paper, *Employment for the 1990s* (Department of Education, 1988), made great play of the importance of standards, developed through consultation with employers, in order to underpin a modern VET system of qualifications. As Debling (1991, p 6) notes:

It was more explicit about the nature of the new standards:

Our training system must be founded on standards and recognized qualifications based on competence – the performance required of individuals to do their work successfully and satisfactorily.

It was also explicit about who should identify the standards:

The standards must be identified by employers and they must be nationally recognized. Thus we need a system of employer-led organizations to identify and establish standards and secure recognition of them, sector by sector, or occupational group by occupational group.

The White Paper also expressed the expectation that the standard-setting organizations would provide the lead in establishing arrangements for assessing and accrediting learning achievements; have the ability to influence a significant part of the sector, and be seen as a body which can deal with government on training and vocational education matters.

The new qualifications were intended, therefore, to be 'employer-led' – the qualification was supposedly designed in consultation with employers and had employer requirements in mind. It was believed that the more ownership employers felt, the more successful this new initiative would be. However, the reality in the catering industry, as evident in the development of the CATERBASE project, suggests that employers were told that they needed standards and directed as to what these standards were to look like. Thus, even though the official documents argue that CATERBASE was developed "very much in accord with the *needs* identified by the hotel and catering industry itself" (HCTB, 1988, p 5, our emphasis), the majority of the people on the CATERBASE project Steering Group and the Industry Advisory Group were from large organisations in the catering and hospitality industry and only one was a chef (see Appendix). Very few people on this list could be classified as small- to medium-sized employers, who make up the majority of employers within the catering industry. The ways in which, and the extent to which, the NVQs that emerged from the CATERBASE project captured any of the reality of the social practices that form the valued culture of learning in kitchens is, therefore, open to serious doubt.

The new occupational standards were supposed to guide the development of training programmes and underpin the assessment of competence in the workplace. However, the documentation of the National Occupational Standards, and the arcane language used in the specification of the NVQs developed from the standards, were far removed from anything that the chefs in our study had experienced in their own apprenticeship, when they had taken the City and Guilds Craft Certificates in catering or the French equivalent. Adopting the new standards in any meaningful way would, therefore, require the chefs to undertake considerable learning in order to understand them and their implications for the training needs of their apprentice chefs. In the absence of strong employer groups to which the chefs felt strong affiliation, and who would therefore be trusted to develop the standards on their behalf and set out in detail what they meant in terms of training, the new standards were sidelined by the chefs in our study with respect to the on-the-job learning of the apprentices. Furthermore, small- to medium-sized employers cannot employ people specifically trained as assessors as part of their staff. Consequently, the chefs in the ethnographic study were offloading the assessment of competence, and thereby the use of the standards, either to the college tutors or the PTP.

This has a number of unfortunate side effects for the project of modernising "training in occupational skills (including apprenticeships) particularly to replace outdated age limits and time serving with training to agreed standards of skill appropriate to the jobs available" (HCTB, 1988, p 5), as set out in the aims of the CATERBASE project. The standards, as operationalised in the language of the NVQ, do provide a useful checklist that specifies the range of experiences and learning opportunities that an apprentice needs to have in order to complete the qualification. Such a checklist is essential if the on-the-job component of learning is going to be used effectively to develop the apprentice's portfolio of work that provides part of the evidence used to judge whether or not they are competent. Constructing this portfolio means that apprentice chefs have to work systematically through each of the different sections that make up a kitchen, such as vegetable preparation, pastry and the grill. However, in the absence of a detailed understanding of these requirements, the rules that guide where an apprentice works, and on what tasks, are overwhelmingly determined by the production needs of the kitchen on a particular day, and the preferences of individual chefs and apprentices about whom they work with, rather than the training needs of the apprentice. As Table 12.1 illustrates, there was an informal curriculum in play that identified the need for the apprentice to work more or less systematically through a range of tasks of growing complexity in different parts of the kitchen. However, the structure of this curriculum was determined primarily by the head chef's own ontogeny and experiences as an apprentice, rather than any recognition of external standards through which to guide the construction of the on-the-job training curriculum.

An additional problem, we suspect, is that the hospitality and catering industry does not work nor is it organised in the way assumed by those advocating the development and dissemination of standards by employer bodies. For example, each catering establishment is, to some extent at least, unique. Thus, while there are undoubtedly some skills that are generic and transferable across establishments, for example, knife skills and basic cooking techniques, the use of other skills and techniques will depend upon aspects such as the type of food being produced by each establishment. Consequently, training on the job to standards agreed nationally, primarily by large employers, may not be possible if parts of those standards, for example, making bread, are not required in a particular workplace because they buy in that component of their menu.

In our judgement, then, the impact of the development of occupational standards on the training received by apprentice chefs in the workplace has been minimal despite the extravagant claims made to support the introduction of this new approach. The major impact of the 'new kinds of standards' that are being introduced is that they make explicit the outcomes sought in education and training programmes. This contrasts with most previous forms of education and training provision which has been defined in respect of learning 'inputs' in the form of syllabuses, courses, training specifications and so on. The requirements of qualifications have also been based primarily on the content of the syllabuses and training specifications, and not the other way around. This shift from an input-led system to an outcome-led system has fundamental implications, both in defining the content of education and training and in opening access to different modes of learning. The specification of outcomes provides the key to unlocking the education and training system (Jessup, 1991, p 11).

The evidence produced in this section suggests that ensuring an industry or occupational group adopts a standards-based approach to training is somewhat more problematic than the top-down planners appreciated. It is now nearly twenty years since the development and implementation of the CATERBASE project, and the approach to defining and assessing standards endorsed both in that project, and in the subsequent development of NVQs. However, this standards-based approach seems to have had little impact on the on-the-job element of the training received by the apprentices in the three kitchens we researched. We think the adoption of such standards, in such a way that they influence the invisible curriculum of on-the-job training provided in the kitchens involved in this study, would require strong mediation by trusted and respected employer bodies. In the absence of such mediational processes, which were assumed to exist in the 1988 White Paper, the adoption of a standards-based approach to training may prove to be less effective than is deemed desirable in raising the quality and standard of training.

Judging competence

Specifying appropriate occupational standards is only the first step in developing a VET qualification system that focuses on competence. It is arguably the notion of competence that has generated the most heat (and possibly the least light) in the debates over the adequacy of NVQs as VET qualifications. A NVQ is defined as:

A statement of competence clearly relevant to work and intended to facilitate entry into, or progression in, employment and further learning, issued to an individual by a recognized awarding body.

The statement of competence should incorporate specified standards in:

– the ability to perform in a range of work related activities

and

– the underpinning skills, knowledge and understanding required for performance in employment. (NVQ Criteria and Procedures, NCVQ, 1989, cited by Jessup, 1991, p 15).

Jessup (1991, p 25) justified using competence as the assessment measure in NVQs as follows:

[W]e should perhaps clarify that the term 'competent', as used here, does not refer to a lowish or minimum level of performance. On the contrary, it refers to the standard required successfully to perform an activity or function. In manufacturing this would relate to quality control standards required to produce a satisfactory product. In the performance of a service, it means meeting the requirements of a customer or client. In most employment areas, unlike education, there is a recognized standard of performance related to the concept of 'quality'. Being competent means performing to professional or occupational standards. In most professional and occupational areas there is no scope for 'second best' standards.

As NVQs are a workplace-based qualification, it is the employer or the trainer who are most likely to be assessors and are therefore the ones 'interpreting' evidence and 'inferring' competence. The problematic nature of this assessment process is evident from the work of Eraut (2001). Even Jessup (1991, p 53) admits:

The credibility of assessment at work still needs to be established despite considerable progress made in the last four years. The belief that it refers to the rather casual and subjective practices that have prevailed in the past is still widespread. Even those who understand something of recent developments, doubt whether supervisors can or will be objective in their assessment of trainees and employees.... The openness of the process, with assessors and employees all knowing the standards by which performance is judged, will help to deter bad practice. At least it will be difficult to hide.

However, the 'openness of the process' relies on all assessors and employers holding the same understanding and using the same notion of competence.

Underpinning the notion of competence as used in the NVQ system is a form of occupational behaviourism and a process of defining competence in an occupational role that advocates 'divisive specialisation' (Moore, 1988; Young, 1998). The methodology underpinning the development of NVQs, functional analysis, involves:

> First, the key purpose of the overall area of competence is stated; this is then broken down into the primary functions which need to be carried out in order for the key purpose to be achieved. The primary functions are further divided into sub-sections, and they in turn are further sub-divided, and so on.... The basis on which a function is divided into sub-functions has significant effects on the statements of competence and the form of qualifications and training which result. (Jessup, 1991, p 36)

This process of "breaking the work role for a particular area into purposes and functions" (Mitchell, 1989, p 58) results in the identification of "'key purposes' in the various occupational sectors, and on this basis, key 'units' and constituent 'elements' of competence are constructed, each accompanied by the appropriate performance criteria, range statements and assessment guidance" (Hyland, 1994, p 6). Such a process is intended to lead to a specification of what is to count as competence that is supposed to be so clear, that competence in a work role can be judged with great validity thereby enhancing the credibility of the assessment of NVQs because everybody is supposed to know what it signifies.

However, perhaps ironically given their supposed role in the development of NVQs, employers, it seems, seriously question what an NVQ means (Eraut, 1994; Eraut et al, 1996, 1998, 2001; Grugulis, 2002). Such uncertainty is not surprising considering the wide array of definitions of competence offered by key players in the development of NVQs. Hyland, (1994, pp 22-3), for example, identifies no fewer than eight differing versions of competence in use by those involved in developing NVQs.

Far from being clear, then, the meaning of the term 'competence' appears to be rather opaque. However, for our purposes here we need to distinguish between two competing versions of competence and identify which are in play, and how the terms are used, in making judgements about the developing competence of apprentice chefs. Hyland (1994, p 20) perceptively notes the "troubling, and largely unnoticed though highly significant, tendency to confuse and conflate the terms 'competence' (plural: 'competences') and 'competency' (plural: 'competencies')". This distinction becomes critical when applying the meaning of competency to the achievement of outcomes. Carr's distinction "between competence as a *capacity* and competence as a *disposition*" (1993, p 256, emphasis in original) highlights the influence of an individual's personal characteristics and the role they play in achieving a standard of competence – something that seems unaccounted for in the NCVQ definition of competence. Hyland (1994, p 21) writes:

In the capacity sense (what I have called the 'holistic' version of competence, Hyland, 1993[c]), the term is employed broadly when we 'evaluate individuals as more or less successful in realising their aspirations to the standards of whichever professional activity they are engaged in' (Carr, 1993, p. 256). This is the sense in which we might speak of a competent electrician, plumber, lawyer or doctor. There is, however, the narrower or more atomistic dispositional sense of competence in which the term is used 'to label particular abilities or mark episodes of causal effectiveness with respect to these abilities' (p. 257). In this more restricted sense we might speak of a competent piece of driving or writing, or the competent performance or handling of a situation.

The first sense of competence – the capacity sense – relates more to the assessment of an individual ('connective specialisation') whereas the latter accounts for the activities an individual performs ('divisive specialisation') (Young, 1998). Moreover, and in line with Hyland (1994), competences align with an individual, while competencies characterise tasks. This latter understanding of competency matches the NCVQ definition of competence, which concentrates on the breakdown of occupations and jobs into units and elements but marginalises an individual's characteristics. Yet an individual's characteristics – one's disposition, motivation and interest (Prawat, 1989; Tobias, 1994; Billett, 1996) – are clearly integral to the ways in which one learns to perform tasks, and are therefore also integral to understanding how knowledge and skill are constructed in the workplace.

In the context of the kitchens involved in our study, the evolving competence of the apprentices is continually monitored, nearly always in a tacit way, by the more experienced chefs who provide more or less explicit feedback to the apprentices. However, their developing competence is not judged just by their ability to use a knife appropriately or to grill chicken correctly or prepare desserts through the individual performance of tasks. Rather, in addition, a more holistic judgement is made about their ability to cope and make a useful contribution, particularly when the action is at its hottest (Beckett and Hager, 2002), during service time. Such full participation in the activity system that is a kitchen relies on more than just having the basic technical skills – it also involves important aspects of attitude, values, motivation and identity.

Thus, the version of competence being used by the chefs in our participating kitchens is the more holistic kind that emphasises connective specialisation rather than the more fragmented kind as suggested by the NVQ assessment mechanism. However, the apprentices do meet the alternative definition of competence when they are assessed either by their college tutors or by the PTP. However, no support is given to help the apprentices rationalise this difference. Consequently, for them the qualification becomes sidelined as they place greater emphasis on fitting into the activity system of the kitchen, and winning the approval of their more experienced colleagues who use the holistic judgement of competence.

Ironically, this was not the intention of the initial CATERBASE project. In developing the CATERBASE modules, it was decided that the assessment needed to be a tool that could assess the achievement of elements while on work experience and to cover all four outcomes of youth training schemes (YTS) (HCTB, 1988, p 21):

1. competence in a job and/or range of occupational skills;
2. competence in a range of transferable core skills;
3. ability to transfer skills and knowledge to new situations; and
4. personal effectiveness.

However, the developers of CATERBASE also wrote:

> It appeared unlikely that a qualification which gave high prominence to the final three outcomes would be meaningful to employers and trainees. Difficulties could be anticipated in gaining acceptance and credibility. The visible aspects of the system therefore establish relevance by concentrating on competence in a job or a range of occupational skills. (HCTB, 1988, p 21)

While core skills, transfer and personal effectiveness were not emphasised, they are nevertheless implicit within the assessment system.

In their more holistic judgements, it is these latter three characteristics that the more experienced chefs are recognising and valuing. Developing the qualification from the ground up, as suggested by Eraut (2001), would have avoided this lost opportunity to have developed a more holistic concept of competence relevant to the demands of learning to be a chef. Stasz's (1997) research indicates that the criteria adopted for YTS (listed earlier) are indeed exactly what employers want. But in the development of CATERBASE (and subsequently NVQs) these criteria were ignored, even though the assessment scheme was supposedly developed by employers.

In addition to marginalising individual characteristics, the NVQ definition of competence means that an apprentice is classified as either competent or incompetent. This binary understanding of competence can be juxtaposed with the more nuanced concept put forward by Eraut (1994, pp 166-7) whereby a worker may be judged competent on a scale befitting the circumstances:

> An ambitious company would not employ an architect to design its new headquarters building who was described as 'competent', and a rich woman might look for rather more than competence in her tax adviser. Where there is a need for extra quality or expertise the description 'competent' is tantamount to damning with faint praise; but for routine tasks competence might be preferred to excellence if it resulted in quicker and cheaper service. This difference in connotation stems from whether the judgment is being made on a binary scale, where a person is judged to be either competent or

not competent, or on a graduated scale where 'competent' is a position on a continuum from 'novice' to 'expert'.

Eraut's concept is in line with the 'capacity' sense of competence, referring to a person as 'competent', rather than the 'competent' performance of certain tasks[1]. The capacity sense of competence implies the possibility for improvement and refinement of performance through personal construction of knowledge and skill. As Pearson (1984, p 32, cited by Eraut, 1994, p 167) states:

> If we can think of a continuum ranging from just knowing how to do something at the one end to knowing how to do something very well at the other, knowing how to do something competently would fall somewhere along this continuum.

The notion of competence being used by the experienced chefs in making judgements about the apprentices takes the form of the continuum from novice to expert identified by Eraut. Traditionally, the process of learning to be a chef has involved an arduous apprenticeship lasting four or five years. This included both an on-the-job component, with the cheaper labour power being offered by the apprentice constituting a crucial component of the productive capacity of the kitchen, and an off-the-job component of the day-release programme to the local FE college, during which apprentices learnt the theoretical knowledge underpinning their craft. In addition, the off-the-job component provided the opportunity for the apprentices to practice techniques and skills away from the hot action of the kitchen, and to develop additional knowledge and skills not used in the kitchen they worked in, for example, bread making. This off-the-job component ran through the whole of their apprenticeship and culminated with formal examinations needed to pass the craft certificate.

Under the Modern Apprenticeship (MA) arrangements, this off-the-job component now lasts only one year – the time deemed necessary to gain the NVQ Level 2 qualification – or does not exist at all with a PTP being used to assess developing competence in the workplace. However, an apprentice chef would never be judged competent by the more experienced chefs in the kitchens used in the ethnographic study after only one year. The process of time serving is still deemed crucial to developing competence, not least because of the time needed to master the work in the various sections of a kitchen, such as to develop expertise over a range of functions, as intimated by the head chef in one of the kitchens:

> He is starting to. He is heading in the right direction definitely. But when he starts to do other sections in the kitchen, is when you know they are worth their money. You can actually train somebody to do that section – no problem – but when they start doing other parts of the kitchen, 'Okay, you know what you are doing now', and when I throw him back over there [the first section]

after four weeks and he can switch straight onto it, I thought okay, you know your stuff now. (Barry, *Gastronomique*, lines 203-18, 7 May 2002)

Since 1986, the NVQ qualification has been used as an official signifier of competence in the workplace, yet the NVQ definition is very different to the concept of competence that the experienced chefs in this study use. Clearly, assessment of competence in the workplace has always been a part of apprenticeship and training. However, under the NVQ framework, assessment is exclusively focussed on competent *performance* of tasks as 'evidence', while in the kitchens in this research the chefs appear to look for evidence of competence in their apprentices, at least partially, on the basis of competence as a personal characteristic (the 'capacity' sense). The regulatory authorities would argue (rightly in our view) that NVQs were developed to recognise competency in the workplace, and employers are therefore prime candidates for assessing standards of competency in the workplace. However, the problem of multiple definitions of competence, and how to apply the different meanings of competence, was not addressed and this again means the impact of the reforms on learning in kitchens has been limited. Ironically the major impact has been on the curriculum of the FE College, which has been realigned with the needs to assess the apprentice chefs in order to gain the funding for completing the NVQ.

The process of constructing knowledge and skill

The occupation of chef has a long history and the process of becoming a chef typically involved a long and gruelling apprenticeship that stretched over many years. In the UK context, this apprenticeship took the form of an extensive period, usually four or five years of on-the-job learning supplemented by off-the-job learning via day-release in a local FE college. Certification of skills took the form of a craft certificate achieved by passing formal examinations. Traditionally, then, learning to be a chef involved participating in a time-honoured set of practices that emphasised the importance of process in the construction of knowledge and skill.

However, as NVQs are concerned primarily with outcomes, it is not surprising that the *process* of constructing knowledge and skill is not a priority. In fact, Jessup (1991, p 48) vehemently states in his book, *Outcomes: NVQs and the emerging model of education and training*:

> When the outcomes of learning are clearly specified, as they are in NVQs, assessment must logically be based directly on those outcomes. Statements of competence or attainment lay down what learners are expected to learn, or more precisely what they are expected to be able to do having learnt, and also what should be assessed to confirm that the required learning has been achieved.

This statement negates the varied and complex processes through which knowledge and skill are constructed. These learning processes can be both positive and negative as evidenced by Billett (2001) and Fine (1996). Jessup seems unconcerned with the way learning occurs, so long as the desired outcomes are reached: the employee must eventually prove to be a competent worker. Jessup (1991, p 121) does, however, make one significant statement about knowledge and skills in the above-mentioned book, although notably in a section entitled 'Outstanding issues which have yet to be resolved':

> The place of knowledge in an outcome-led system of education and training, as implied by NVQs, has recently emerged as a major issue. The term 'knowledge' is used in the broad sense to include the understanding of concepts, principles, theories, and relationships-in fact all the cognitive structures which underpin competent performance. In simpler language we might say we are here concerned with what people need in their heads to perform effectively with their hands, feet, voice, eyes, and so on.

A distinction is normally made between the knowledge and the skills which also underpin competent performance. Skills can only be demonstrated through their application in performance (doing something), while knowledge can be elicited through more abstract means of conversation, questioning and writing. The distinction becomes less clear when we consider cognitive skills (such as problem solving skills, perceptual skills) but skills refer to a process that leads to an outcome, while knowledge may be elicited as an abstraction from behaviour (for example, facts, principles, theories).

The following statement, however, makes clear Jessup's debt to the field of behavioural psychology, which has a long history in the study of competence-based education and training (Hyland, 1994). So long as a worker exhibits appropriate behaviour (performs competently) on the job, then he/she has acquired the necessary knowledge and skills:

> [It is] not necessary to define what we mean by 'knowledge and understanding' or to distinguish it from other attributes.... Along with, and in combination with, other basic skills ... it comprises the repertoire of attributes a person might possess which underpin competent performance. Occupational competence is being able to *apply* these attributes in various combinations to the successful performance of work functions. (Jessup, 1990, p 39, emphasis in original)

However, the evidence from both our ethnography of apprentice chefs and the evaluation of the CATERBASE project speaks to the value placed by more experienced chefs on both theoretical knowledge and the process of constructing knowledge. Apprentice chefs, who are usually 16 years of age when they start their apprenticeship, start their learning trajectory as legitimate peripheral participants to then become full members of a community of practice (Lave andWenger, 1991;Wenger, 1999) in exactly the same way as the more experienced chefs they are working with did. Much of their learning involves long periods of repetition of the same basic tasks until they are accomplished automatically. In so doing, they are of course not just learning, but are also making an essential contribution to the work of kitchens; they learn in the midst of accomplishing useful, productive work. Furthermore, an apprentice will find themselves continuing to work in a particular section of a kitchen long after they have mastered the tasks involved in the work of that section because their work is essential to the overall functioning of the kitchen. The tasks the apprentices complete in the first 18 months of their trajectories are illustrated in Table 12.2.

The physical structure of the kitchen, the tasks that comprise the work of chefs, and the more experienced chefs, all provide affordances for the learning of the apprentices through processes of co-participation (Billett, 2002, p 466):

> [E]ngagement at work is held to be co-participative: a relationship constituted between the affordances of the work practice and how individuals elect to engage in the work practice. The participatory practices are a product of the evolving social practice of the workplace, which is historically, culturally and situationally constituted, and the socially constructed personal history of the individual.

Developing the personal dispositions and characteristics needed to become a full participant in these social practices is seen as being just as important as developing the technical skills, and the process of time serving is deemed crucial by the more experienced chefs for the apprentice's development.

In addition, the evaluation of the CATERBASE project, though mainly positive (PRD, 1988, p 12), indicated the value placed by chefs on the development of theoretical knowledge through college placement:

> A more problematic criticism, and one which relates to the issue of standards and off-the-job training provided as part of CATERBASE was the feeling expressed that while CATERBASE modules were splendid for practical work, there was too little emphasis on theory. (PRD, 1988, p 11)

> Issues identified by the evaluators/PRD regarding assessment concern the element of time-serving, as show in the time taken to reach basic standard/ performance criteria before assessment occurs on the module itself and the need for additional testing, to check knowledge (theory). (PRD, 1988, p 12).

> While they [employers] appreciated the value of CATERBASE modules as training documents and the scheme as a whole, it was nevertheless "not as good as" college training, which has become the accepted way of qualifying to work in the industry. Even the carrot of joint certification with City & Guilds did not reassure them, since holders of such a certificate may still lack the theoretical background prized so highly. (PRD, 1988, p 14; emphasis in original)

Table 12.2: Trajectories of apprentices

Trajectory Apprentice	Two months	Six months	16 months	18 months
Jack (Chives)	• breakfast • vegetable preparation	• breakfast • vegetable preparation • main kitchen	• breakfast • vegetable preparation • main kitchen	• breakfast • vegetable preparation • main kitchen
Daniel (Chives)	• breakfast • vegetable preparation	• breakfast • salad preparation • some main kitchen		
Lawrence (Gastronomique)	• vegetable preparation • garde manger	• vegetable preparation • garde manger	• vegetable preparation • garde manger • dessert section • about to begin on entremetier	
Clint (Sebs)	• salad preparation • vegetable preparation • parts of dishes from the main kitchen • pastry section			

The issues of the development of theoretical knowledge, experience and time serving, identified in the above extracts of the report, are elements inherent in the processes of learning in traditional apprenticeship, and were the aspects that remained in the apprenticeships young people were undertaking at the same time YTS was running. The new CATERBASE assessment framework being imposed on the hospitality and catering industry was therefore, not only contrary to the culture and history of that industry, but also antithetical to the philosophy of the training scheme it was being fitted into, the YTS.

The learning of apprentice chefs is therefore located in a set of time-honoured social practices that involve a well-defined community structured by a hierarchy, the kitchen brigade system introduced by Escoffier (www.escoffier.com/great_chefs.html), a clear division of labour, participating fully in a daily cycle of work that involves significant shifts in tempo as service periods come and go and largely tacit rules that are learnt through the work process. Within this activity system the learning trajectory of the apprentice is largely structured by the ontogeny of the more experienced chefs, particularly the head chef. Judgements about the competence of the apprentice are made largely intuitively and in a holistic way (Carr, 1993; Hyland, 1994) – can they hold their own in a particular section of the kitchen when the going gets tough?

It is this set of social practices that constitute the culture of learning in these kitchens and they matter in terms of judging the competence of the young apprentices:

> On being questioned, employers said that they would be happy to accept completed Passbooks as indicators of experience, although they would want to know where someone had been working before. (PRD, 1988, p 13)

It is apparently not enough to just tick off a list of competences to be considered competent, it is where and how you trained that is also deemed important. Thus, identifying standards and competences is not enough for producing the competent chef: participating in and becoming accepted as being part of an existing set of practices is equally important. To pretend otherwise is to fail to understand the full nature of becoming a chef.

Conclusion

Now, it is not our purpose here to valorise the particular learning cultures of kitchens. In many ways, these kitchens, because of economic necessity, are such that the apprentices become deeply embedded in production processes from the very beginning of their apprenticeship, have many of the hallmarks of what Fuller and Unwin (2003a, 2003b; Chapter Six of this volume) would describe as restrictive learning environments. Indeed, we would suggest that adopting a standards-based approach to the on-the-job training of these apprentices would likely result in an improved learning environment. Our intention was to counterpoise this culture of learning against the technology of assessment that underpins the qualification these young people were working towards – a Level 2 NVQ – in order to better understand the challenges of developing the next round of outcomes-based qualifications.

The use of NVQs in the catering industry represents an important case study from which those advocating the development of new types of competence-focused qualifications can learn. For example, even though NVQs were supposedly developed for employers in conjunction with their Industry Training Organisations (ITOs), and despite a 20-year history, the chefs in our kitchens have not embraced the attempt to certify the knowledge and skill constructed in the workplace through NVQs. This speaks to the need for strong mediational processes through which new systems of qualifications become incorporated into existing occupations. Indeed, it speaks to the need to decide on the nature of an occupation, defining its *'berufness'*, as an integral part of developing new vocational qualifications. Ensuring that appropriate systems and structures are in place to mediate new definitions of qualifications so that they are adopted by employers, and to decide on the nature of occupations, will take more time than was devoted to the development of NVQs.

Furthermore, it can be seen that the constant attempts to move away from the model of traditional apprenticeship has not been successful, and many industries and the workers in them still follow, and revere, aspects of the traditional apprenticeship (Unwin, 1996; Fuller and Unwin, 2004). In fact, traditional approaches to apprenticeship, in industries with long histories of apprenticeship such as engineering, construction, manufacturing and catering, persisted throughout the turmoil of the various youth training initiatives in the 1970s and 1980s, and ran alongside YTS. Modern Apprenticeships represent both an attempt to appropriate the cachet of this older tradition and an attempt to rework existing cultures of learning to meet newer political ends.

Recent research on workplace learning highlights the social and situational nature of knowledge and skill construction (for example, Engeström, 1987, 1993; Lave and Wenger, 1991; Billett, 1995, 2001; Saxe, 1997; Scribner, 1999; Rogoff et al, 2002; Fuller and Unwin, 2003a, 2003b). The MA programme incorporates NVQs, an outcomes-based assessment mechanism, to formalise and qualify these processes of knowledge and skill construction. However, this chapter has sought to demonstrate that the NVQ emphasis on outcomes, and the underlying notion of competence on which NVQs are based, clash with both the values of traditional apprenticeship and the training practices of employers, who continue to believe an apprentice chef must serve time in the industry before developing competence in the 'capacity' sense. The identification of a worker as either competent or not competent, the basis on which an NVQ is awarded or withheld, does not do justice to the depth and breadth of knowledge and skill that is constructed in the workplace.

As a consequence apprentices must constantly negotiate between two contradictory commitments: process-based outcomes in the workplace and an outcomes-based process of assessment in NVQs. *Becoming* competent holds value to a kitchen, while *being* competent holds formal value in the guise of an

NVQ. The disjuncture between a qualification (ostensibly developed by the industry) that grounds its own products in *being* on the one hand, and an industry (ostensibly served by the qualification system) that prizes *becoming* on the other hand, means that the apprentices, in developing their knowledge and skills, are positioned between the values of the workplace and the requirements of the NVQs. They are left to make sense of the static description of their 'being' as laid down in the NVQ competencies in relation to the more dynamic process of 'becoming' that they experience as they construct their knowledge and skill in the production environment of the kitchen. In the wake of this tension, and in the daily complex working environment of professional kitchens, it is the *process* of learning to become a chef that takes priority, and the qualification falls by the wayside.

Appendix: Industry Advisory Group

Chairman	Mr J. Lomas	Personnel Director, Embassy Hotels
Members	Mr T. Blumenau	Director, Personnel and Training, Kennedy Brookes
	Ms C. Bailes	Head of Catering Training and Technical Standards Group, British Telecom Catering College
	Mr C.N. Bone	Contracts Director, Gardner Merchant
	Mr K. Smith	Personnel Manager, Swallow Hotels
	Mr M.E.G. Hawkes	Hospital Caterers Association, Management Services Department
	Mr G.E. Reeks	Head of Catering, The Post Office Headquarters
	Mr A.H. Roux	Managing Director, Roux Restaurants Ltd
	Mr E. McNally	Personnel Director, Commercial Catering Group
	Mr P. Hamilton	Training Director, Trusthouse Forte Hotels
	Mr B. Henson	Controller, Education & Training Services, City & Guilds of London Institute
	Mr R. Perrett	The Cookery and Food Association c/o Craigmiller
	Mr C. Ripper	Company Personnel Manager, Thistle Hotels
	Mr I.M. Tyers	Manager, The Automobile Association

Note

[1] Young (1998, p 77) also notes that, "the broad notion of skills that is being sought after in potential employees by leading edge companies (British Telecom, 1993) is very different from the narrowly defined job specific concept of NVQs".

References

Ainley, P. (1990) *Vocational education and training*, London: Cassells Education Limited.

Beckett, D. and Hager, P. (2002) *Life, work and learning: Practice in postmodernity*, London: Routledge.

Billett, S. (1995) 'Structuring knowledge through authentic activities', unpublished PhD, Brisbane: Faculty of Education, Griffith University.

Billett, S. (1996) 'Constructing vocational knowledge: history, communities and ontogeny', *Journal of Vocational Education and Training*, vol 48, no 2, pp 141-54.

Billett, S. (2001) *Learning in the workplace: Strategies for effective practice*, Sydney: Allen & Unwin.

Billett, S. (2002) 'Workplace pedagogic practices: co-participation and learning', *British Journal of Educational Studies*, vol 50, no 4, pp 457-81.

British Telecom (1993) *Matching skills: Report of a collaborative project*, London: British Telecom.

Carr, D. (1993) 'Questions of competence', *British Journal of Educational Studies*, vol 41, no 3, pp 253-71.

Debling, G. (1991) 'Developing standards in change and intervention: vocational education and training', in P. Raggatt and L. Unwin (eds) *Change and intervention: Vocational education and training*, London: The Falmer Press, pp 1-21.

Department of Employment (1988) *Employment for the 1990s*, Cm 540, London: HMSO.

Edexcel (1999) *Level 1/Level 2 BTEC NVQ Catering & Hospitality generic candidate guidance and log book*, Mansfield: Edexcel Publications.

Engeström, Y. (1987) *Learning by expanding. An activity-theoretical approach to developmental research*, Helsinki: Orienta-Konsultit.

Engeström, Y. (1993) 'Developmental studies of work as a testbench of activity theory: the case of primary care medical practice', in S. Chaiklin and J. Lave (eds) *Understanding practice: Perspectives on activity and context*, Toronto: Cambridge University Press, pp 64-103.

Eraut, M. (1994) *Developing professional knowledge and competence*, London: Falmer Press.

Eraut, M. (2001) 'The role and use of vocational qualifications', *National Institute Economic Review*, vol 178 (October), pp 88-98.

Eraut, M., Alderton, J., Cole, G. and Senker, P. (1998) *Development of knowledge and skills in employment*, Brighton: Institute of Education, University of Sussex.

Eraut, M., Steadman, S. and James, J. (2001) *Evaluation of higher level S/NVQs, research report*, Sussex: University of Sussex Institute of Education.

Eraut, M., Steadman, S., Trill, J. and Parkes, J. (1996) *The assessment of NVQs: Research report 4*, Sussex: University of Sussex Institute of Education.

Fine, G. (1996) *Kitchens: The culture of restaurant work*, Berkeley, CA: University of California.

Fuller, A. and Unwin, L. (2003a) 'Learning as apprentices in the contemporary UK workplace: creating and managing expansive and restrictive participation', *Journal of Education and Work*, vol 16, no 4, pp 407-26.

Fuller, A. and Unwin, L. (2003b) 'Creating a "modern apprenticeship": a critique of the UK's multi-sector, social inclusion approach', *Journal of Education and Work*, vol 16, no 1, pp 5-25.

Fuller, A. and Unwin, L. (2004: forthcoming) 'Expansive learning environments: integrating personal and organisational development', in H. Rainbird, A. Fuller and A. Munro (eds) *Workplace learning in context*, London: Routledge, pp 126-44.

Grugulis, I. (2002) *Skill and qualification: The contribution of NVQs to raising skill levels*, SKOPE Research Paper 36, Oxford: Oxford and Warwick Universities.

Hayward, G. (1997) *British vocational qualifications*, (2nd edn), London: Kogan Page.

HCTB (Hotel and Catering Training Board) (1988) *The CATERBASE project: Workplace assessment and accreditation for the hotel and catering industry. Report on the first two years to the MSC*, London: MSC.

Hyland, T. (1994) *Competence, education and NVQs: Dissenting perspectives*, London: Cassell.

James, S. (2004) *Learning to cook: Knowledge and skill construction in the workplace*, Unpublished D.Phil Thesis, Oxford: University of Oxford.

Jessup, G. (1990) *NVQ framework: A proposed system of classification of NVQs by areas of competence. Note for informal consultations*, London: NCVQ.

Jessup, G. (1991) *Outcomes: NVQs and the emerging model of education and training*, London: Falmer Press.

Lave, J. and Wenger, E. (1991) *Situated learning: Legitimate peripheral participation*, Cambridge: Cambridge University Press.

Mitchell, L. (1989) 'The definition of standards and their assessment', in J. Burke (ed) *Competency based education and training*, Lewes: Falmer Press, pp 54-64.

Moore, R. (1988) 'The correspondence principle and the radical sociology of education', in M. Cole (ed) *Bowles and Gintis revisited: Correspondence and contradiction in educational theory*, London: Falmer Press, pp 51-85.

NCVQ (National Council for Vocational Qualifications) (1989) *The NVQ criteria and related guidance*, London: NCVQ.

Pearson, H. (1984) 'Competence: a normative analysis', in E. Short (ed) *Competence: Inquiries into its meaning and acquisition in education settings*, Lanham, MD: University Press of America, pp 31-8.

Prawat, R. (1989) 'Promoting access to knowledge, strategy, and disposition in students: a research synthesis', *Review of Educational Research*, vol 59, no 1, pp 1-41.

PRD (Psychometric Research and Development) (1988) *The PRD evaluation of CATERBASE: Early delivery in hotel and catering YTS schemes*, London: MSC.

Rogoff, B., Topping, K., Baker-Sennett, J. and Lacasa, P. (2002) 'Mutual contributions of individuals, partners, and institutions: planning to remember in girl scout cookie sales', *Social Development*, vol 11, no 2, pp 266-89.

Ryan, P. and Unwin, L. (2001) 'Apprenticeship in the British "training market"', *National Institute Economic Review*, vol 178 (October), pp 99-115.

Saxe, G. (1997) 'Selling candy: a study of cognition in context', in M. Cole, Y. Engeström and O. Vasquez (eds) *Mind, culture and activity*, Cambridge: Cambridge University Press, pp 330-6.

Scribner, S. (1999) 'Knowledge at work', in R. McCormick and C. Paechter (eds) *Learning and knowledge*, London: Paul Chapman Publishing in association with The Open University Press, pp 103-11.

Stasz, C. (1997) 'Do employers need the skills they want? Evidence from technical work', *Journal of Education and Work*, vol 10, no 3, pp 205-23.

Tobias, S. (1994) 'Interest, prior knowledge and learning', *Review of Educational Research*, vol 64, no 1, pp 37-54.

Unwin, L. (1996) 'Employer-led realities: apprenticeship past and present', *Journal of Vocational Education and Training*, vol 48, no 1, pp 57-68.

Wenger, E. (1999) *Communities of practice: Learning, meaning and identity*, Cambridge: Cambridge University Press.

Young, M. (1998) *The curriculum of the future: From the 'new sociology of education' to a critical theory of learning*, London: Falmer Press.

Index

Page references figures and tables are in italics; those for notes are followed by n

Social capital and lifelong learning
John Field, Division of Academic Innovation and Continuing Education, University of Stirling

This book confirms the significance of social capital as an analytical tool, while challenging the basis on which current policy on lifelong learning is being developed.

Paperback £24.99 US$39.95 ISBN 1 86134 655 7
Hardback £55.00 US$79.95 ISBN 1 86134 543 7
234 x 156mm 176 tbc pages May 2005

Learning for life
The foundations for lifelong learning
David H. Hargreaves, Fellow of Wolfson College, Cambridge

This book challenges the myth that lifelong learning can or should be separated from school education. It asks the critical question: what changes in thinking, policy and practice are needed for the culture and process of lifelong learning to become a reality?

Paperback £14.99 US$25.00 ISBN 1 86134 597 6
234 x 156mm 128 pages June 2004

Learn to succeed
The case for a skills revolution
Mike Campbell, Sector Skills Development Agency

This is the first book to draw together the evidence on the 'case' for skills and to examine the policies appropriate to achieving 'skills for all'.

Paperback £19.99 US$29.95 ISBN 1 86134 269 1
Hardback £50.00 US$79.95 ISBN 1 86134 392 2
234 x 156mm 128 pages May 2002

Creating a learning society?
Learning careers and policies for lifelong learning
Stephen Gorard and **Gareth Rees**, School of Social Sciences, Cardiff University

This book presents a highly innovative study of participation in lifelong learning and the problems which need to be overcome if lifelong learning policies are to be successful.

Paperback £19.99 US$32.50 ISBN 1 86134 286 1
Hardback £50.00 US$75.00 ISBN 1 86134 393 0
234 x 156mm 208 pages May 2002

Differing visions of a Learning Society
Research findings Volume 1
Edited by **Frank Coffield**, Department of Education, University of Newcastle upon Tyne

This first volume explores the ways lifelong learning can contribute to the development of knowledge and skills for employment, and other areas of adult life. It addresses the challenges to social science researchers to study issues that are central and directly relevant to the political and policy debate, and to take into account the reality of people's lives.

Paperback £21.99 US$37.50 ISBN 1 86134 230 6

Hardback £50.00 US$75.00 ISBN 1 86134 246 2

216 x 148mm 288 pages July 2000

ESRC Learning Society series

Differing visions of a Learning Society
Research findings Volume 2
Edited by **Frank Coffield**, Department of Education, University of Newcastle upon Tyne

This second volume presents findings from a national survey of the skills of British workers. It discusses both the meaning of the Learning Society for adults with learning difficulties, and the use of social capital to explain patterns of lifelong learning. The book also presents five different 'trajectories' of lifelong learning, explores the determinants of participation and non-participation in learning, and examines innovation in Higher Education.

Paperback £18.99 US$29.95 ISBN 1 86134 247 0

Hardback £50.00 US$75.00 ISBN 1 86134 248 9

216 x 148mm 248 pages November 2000

ESRC Learning Society series

To order further copies of this publication or any other Policy Press titles please contact:

In the UK and Europe:
Marston Book Services, PO Box 269, Abingdon, Oxon, OX14 4YN, UK
Tel: +44 (0)1235 465500
Fax: +44 (0)1235 465556
Email: direct.orders@marston.co.uk

In the USA and Canada:
ISBS, 920 NE 58th Street, Suite 300, Portland, OR 97213-3786, USA
Tel: +1 800 944 6190 (toll free)
Fax: +1 503 280 8832
Email: info@isbs.com

In Australia and New Zealand:
DA Information Services, 648 Whitehorse Road Mitcham, Victoria 3132, Australia
Tel: +61 (3) 9210 7777
Fax: +61 (3) 9210 7788
E-mail: service@dadirect.com.au

Further information about all of our titles can be found on our website:

www.policypress.org.uk